THE ETHICS OF STAR TREK

Also by Judith Barad, Ph.D.

Consent: The Means to an Active Faith According to Thomas Aquinas

Aquinas on the Nature and Treatment of Animals

Also by Ed Robertson

The Fugitive Recaptured

Maverick: Legend of the West

This Is Jim Rockford/The Rockford Files

THE ETHICS OF

STAR TREK

JUDITH BARAD, Ph.D., *with* ED ROBERTSON

HarperCollins*Publishers*

HarperCollins books may be purchased for educational, business, or sales promotional use. For information, please write: Special Markets Department, HarperCollins Publishers Inc., 10 East 53rd Street, New York, NY 10022.

FIRST EDITION

Designed by Lindgren/Fuller Design

Printed on acid-free paper

Library of Congress Cataloging-in-Publication Data

Barad, Judith A.
    The ethics of Star Trek / Judith Barad, with Ed Robertson.—1st ed.
        p. cm.
    Includes index.
    ISBN 0-06-019530-4
        1. Star Trek television programs—Moral and ethical aspects. I. Robertson, Ed. II. Title.
    PN1992.8.S74 B37 2000
    791.45'72—dc21   00-033429

00 01 02 03 04 ❖ 10 9 8 7 6 5 4 3 2 1

To Justice,
with hope for the future
J.B.

To Mrs. Colby,
from Mr. Colby
E.R.

CONTENTS

PART FOUR

WHEN DUTY CALLS

PART FIVE

RECEPTACLES,

RESPONSIBILITY, AND

RECONCILIATION

ACKNOWLEDGMENTS

Thanks to Pete Dean for suggesting I write this book; Jake Jakaitis for his help with the first two chapters; Rocco Gennaro, for reading a draft of the book; and my agent, Winifred Golden, for her useful suggestions, constant encouragement, and believing in the project from the start. Above all, my deepest appreciation to my mentors, role models, and friends for their inspiration and abiding faith in me, and to Indiana State University for granting me a sabbatical so that I could write this book in the first place.

J.B.

My thanks go to D. Patrick Miller, who originally steered me toward this project; my agent, Tim Seldes, for his good cheer and sage counsel; Larry Ashmead at HarperCollins, for his vision; Allison McCabe, my editor at Harper, for her encouragement; John Ali, *Star Trek* expert nonpareil; my sister Jo-Ann Collins and her friends at the San Francisco Public Library; and Chloe Rounsley, my partner, best friend, personal editor, the driving force in my life, and the brightest star in the galaxy.

E.R.

PICARD: There is no greater challenge than the study
   of philosophy.
WESLEY: William James won't be on my Starfleet exams.
PICARD: The important things never will be.

> "Samaritan Snare"

Star Trek is an unparalleled phenomenon that has fascinated, challenged, inspired, and of course entertained us for nearly 35 years. With a view of the future that began with the voyages of the original *Enterprise, Star Trek* imagines a universe of advanced technology, adventure on a galactic scale, and unbridled optimism for humanity's ethical progress. And yet, though set in the future, the attitudes, politics, and culture depicted in each series and film have always reflected the mores of contemporary society—be they those of the mid-1960s (in the case of the Original Series) or the era of the new millennium (*Voyager*).

One reason why *Star Trek* has endured from one generation to the next is that most of the stories themselves are indeed moral fables. Though the episodes are obviously self-contained, when taken as a whole they constitute a harmonious philosophy filled with hope. While our *Star Trek* heroes are far from perfect, they are nonetheless essentially decent beings whose interaction with "new life and new civilizations" is always guided by nobility and morality. This morality is based on a fundamental ethics that was inherent (at least implicitly) when the franchise was initially conceived.

From portraying television's first interracial kiss to dramatizing the issues of homelessness, homosexuality, and religious intolerance, the ethics of *Star Trek* has generated a world that strives to be free of the racist, sexist, and xenophobic attitudes that are, unfortunately, still all too common today. By raising these issues, each series challenges us to examine our own values and ask ourselves whether they are defensible, let alone reasonable.

In addition, the ethical dilemmas of the *Star Trek* universe also enable us to better understand our own society and the presuppositions that govern it. Sometimes, for example, we can get so caught up in the values of our commerce-driven society that we develop a kind of "ethical myopia" about it. By dramatizing these values in a 24th-century setting (even to the point of exaggeration), *Star Trek* provides us with a forum that's informative as well as entertaining. In laughing at the Ferengi, we can also laugh at ourselves—thus attaining the kind of perspective we all need from time to time.

As we complete the first year of the new millennium, there is a growing concern over the ethical direction—or lack thereof, depending on how you see it—our society appears to be taking. It no longer shocks us to learn about the lies, corruption, sexual peccadilloes, or other scandals that characterize all too many of those who hold public office. In fact, many of us are willing to overlook the character flaws of our elected leaders, so long as they do their job (and the economy stays on the upswing). Meanwhile, our court dockets have become inundated with lawsuits that belie common sense, filed by litigants attempting to avoid responsibility. At the same time, the improvements made possible by our ever-changing technology have raised additional questions about the morality of cloning, genetic engineering, fertility drugs, life support, and other important issues. *Star Trek* reminds us that basic ethical problems, responses, and theories can still exist in societies far more technologically advanced than ours.

In fact, its overall principles form an impetus powerful enough to provide direction for our own future.

But what exactly are the ethics of *Star Trek*? Are these principles basically the same from series to series? Are they even consistent within the same series? Take the idea of self-sacrifice, for example. No Trekker could possibly forget the words Spock utters before he gives up his life so that the crew might live in *Star Trek II: The Wrath of Khan*: "The needs of the many outweigh the needs of the one." A leader (at least in the eyes of Starfleet) should always serve his people to the very end. Kirk himself on umpteen occasions has put the safety of his crew before his own. That would strongly suggest that self-sacrifice, as *Star Trek* sees it, is a good thing. But if that's the case, why does the captain try to stop the alien woman in "The Mark of Gideon" from sacrificing her life for the good of her people? Not only that, how do we account for Kirk's rationale for risking his career to save Spock in *Star Trek III: The Search for Spock* ("The needs of the one outweighed the needs of the many")? Though the captain's actions in both instances are clearly portrayed as heroic, wouldn't you say they also contradict the show's overall position on self-sacrifice?

Before delving into these and other pressing questions, though, we need to differentiate between what ethics is and what it isn't. For one thing, ethics is not just the folk wisdom dispensed by your parents when you were a kid. It can't be learned in a single lecture or reduced to glib slogans. Nor is ethics simply that which reflects the particular laws or etiquette of a given society. Ethics, as a matter of fact, is quite independent of the law. As unethical as it may be to backstab your friends or colleagues to advance your career, it's certainly not illegal.

So where do we turn? Well, at this point, we have two options: religion or philosophy. But if we're talking about the ethics of *Star Trek*, religion would seem to be out of the question, especially considering the longtime personal weltanschauung of series creator Gene Roddenberry. As many of us know, Roddenberry for years associated himself with humanism, a vague philosophical view that emphasizes a move away from God and toward the importance and achievements of the human being. Linked with agnosticism and atheism, humanism contains an appeal to reason that is decidedly in contrast to religious authority or revelation. Humanism also encourages us to discover the universe as well as the nature and destiny of the human being through our own efforts. Both the appeal to reason and the impulse to discovery certainly permeate *Star Trek*, especially the Original Series and *The Next Generation*. Therefore, if we are to remain true to the spirit of the creator, reason would suggest looking for ethics in philosophical writings.

Wait a minute, you say. Isn't religion an integral part of the Bajoran people, who in turn are an integral part of *Deep Space Nine*—which in turn is an integral part of the *Star Trek* fabric? Are not the Bible, the Torah, and the Koran also books of philosophy that might tell us what ethics is? Good questions, both of which we'll address in short time. For now, though, let's define "philosophical ethics" as the systematic inquiry into human conduct designed to discover the rules that should guide our actions, as well as the good we seek in life. I realize this sounds a little academic, but that can't be helped. You see, the term "ethics" itself refers to theory, rather than practice. Nevertheless, an understanding of ethical theory can provide us with practical guidelines to live our everyday lives, be it here and now on Earth, or in the far reaches of the galaxy.

In order to successfully understand ethics, we need to approach each ethical theory we encounter with the same spirit of objective open-mindedness with which our friends on *Star Trek* approach new civilizations. At the same time, however, our examinations must remain critical, so that our final judgment of each theory is based solely on the weight of the arguments. These basic two facts are important to bear in mind because ethics is quite different from, say, physics. I'll bet that most of us who read *The Physics of "Star Trek"** had few if any preconceived notions about physics when we started the book, because most of us have little if any idea of what physics is even about. I'll also bet that isn't the case as you start reading this book, because most of us have *a lot* of preconceptions of what ethics is about. True, ethics is not an exact science like physics. It does, however, contain theories and principles that can be tested by Mr. Spock's favorite subject—logic. Because it provides ethics with some objectivity, logic is as indispensable to ethics as scientific method is to physics. We'll look closely at the important role logic plays in ethical inquiry in our first two chapters.

The Ethics of "Star Trek" provides a brief introduction to just about every major ethical theory from the time of the ancient Greeks though 20th-century existentialism. Each chapter will present the ethical dilemmas of a particular *Star Trek* episode or two, show how someone such as Plato or Aristotle might have treated the problems, and compare the course of action taken by the *Star Trek* characters to what our various ethicists have to say. We'll probe such matters as our moral duty (what it is, how to measure it, and what to do when duties conflict); the significance of virtue, individualism, and responsibility in *Star Trek*; the morality of assisted suicide, the use of animals in science and commerce, and other controversial issues; the age-old debate over what's more important, the intentions of our actions or the results they yield; and practical advice on how to pull ourselves together when we find ourselves split in two.

We'll also see how *Star Trek* answers such eternal questions as (1) Does absolute power tend to corrupt absolutely? (2) Are

---

*Lawrence M. Krauss, *The Physics of "Star Trek"* (New York: Basic Books, 1995).

rational beings the only life forms entitled to our respect? (3) Does might indeed make right? (4) What would it mean if, deep down, everyone really were a Ferengi? and finally (5) If the Prime Directive is so inviolable, why does Kirk always seem to breach it?

Interestingly enough, we'll find that our *Star Trek* friends not only tackle many of the same issues raised by our prominent ethicists, they often speak the same language. In many cases, we'll use dialogue from the episodes incorporating terms and phrases originally associated with each of our various theories, so as to highlight the deeply ethical nature of the *Star Trek* universe.

Part One focuses on what role, if any, religion and culture play in determining ethical values, as well as the importance of logical principles to ethical reasoning. Part Two explains how virtue ethics, hedonism, and Stoicism manifest themselves in the *Star Trek* universe. In Part Three we'll look at *Star Trek* from polar opposite extremes: the spiritual challenges raised by Christian ethics versus the decidedly capitalistic values of Hobbes' social contract theory. Part Four introduces three variations of duty-based ethics—a philosophy that resonates throughout the *Star Trek* series and films. Finally in Part Five, we'll illustrate how utilitarian thought and existentialist principles operate in *Star Trek*. Then, after examining the ethical bias of each of the four series, we'll see if we can come up with an overall ethics of *Star Trek* that can indeed stand to reason.

One final note before we begin. As much as I'm looking forward to exploring these and other questions over the course of our journey, my goal is not merely for us to discover the ethical foundation of *Star Trek*. Nor do I simply want to introduce people to ethical reasoning. If along the way we achieve both these goals, that would be great. But my "prime directive" for this book is to stimulate greater awareness of the many ethical issues and concerns in our daily lives. After all, only with greater ethical awareness and compassion can we bring *Star Trek*'s optimistic view of the future closer to reality.

PART ONE

BEGINNING THE ETHICAL ENTERPRISE

"The mind opens! In creeps wisdom."
—Lwaxana Troi to Alexander,
"Cost of Living"

CULTURAL
RELATIVISM

"Cost of Living"
TNG: Episode 120*
Stardate: 45733.6
Original Air Date: Week of April 20, 1992

Ship psychologist Deanna Troi's efforts to help Lieutenant Worf teach his young son, Alexander, the value of responsibility are immediately undermined by her irrepressible mother, Lwaxana, who spirits the young impressionable boy off to a holodeck community "where there are no rules." Deanna barely recovers from the havoc her mother wreaked when Lwaxana drops a bombshell: she's marrying Minister Campio of Kostolain—a man she's never actually met. Lwaxana also announces that she will be going against her own Betazoid wedding customs by wearing a traditional Kostolain wedding gown at the ceremony. That shocks Deanna even more. After all, in an orthodox Betazoid wedding ceremony, the bride appears completely nude.

If you were Lwaxana Troi, what would you have done? Should you "go the full monty," just because that's what your family

---

*Abbreviations for the four *Star Trek* TV series are as follows: *TOS* = the Original Series; *TNG* = *The Next Generation; DS9* = *Deep Space Nine;* and *VGR* = *Voyager.* Episode numbers are based on those provided by Michael Okuda and Denise Okuda's *The "Star Trek" Encyclopedia,* 2nd ed. (New York: Pocket Books, 1997), which lists the episodes of each series in the order of their production.

expects you to do? What if you knew it would make your husband-to-be feel uncomfortable? What if it made *you* feel uncomfortable? What's more important, honoring a wedding tradition or laying the groundwork for a happy marriage?

We all know that from ancient times right on through to the 24th-century world of *Star Trek,* ideas of love, marriage, and right and wrong in general have differed from culture to culture. Many people happen to believe that the customs of diverse cultures are what forms the basis of morality for those cultures. This is known among ethicists as "cultural relativism." No one culture's customs can ever be evaluated as right or wrong, the theory goes, as that would suggest the existence of some universal standard of morality independent of people's opinions. Because ethical judgments do not have a standard of morality, any belief about right or wrong is entirely arbitrary and therefore relative.

Cultural relativism has its good points. For one, it warns us against the danger of ethnocentrism, an attitude that assumes the values of our own particular society are also best for everyone else. There's a lot of ethnocentric thinking going on in "Cost of Living," mostly on the part of the Kostolains. It's not enough that Lwaxana is abandoning ancient Betazoid tradition for her upcoming nuptials—they expect her to adopt all of their customs without giving any consideration to her own.

Cultural relativism also tells us that a custom that we personally find offensive is not necessarily immoral. Perhaps some of you who are parents were momentarily put off by the erotic dancer who entertains Lwaxana, Alexander, and the other "free spirits" at the end of the "mud bath" scene in "Cost of Living." Not that you have anything against erotic dancers or communal mud baths. It's just that the idea of an impressionable young boy lounging buck-naked with several equally nude adults might strike you as odd. Fair enough. But just because it's odd to you, a cultural relativist would say, doesn't necessarily make it wrong for everyone.

Which, in a sense, is basically what *Star Trek* is all about. Gene Roddenberry, a man who was very open-minded about the customs of different cultures, said so himself: "[By the 23rd century, we] will have learned to take a delight in the essential differences between men and between cultures. [We] will learn that differences and attitudes are a delight, part of life's exciting variety, not something to fear."*

FACTS VERSUS VALUES

Now, you might say, "Sure, some aspects of cultural relativism are a recurring theme on *Star Trek*. But does that make cultural relativism the basis of the ethics of *Star Trek*?" It would certainly appear to be. Perhaps the best way to find out for sure is to look at what cultural relativism really is, so that we can easily identify it when we see it.

According to James Rachels, a contemporary American ethicist, cultural relativism is a theory that makes six basic claims:

1. *Different societies have different moral codes.*
2. *There is no objective standard that can be used to judge one societal code better than another.*
3. *The moral code of our own society has no special status; it is merely one among many.*
4. *There is no "universal truth" in ethics—that is, there are no moral truths that hold for all peoples at all times.*
5. *The moral code of a society determines what is right within that society; that is, if the moral code of a society says that a certain action is right, then that action is right, at least within that society.*

---

*Stephen Whitfield and Gene Roddenberry, *The Making of "Star Trek"* (New York: Ballantine Books, 1968), p. 40.

6. *It is mere arrogance for us to try to judge the conduct of other peoples. We should adopt an attitude of tolerance toward the practices of other cultures.*

According to Rachels, these six propositions are independent of one another, in that some of them might be true even if others are false. Using "Cost of Living" as our model, let's see how each claim is important in not just understanding but also evaluating cultural relativism.

1. *Different societies have different moral codes.* We see at least three examples in this story alone: the Betazoids, with their unique wedding custom in which the bride appears nude; the Kostolains, with their rigid adherence to protocol, procedure, and ceremony; and the colony of free spirits, where no rules apply (other than the pursuit of happiness).

   It's important to note that the claim itself ("Different societies have different moral codes") is a *descriptive* statement— that is, a statement that addresses the facts without making any value judgments. When Lwaxana tells Deanna she's adapting to Kostolain custom because she knows Campio would not approve of a traditional Betazoid wedding, she's merely stating a fact about Campio to Deanna. Sociologists, anthropologists, psychologists, and others trained in the social sciences rely on descriptive statements because they provide important clues in learning how different people behave in a given society. Ethicists, on the other hand, use *prescriptive* statements to tell us what ought to be. (We use descriptive statements, too, but we'll get into that in a second.) Prescriptive statements are concerned not with facts but with values: "You ought to follow the Prime Directive." "A woman should never wear white shoes after Labor Day." "A Betazoid bride should always be nude at her own wedding ceremony." Going back to our "Cost of Living" example, it is

Deanna who assesses value to Lwaxana's statement, "Campio is from a different planet with different traditions...," by voicing concern over her mother's decision.

2. *There is no objective standard by which to judge one society's code better than another's.* That doesn't stop the Kostolains from trying, though. From the moment Campio meets Lwaxana aboard the *Enterprise*, he and his protocol master/flunky Erko do everything they can to impose their ways on the bride-to-be. When Lwaxana leans in to kiss her intended, she is halted by the outstretched hand of Erko ("We don't wish to be too familiar at this early juncture," he explains). Campio, to Lwaxana's surprise, agrees with his aide, explaining that it would be "unpardonable for us to simply abandon ourselves to the moment." Lwaxana then calls Campio by his first name, which Erko finds even more "unacceptable." He insists that Lwaxana address Campio by his proper title at all times, even after they are married.

3. *The moral code of our own society has no special status; it is merely one among many.* Let's say Klingon culture teaches that a child should never question his parents. That would in part explain why Worf bristles at the notion of entering into a parent-child contract, a course of action Deanna suggests in "Cost of Living" to help him teach his son, Alexander, the value of responsibility. (The warrior in him, accustomed to giving orders without resistance, probably has a lot to do with it, too.) Worf resists the idea because it goes against the grain of what he was taught as a child, and what he understands to be custom. However, as Deanna effectively tells him in this episode, there's more than one way to raise a child. If you want to foster a happy, healthy, mutually beneficial relationship with your child—or simply teach him how to pick up after himself—and what you're doing right now prevents you from attaining that goal, then perhaps you ought to try something else.

4. *There are no moral truths that hold for all peoples at all times.*
   Marriage may prevent loneliness, but it doesn't necessarily
   promise happiness, as Lwaxana (with a little help from
   young Alexander) ultimately finds out.

5. *The moral code of a society determines what is right within
   that society.* Again, this cuts to the basic conflict of "Cost of
   Living": while Deanna is troubled by Lwaxana's plans to
   marry a man she's never met, she's even more concerned
   by her mother's plans to abandon Betazoid custom by actually wearing a wedding dress. (One look at the gown, and
   it's certainly easy to understand why—at least, aestheti-
   cally speaking. The outfit the Kostolains provide—a staid,
   Victorian-looking garment—transforms the ordinarily viva-
   cious Lwaxana into Barbara Bush.)

   Other examples of this claim are illustrated in this
   episode. "Only those whose hearts are joyous may enter
   the colony of free spirits," Lwaxana explains to Alexander.
   Enforcing that rule (the only one, apparently, in a place
   where rules otherwise don't exist) is the guardian Wind
   Dancer, a disembodied multicolored harlequin's head
   encased in a blue bubble. Later in the story Worf and
   Deanna follow Lwaxana and Alexander into the colony.
   While Deanna slips through, the humorless Worf finds his
   way blocked (momentarily, at least) by the perceptive
   gatekeeper.

6. *It is arrogant to try to judge the conduct of other peoples. We
   should adopt an attitude of tolerance toward the practices of
   other cultures.* We see both extremes of this claim illustrated
   in the climactic wedding sequence. Lwaxana decides a marriage to Campio would be unacceptable once she realizes
   he expects to her to adhere completely to his customs without any regard to her own. To make sure he gets the message, she arrives at the wedding wearing nothing but a
   smile—as a traditional Betazoid bride would do. While

Campio and Erko stand predictably horrified ("This is infamous!" shrieks Erko as he shields Campio's eyes with his hand), the crew of the *Enterprise,* long familiar with the customs of diverse peoples, respect Lwaxana's nudity (and in the case of Commander Ryker, clearly admire it).

IS CULTURAL RELATIVISM LOGICAL?

Rachels' first claim, "Different societies have different codes," is certainly a theme common to many of *Star Trek*'s story lines. Could we therefore conclude it's also the basis of *Star Trek*'s ethics? Before we can, an ethicist would say, we must first subject the theory to rational scrutiny. We'd have to analyze all the arguments the theory poses and see if they hold up against any faulty reasoning. If they fly, then there's our answer. If they don't, we look elsewhere.

How would we determine whether a theory flies? By testing the logic of its arguments. This is where someone like Mr. Spock would come in. *Logic,* as we know, is the study of correct and incorrect reasoning; complete adherence to logic, of course, is the primary motivating factor in the Vulcan mind. Logic provides ethicists with a means of distinguishing good arguments from poor ones. In logic, an argument consists of two or more *propositions,* one of these propositions is claimed to follow from the other(s). The *conclusion* of an argument is the proposition that is affirmed or denied on the basis of the other propositions (also known as *premises*) in the argument.

Here's a classic example of an argument that Captain Kirk used to defeat a computer with a mind of its own in *TOS:* #53, "The Ultimate Computer":

All who commit murder must die. (*premise*)
The M-5 has committed murder. (*premise*)
The M-5 must die. (*conclusion*)

As you recall, the *Enterprise* agreed to participate in an ambitious experiment to determine whether a sophisticated multitronic computer, the M-5, could actually run a starship more efficiently than humans. Much to Kirk's chagrin, the answer at first appears to be a resounding yes. Eventually, however, the M-5 runs amok, attacking several starships, and killing numerous crewmen (including one member of the *Enterprise*). Efforts to unplug the M-5 are thwarted by the computer's self-generated force field, which prevents anyone from getting near it. Upon learning that the M-5 was patterned after not just the mind but the very conscience of its creator, Dr. Richard Daystrom, Kirk finally determines how to outwit the computer. Knowing that Daystrom is a man who abhors murder—and that, by extension, so should the M-5—Kirk uses the logic of the "All who commit murder must die" argument to convince the computer it should atone for the lives it took when it attacked the other starships. Recognizing the premise as something it inherently believes in (for its beliefs are based on those of its creator), the M-5 knows there can only be one course to follow. It immediately deactivates itself.

Cultural relativism also involves a certain form of argument, which Rachels dubs, appropriately enough, the "Cultural Differences Argument." Using the Betazoid wedding custom from "Cost of Living" as an example, this argument begins with the following descriptive statement:

> The Betazoids believe it is right for the bride to appear nude at her wedding, whereas the Kostolains believe it is right for the bride to wear a traditional gown at her wedding.

This statement is meant to provide support for accepting the conclusion, the prescriptive statement given below:

Therefore, whether a bride appears nude or clothed at her own wedding is neither objectively right nor objectively wrong. It is merely a matter of opinion, which varies from culture to culture.

If we generalized this argument, it would look something like this:

Different cultures have different moral codes. (*premise*)

Therefore, there is no objective "truth" in morality. Right and wrong are only matters of opinion, and opinions vary from culture to culture. (*conclusion*)

The problem with this argument is that it's invalid: the conclusion does not follow from the premise. (Or, as Mr. Spock would say, "It is not logical.") The premise concerns what people believe: Deanna believes her mother should honor Betazoid wedding custom, while Lwaxana believes she should adapt to Kostolain custom by wearing the dress. But the conclusion doesn't follow from that premise; it merely describes what is actually the case (different cultures have different ideas as to what a bride should wear at her own wedding ceremony).

What's the difference between a valid and an invalid argument? In a word, the valid arguments are the good ones, where the conclusion always follows from the premise(s). Once the M–5 realized it had committed murder, it knew it had to die. Invalid arguments are bad arguments, where the conclusion does not follow from the premise(s). It would have been a much different story (and *Star Trek* a much shorter series) had Kirk tried to outsmart the M-5 with, say, the Cultural Differences Argument. A sophisticated-thinking computer such as the M-5 would know that even if the premise were true, the conclusion might still be false. The argument is invalid because it tries to obtain a conclusion about morality merely from the fact that people disagree about it.

There's one other item we should consider. Unlike arguments, which are evaluated as valid or invalid, a single proposition can be evaluated as true or false. To an ethicist, truth and validity are two very different things. An argument can have a true statement yet still be invalid (that is, "illogical"). Here's an example:

All Vulcans have pointed ears. (*premise*)
Therefore, all Ferengi have large ears. (*conclusion*)

There's no logical way you can infer the conclusion "All Ferengi have large ears" solely from the statement "All Vulcans have pointed ears." Therefore, even though both the premise and the conclusion happen to be true, the argument is nonetheless invalid because the conclusion does not follow from the premise.

Consequently, when I point out that the Cultural Differences Argument is invalid, I'm not saying that the conclusion itself is false. What's right and wrong may very well vary from culture to culture. What I *am* saying is that this conclusion doesn't necessarily follow from the premise "Different cultures have different moral codes." The argument is therefore illogical. It doesn't prove anything.

THE POWER OF CONTRADICTION

As long as we're scrutinizing this thing . . . let's say the cultural relativists are right, and that there is no "universal truth" in ethics (Rachels' fourth claim, as you'll recall). That would mean there are no moral truths that hold for all peoples at all times, and that matters of right and wrong are relative to the culture in which we live. But if that's true, then isn't the very idea "there are no universal truths in ethics, therefore all our concepts of right and wrong are relative" itself a universal notion? Wouldn't that seem to fly in the face of cultural relativism to begin with? To put it another way, in 1995 Leonard Nimoy wrote a memoir called *I Am Spock*. At first blush, that's certainly a logical title, since the character of Mr. Spock in both the Original Series and the first six *Star Trek* movies is the role for which Nimoy is best known. And yet, twenty years earlier, Nimoy also published a book called *I Am Not Spock*.* Notwithstanding the fact that one's views about a particular topic can actually change as one grows older, the two titles of Nimoy's books are self-contradictory. Speaking strictly from a logical perspective, he cannot say he's Spock and also say he's not Spock—any more than a theory claiming "there are no universal notions" could itself be based on a universal notion.

Think about it. Cultural relativism can't possibly claim to be true in any objective sense since, according to its beliefs, there is no objective truth. Yet if cultural relativists argued that their theory is true in some objective sense, they'd be contradicting the very foundation that all concepts are relative. In other words, you can't have your cake and eat it, too. When you look outside your window, it can't be raining in front of your house and not be raining in front of your house at the same time. The notion that all concepts are relative, therefore, cannot be an exception to the rule "all concepts are relative" without entailing a self-contradiction.

So what's wrong with basing your theory on a contradiction? Well, it's sort of like embarking on a long drive thinking you have a full tank of gas, only to discover your gas gauge is

---

*In *I Am Not Spock* (Millbrae, Calif.: Celestial Arts, 1975), Nimoy voiced his concern over being typecast and denied "non-alien" roles in movies and TV in the early 1970s, on the heels of *Star Trek*'s emerging status as an international cult hit. However, by the time the actor wrote *I Am Spock* (New York: Hyperion, 1995), he had clearly come to grips with both his eternal identification with Spock and the impact that has had on his career.

defective. You may travel along fine for a while, but eventually you're going to run out of gas.

We've seen this illustrated time and again on *Star Trek*. The crew of the *Enterprise* often uses contradiction as a means of defeating androids and computers that are considerably less bright than the M-5. In "I, Mudd" (*TOS: #41*), for example, Kirk and his officers (along with intergalactic rogue Harry Mudd) use contradictory logic to escape imprisonment on an android-run planet. In one sequence, Spock tells android Alice-27 that he loves her, then immediately tells her android clone, the qualitatively identical Alice-210, that he hates her. The logic that one could both love and hate the same exact person confounds the Alices; they both shut down instantly. Meanwhile, Kirk and the others perform an elaborate pantomime before the rest of the androids. Harry tells Norman, the main android, that Scotty and McCoy have invisible explosives. Scotty and McCoy proceed to set off the "bombs," then act as though they were detonated. Only there is no explosion. This baffles Norman. Kirk and Harry, flanking Norman, then apply the coup de grâce. Harry tells Norman that he lied about the explosives. Kirk counters this by telling Norman, "Everything Harry tells you is a lie." Harry then says, "Now listen carefully, Norman. I am lying." Norman is now completely befuddled: "You say you are lying. But if everything you say is a lie, you are telling the truth. But you cannot tell the truth because everything you say is a lie. But you lie; you tell the truth."* As smoke drifts around his head, the discombobulated android soon goes out of commission, with the other androids following suit.

---

*The ancient Greeks first posed this logical paradox, known as the Liar's Paradox. A logical paradox is any chain of reasoning that uses only meaningful and consistent premises and commits no logical errors, yet nevertheless produces contradictory conclusions.

APPLYING CULTURAL RELATIVISM
TO *STAR TREK*

You can probably imagine why we'd want to avoid contradiction and inconsistency in our search for the ethical foundation of *Star Trek*. A moral theory, after all, strives to provide us with a standard by which we may rationally judge which actions are right and which actions are wrong, so it ought to be consistent.

We've seen that cultural relativism, in principle, is based on a contradiction. We haven't necessarily proven that it's also inconsistent. Let's assume, for argument's sake, that it isn't—that people who advocate cultural relativism are, indeed, consistent. What would that mean on a practical basis? Would societies that consistently practiced cultural relativism in their beliefs and actions be any different from what they are now? What impact would that have on the *Star Trek* universe?

According to Rachels, there are three consequences to applying cultural relativism on an everyday basis: (1) we can no longer criticize the customs of other societies; (2) we can no longer criticize the customs of our own society, since the very essence of cultural relativism claims that "whatever the culture thinks is right, is right for that culture"; and (3) it makes moral progress impossible. Again, using "Cost of Living" as our primary model, let's look at these consequences individually and see how they compare to the ethics of *Star Trek*.

1. *We can no longer criticize the customs of other societies.* This consequence is derived from the second, third, and sixth claims, respectively, of Rachels' theory: there is no objective standard that can be used to judge one societal code better than another; the moral code of our own society has no special status, but is merely one among many; and it is arrogant for us to try to judge the conduct of other peoples—we should tolerate their practices instead.

If these claims are true, both we and the *Star Trek* characters would have to stop condemning other cultures just because they are "different." If morality within a society is confined to the customs of that society, we'd have no grounds for judging the moral practices of another culture. If two cultures disagree about what is morally right but there is no disagreement about the facts, then there is no rational means for reaching agreement or continuing the discussion. What we'd have is a scenario very much like the sequence in "Cost of Living" where the episode's two story lines converge. At one point there are three separate conversations taking place simultaneously: Deanna and Worf confront Lwaxana about spiriting Alexander away from his scheduled family counseling appointment; Alexander wants Lwaxana to take him to the mud baths again, as she promised; Campio and Erko insist that Lwaxana be briefed on the details of the upcoming wedding. There's a lot of talking going on, but absolutely no communication.

Now, if we limited ourselves to not criticizing such customs as, say, what a bride wears (or rather, doesn't wear) at a traditional Betazoid wedding, that's one thing. But we can't do that—not if we're going to practice cultural relativism on a consistent basis. We'd have to accept and respect all customs and values of a particular society equally, whatever they happen to be.

But are customs pertaining to wedding ceremonies, dining etiquette, burial customs, and preferences in fashion and weather really on the same level as moral values such as honesty, justice, and courage? By identifying morality with custom, cultural relativists include behavior in the moral realm that is actually outside the scope of morality. If that's the case, not only would we have to stop criticizing the customs of other cultures, we wouldn't be able to criticize other, more violent practices either.

In "Patterns of Force" (*TOS: #52*), the *Enterprise* visits a planetary system containing an inner planet, Ekos, and an outer planet, Zeon, in order to find a lost researcher named John Gill. Kirk and Spock discover that the Ekosians have patterned their society after 20th-century Nazi Germany and are carrying out a policy of genocide against the citizens of Zeon. The Ekosians think they are right to wipe out the "Zeon pigs." But the Federation strongly opposes genocide. Does it follow, from the mere fact that the Ekosians and the Federation disagree, that there is no "objective truth" about genocide? As open-minded as it appears to be, the Federation finds this conclusion unacceptable. So do we, since we know from history that the actions of some societies, such as those of the Nazis, were absolutely wrong.

Yet if we and the Federation were consistent cultural relativists, neither we nor they could say that the genocide of the Zeons is wrong. Neither we nor the *Star Trek* characters could even affirm that a society tolerant of its neighboring planet is better than a society that seeks to annihilate a neighboring planet, since that would imply an objective standard of comparison. We could not criticize another culture's practice of genocide due to our belief that what cultures do is good only for them (Rachels' fifth claim). But let's say in our hearts we believe genocide is wrong. If the failure to condemn genocide does not seem right, then a central belief of cultural relativism is mistaken.

Restricting moral values to the conventions of specific cultural groups has another unfortunate effect—it forces us to yield to majority rule. Which leads us to Rachels' second consequence...

2. *We can no longer criticize the customs of our own society.* We would have no grounds for disagreeing with our own cul-

ture, since our culture is the source of our moral values. This stems from Rachels' fifth claim of cultural relativism: if the moral code of a society says that a certain action is right, then that action is right, at least within that society. The fact that Lwaxana decides to get married in the first place shows her inherent belief in the idea of marriage, at least as seen in Betazoid culture. As she explains to Alexander, people get married because they "want to spend the rest of their lives with someone." "They must have to like that person a lot," replies Alexander. "If you're young and lucky," says Lwaxana, "it'll be someone you like a lot. If you're older... or alone... and you can no longer pick and chose from what comes your way, you compromise. That keeps you from being afraid." Lwaxana therefore chooses marriage—even to a man she hasn't met—because she's afraid of growing old alone.

Now suppose you disagree with the rules of the culture in which you live. Cultural relativism's test for determining what is right and what is wrong is that you ask whether the action is in accordance with the customs of your culture at this point in history. Imagine Rom, the brother of the Ferengi owner of the gambling casino on *Deep Space Nine,* questioning whether Ferenginar's policy of preventing females from owning property or wearing clothes and keeping them homebound, doing household chores, and tending to the males' every need (including chewing their food until tender) is morally correct. If he were a cultural relativist, all he'd have to do is ask whether this policy conforms to Ferenginar's moral code— if it does, then the policy is morally correct and he would be wrong to disagree. If he were a consistent cultural relativist, he would therefore have to treat his Bajoran wife, Leeta, in the customary Ferenginar way. (Of course, their relationship would face some very rocky times ahead.)

Happily for their marriage, Rom is not a cultural relativist: he treats Leeta in a way that transcends the standards of Ferengi culture. Neither, for that matter, is Lwaxana Troi. When she realizes that a marriage to Campio would be one in which she would have to do all the compromising, she decides it's far better to be alone yet happy than married and miserable.

As we see from both these examples, cultural relativism can become oppressive since it does not need to offer any rational justification for imposing a particular cultural value on people. If it is the majority practice of a society, cultural relativism may end up demanding conformity in ideology, speech, and dress—an implication completely contrary to the individualism celebrated in *Star Trek*.*

3. Finally, let's consider what the cultural relativist would say about the possibility of moral progress. Since cultural relativism makes it impossible to disagree with any practices that are in effect, the idea of moral progress is out of the question. After all, to progress is to move forward, and to move forward involves change. And why would anyone want to change a society's value structure if that structure cannot be judged as deficient? As Commander Chakotay put it in "Distant Origin" (*VGR:* #65), "I know from the history of my own planet that change is difficult. New ideas are often greeted with skepticism... even fear. But some-

---

*Of course, sometimes yielding to majority rule can be a good thing, as "Cost of Living" also illustrates in a humorous way. The episode is, after all, about compromise. Sometimes we must meet the other side on their ground in order to reach a mutual understanding, as we see when Deanna and Worf join Lwaxana and Alexander in a communal mud bath in the final scene of the show. Deanna clearly revels in giving in to the pleasure of the moment, much as her mother would. While Worf doesn't understand that concept as easily ("You're just supposed to sit here?"), his presence in the tub serves a greater purpose: it shows Alexander if Dad can make the effort to compromise, so can he.

times those ideas are accepted . . . and when they are, progress is made . . . eyes are opened."

Because not of all of us are cultural relativists, because some of us have thought our society was flawed and actually tried to change it, moral progress has occurred. Throughout time, many societies have evolved in ways that constitute not just differences but improvements. These improvements can be explained mainly in terms of a progressive recognition of superior values. If our conceptions of right and wrong were based solely on our culture's practices, it would be pretty hard to account for the ethical advances of both our current civilization and the Federation. Even the civilization of recent centuries is generally higher in ethical character than that of earlier ages. Slavery has been virtually abolished. Rules of war have been adopted so that when one nation vanquishes another, the women and children are not murdered or taken as spoils. Human sacrifice is no longer practiced as a religious ritual. Racial segregation is no longer the norm. All of which, most would agree, are good things, and that we're better for it. None of these things would have come about were it not for those who had the courage to question the wisdom of the prevailing standards and to change the status quo in accordance with their vision of a better society. Instead of encouraging others to be more "culture-retentive," most social reformers insist that cultural rules are morally binding only when they respect and nurture human dignity or, more broadly, all sentient life. In so doing, social reformers claim that they are judging their culture against a standard of the ideal society that transcends culture.

THE POWER OF TRUTH

Now that we've carefully looked at this theory, we can finally ask the $64,000 question: Does *Star Trek* embrace cultural relativism? One prominent Vulcan principle, much esteemed in the series, certainly suggests that it does. The cornerstone of Vulcan philosophy is Infinite Diversity in Infinite Combinations, referred to by its acronym, IDIC. Because IDIC teaches acceptance and respect of other cultures, it would seem at first to be the Vulcan equivalent of cultural relativism.

Yet the meaning of IDIC goes far beyond that. A union of a plain circle and triangle forming a beautiful gemstone in the middle, the IDIC symbol (designed by Gene Roddenberry himself, and first worn by Spock in *TOS:* #62, "Is There in Truth No Beauty?") represents a Vulcan belief that beauty, growth, and progress result from the union of the unlike. The idea is that any two diverse things can come together to create truth. The circle represents things such as woman, nature, and infinity, with the triangle representing their diametric opposites (man, art, and the finite). The brotherhood of man is an ideal based on learning to delight in our essential differences, as well as recognizing our similarities. Only then can we know truth. If a culture's beliefs detract from the truth, according to IDIC, those beliefs must ultimately be rejected.

Truth is one value *Star Trek* holds dear. Consider "For the World Is Hollow and I Have Touched the Sky" (*TOS:* #65), wherein Kirk, Spock, and McCoy beam aboard an asteroid/spaceship after discovering that it consists of a hollow outer shell with an inner core. Upon their arrival they are greeted by the priestess Natira. Our heroes soon learn that the inhabitants of the asteroid/spaceship worship a computer known as the "Oracle" and are blithely unaware of the true nature of their world. When the Oracle turns destructive, Kirk tells Natira that her planet is actually a spaceship. When Natira asks the Oracle for the truth, the computer tells her that there is a different truth for the people of her world than there is for others. Assuming that universal truth exists, Natira asks, "Is truth not truth for all?" Indeed it is, and by the end of the episode, Natira finds that truth shattering her preconceptions. (Truth often has a funny way of doing that.) Clearly, though, Natira's plaintive questions about truth reflect the perspective of *Star Trek*.

Now, you might ask, doesn't IDIC, like cultural relativism, promote an understanding and appreciation of other cultures? Sure, it does. But there's an important distinction: IDIC does not tolerate cultural values that oppose diversity. For instance, Spock urged an attack on a Romulan warbird in "Balance of Terror" (*TOS:* #9) because it was the logical thing to do. IDIC does not promote tolerance of any kind of cultural belief simply out of respect for a different culture. Recognizing that there are and should be limits to toleration, IDIC suggests an objective standard of morality. This, of course, runs completely counter to Rachels' second claim, upon which the central argument of cultural relativism is based ("There is no objective standard by which to judge one society's code better than another"). Though the Prime Directive strictly forbids Kirk from intervening in the evolution or politics of other cultures, as we all know, sometimes he does so anyway.* In "The Return of the Archons" (*TOS:* #22), he destroys a culture-controlling computer because it does not allow human beings to exercise their free will. In "A Taste of Armageddon" (*TOS:* #23), two planets fight a computer-controlled war in which people obediently go into disintegrators

---

*Many episodes of the original *Star Trek* made covert references to the Vietnam War, insisting that our country had no business interfering in the internal affairs of other nations. At the same time, it cleverly avoided being subversive not only by having Kirk occasionally intervene, but by setting the proceedings in faraway outer space. With that in mind, it's interesting to note that on the day "A Taste of Armageddon" first aired in the United States (February 23, 1967), the presence of U.S. troops in South Vietnam increased to over 400,000. Source: *www.scifi.com/startrek/*

when they are ordered to do so; Kirk again destroys this computer to show the combatants the true horror of their carnage. In "The Cloud Minders" (*TOS:* #74), Kirk forces the elite, who live in a city floating in the sky far above the bleak surface of their planet, to experience the way their manual laborers live.

Time and again, *Star Trek* shows us that any culture can be held up to universal ethical standards. Genocide is morally wrong. Exploitation is morally wrong. Racism is morally wrong. Tyranny is morally wrong. Slavery is morally wrong. Subsequent episodes continue along the same theme, illustrating that cultures promoting sexism, or that are indifferent to homelessness, or that encourage terrorist solutions, or that dump toxic waste in populated areas, are cultures that should change their ways. That is clearly not an ideology that advocates cultural relativism.

AND IF MORALITY ISN'T RELATIVE...

Generally, cultural relativism is a theory with enormous practical and theoretical problems. It is illogical, contradictory, and fails to offer an explanation of social progress. Because of these inherent problems, it seems clear that culture alone cannot form the basis for a justifiable ethical theory.

But if cultural customs cannot provide the foundation for ethics, particularly the ethics of *Star Trek*, where can a foundation be found? Some people maintain that everything a person needs to know to live an ethical life can be found in religious teachings. They believe that religion alone provides all the answers to whatever perplexities and hurdles we may encounter along the path (or en route to an extraterrestrial destination) of life. They also suggest that ethics, as distinct from religious teachings, is not needed, as it adds nothing to what religion already provides.

What do you think? Do the *Star Trek* characters need to follow the dictates of religion in order to act ethically? Let's find out in our next chapter.

CHAPTER 2

IS RELIGION
ALONE THE BASIS
OF ETHICS?

"Accession"
DS9: Episode 89
Stardate: Unknown
Original Air Date: Week of February 26, 1996

The sole passenger of a spacecraft that emerges from the
wormhole is none other than Akorem Laan, the legendary
Bajoran poet of the 22nd century. Akorem tells Captain
Sisko and Major Kira that he had an accident in space and
was rescued by the ancient Bajoran Prophets. Based on his
understanding of Bajoran scriptures, this leads Akorem to
believe he was chosen to be the Emissary.* Sisko is more

---

*The Emissary is the equivalent of Moses or the Messiah in the Bajoran reli-
gion. According to Michael Okuda and Denise Okuda, *The "Star Trek" Encyclopedia,* 2nd ed. (New York: Pocket Books, 1997), p. 134, the Emissary is the person
prophesied to save the Bajoran people and unite the planet by finding the mysterious Celestial Temple. When Sisko stumbled onto the Bajoran wormhole in
DS9's pilot episode ("Emissary"), he became in the eyes of the Bajoran people
their long-awaited Emissary. Although Sisko rejected the notion, his Starfleet
duties demanded that he nonetheless respect Bajoran beliefs and perform the
duties of the venerated office.

than willing to relinquish his post, since he never accepted the assumption that he was the Emissary to begin with. Sisko quickly regrets his decision, however, once Akorem orders the Bajoran people to return to the D'jarras—a caste system that dictates social status as well as which occupation its members may hold. Among other things, this means that Kira, whose family belonged to the artist D'jarra, must give up her military career and take up an artist's life. Akorem believes returning to the D'jarras is the only way for the Bajorans "to reclaim what we were and follow the paths the Prophets laid out for us." Though Kira has neither the desire nor aptitude to be an artist, her devout faith binds her to follow the word of the Emissary. Meanwhile, Sisko knows Akorem's decree will also have disastrous ramifications for the Bajoran people as a whole—because the Federation charter prohibits caste-based discrimination, it will ultimately cost them member-ship in the Federation. Yet as a Starfleet officer, he is forbidden to interfere.

"Accession" shows us that when the worlds of religion and ethics collide, the results can be polarizing—not just in terms of dividing people into sects (as we see with the D'jarra system), but also by causing inner turmoil in the individual. If you'd spent your entire life in the military (or whatever your chosen craft happens to be), and someone like Akorem popped in from out of nowhere and said, "Oh, by the way, you've been wrong all this time, this is what you really should be doing with your life..."—and you acknowledged his authority but didn't agree with what he believed you ought to be doing—chances are you'd be as devastated as Kira was. Compounding the problem even more is the fact that your faith doesn't allow you room for questioning. You have to put yourself in his hands and hope to God he's right.

That's a tough choice to make: do you follow your religion with all your heart, or do you follow your principles? Isn't it possible somehow to do both? If it isn't, that would suggest that religion and ethics must be distinct.

The problem is, a lot of people think that religion and ethics are one and the same. They're right in the sense that many of the ethical beliefs we hold do, indeed, have their roots in religion. A case in point: whether we learned about them by way of church, school, or Charlton Heston, most of us know what the Ten Commandments are. While some may debate the morality of coveting and adultery, most of us would agree that honoring one's mother and father is a good thing to do. And certainly, given the laws against murder in most countries (not to mention overall human decency and compassion), most would agree that "not killing" is fundamentally right, too.

Consequently, many people tend to believe that religion alone is the basis for ethics. Using "Accession" as our primary source, we'll take a hard look at this pervasive belief and what it means, particularly in terms of the ethics of *Star Trek*. Along the way we'll introduce the philosophy of Plato, and how he specifically handles the issues of religion and morality in his dialogue *Euthyphro*. We'll also see how "Accession" in many ways closely resembles this classic discourse, thematically as well as structurally. In both stories, two characters take opposite sides of the following ethical issue: Do moral codes depend entirely on the divine will, or do they somehow exist independently of it?

FAITH AND INTERPRETATION

Let's face it. If someone like Akorem were to go on CNN live and say he had been dropped out of the sky to provide spiritual guidance to the people of the United States, we might be a little skeptical. While our country was ostensibly founded on

Christian principles, we also have separation of church and state. As a people, we just aren't defined by a sense of religious destiny—certainly not in the same way faith defines Bajoran society.

The Bajorans, as we know, are a deeply spiritual people, almost childlike in their trust and dependence upon their religious leaders. The promise of an Emissary is a critical aspect of their faith; it gave them the strength to survive the Cardassian oppression, as "In the Hands of the Prophets" (*DS9: #20*) previously established. As Kira explains to Sisko in "Accession," the Bajorans would do anything their Emissary tells them to do. Thus they accept Akorem at his word when he exhorts them, at the top of the show, to return to their D'jarras.

According to Bajoran scriptures, the Prophets will name their Emissary by "calling him to them." It is also written that the Emissary will discover the wormhole and that the Prophets will "give him back his life." Given the circumstances of his bizarre encounter in space, it's not surprising that Akorem, a poet and a renowned holy man of his time, would interpret his near-death experience and perceived visitation to mean that he is, indeed, the Emissary. Given Sisko's steadfast disbelief in the Bajoran religion (and, by extension, the Bajoran people's perception of him as their Emissary), it's also not surprising that he accepts Akorem's claim so readily. Though he ordinarily wouldn't read the Bajoran texts that literally (if, indeed, at all), Sisko is perfectly willing to make an exception in this case. Why? Because Akorem's interpretation happens to provide the Deep Space Nine commander with a convenient way out of a responsibility that he thought was mislaid and, consequently, never really wanted in the first place.

The problem with interpretations, particularly when it comes to religious scriptures, is that they're, well, subject to interpretation. We'll address that issue in due time. For now, suffice it to say, certain facets of faith (be it Buddhist, Christian,

Muslim, Jewish, or Bajoran) are hard to comprehend. Kira Nerys is as devout a Bajoran as you'll find, but even she struggles with Akorem's decree to return to the D'jarras. A soldier since she was twelve years old, she knows no other life. Nor, for that matter, does she desire any other. But Kira also knows that if her faith says to put her trust in the Emissary, and the Emissary tells her to abandon her career and become an artist (even though, as we see elsewhere in the episode, she's clearly all thumbs when it comes to sculpture), then ultimately that's what she must do. "Sure, I have some questions," she admits to Sisko. "But it's not our place to question the Emissary. We have to have faith that [Akorem] is guiding us toward something."

If the idea of blind faith—faith without reasoning—is hard to comprehend even for those who ascribe to it, imagine how it must seem for those who don't. Observing Kira's rapt attention to Akorem during his first public address as Emissary, Security Chief Odo doesn't understand how she and the other Bajorans can so readily accept this mysterious visitor as their spiritual leader. After all, he reminds her, "Just two days ago, you believed Sisko was the Emissary."

"But Sisko made it clear that he wanted to step aside," says Kira.

"Does this mean he really never was the Emissary?" asks Odo.

"No," says Kira.

This response puzzles the Spock-like Odo. "But they can't both be," he replies. "I don't mean to be difficult, Major, but your faith has apparently led you to a contradiction."

"I don't see how it's a contradiction."

Again, Odo doesn't understand.

"That's the thing about faith," says Kira. "If you don't have it, you can't understand, and if you do, no explanation is necessary."

THE PARALLEL OF THE *EUTHYPHRO*

This exchange on faith closely parallels Plato's discourse on piety in the *Euthyphro*. The dialogue takes place shortly before Socrates' trial and execution in 399 B.C. Socrates is at the department that prosecutes religious offenses to learn the nature of the charges against him. Here he meets Euthyphro, a religious fanatic who claims to have knowledge of the gods not available to anyone else. Like Akorem in "Accession," Euthyphro claims that he alone knows what the will of the gods truly is.

Euthyphro is at the same department to bring charges of murder against his father, a rich landowner, for causing the death of a slave who had murdered another slave in a brawl. Euthyphro believes wholeheartedly that prosecuting his father for this murder is the only pious or holy thing to do. This, for Socrates, begs the question: does Euthyphro really know the nature of piety? After all, if you're going to accuse your father of murder, and then justify yourself by claiming your actions are pious, you ought to know what piety is. This isn't too much for Socrates to ask, considering he himself has been charged with impiety—a crime so serious in ancient Greece, it could (and, ultimately, would) cost him his life.

Euthyphro tells Socrates that piety is doing precisely what he is doing—prosecuting a wrongdoer for murder, whether he is your father or anyone else. Euthyphro's answer certainly has a great deal of merit to it. In attempting to give the right response to moral issues, we should strive to avoid unquestioned favoritism, lest we risk having our judgment impeded by bias and one-sidedness. From a rational point of view, no one is born more important than anyone else. Logically speaking (as Mr. Spock might say), we should therefore never regard ourselves, our parents, or our friends as being more privileged than anyone else.

Rather than treating a particular group or individual with favoritism, ethics requires that we treat everyone impartially. Besides the fact it will likely cost Bajor membership in the Federation, the main reason Sisko objects to restoring the caste system is that it automatically judges some people as more privileged than others. He sees this firsthand in the commissary when a Bajoran woman, upon seeing Kira and realizing there are no empty chairs left, feels compelled to offer her seat, even though she has not yet finished her meal. Her rationale? Because she belongs to a D'jarra that ranks below Kira's, she must therefore acquiesce to her. Sensing Kira's discomfort with the woman's actions, Sisko tells the major that when he was first promoted to lieutenant, "it took me a while to get used to being called 'Sir' by friends of mine who were still ensigns." But that's different, says Kira: "At least you earned the right to be treated with respect. I haven't done anything."

Impartiality is central to the formal principle of justice, which holds that justice is the similar treatment of similar individuals, while injustice is dissimilar treatment. As Odo observes in "Necessary Evil" (*DS9: #28*), "There's no room in justice for loyalty or friendship or love.... Justice, as the humans like to say, is blind."* Failure to comply with the formal principle of justice is a symptom of prejudice, a rational flaw that must be recognized and corrected if we are to approach ethics in the right way. In short, we should not treat one individual differently from another when there's no good reason to do so.

Despite the merits of Euthyphro's response, it doesn't really answer the question. Socrates doesn't want an example of piety but rather a definition of it. Like Odo, he doesn't mean

---

*The statue representing Justice as a woman holding a scale depicts her as blindfolded. As the statue suggests, it is an essential feature of justice to avoid partiality.

to be difficult—he just knows that for us to know a concept, recognizing examples of it isn't enough. We need to know the meaning of a concept before we can identify it. If the meaning of the concept we're discussing (be it piety or the Prime Directive) is not clear, the result will almost certainly be confusion. And if we're not clear on the concept, we may act indecisively—or worse yet, incorrectly—at the moment of truth. Therefore, Socrates explains to Euthyphro, we need a definition of piety so that we can use it to determine whether prosecuting your father for murder is indeed pious or impious.

DOES MORALITY EXIST BECAUSE OF THE DIVINE?

Understanding this distinction, Euthyphro tries again: "What is loved by the gods is pious, and what they hate is impious." Good answer, except that Euthyphro overlooks the fact that the gods of ancient Greece constantly disagreed with each other. For example, Hera, the goddess of marriage, condemned Paris, the son of Priam, for kidnapping Helen, wife of Menelaus, and carrying her off to the walled city of Troy—the act that eventually triggered the Trojan War. On the other hand, Aphrodite, the goddess of love and beauty, saw Paris' actions as a dramatic act of passion, so she thought it was just dandy! By Euthyphro's definition, Paris' act would be both pious and impious. That, points out Socrates, is a contradiction, and a contradiction by definition cannot possibly be true. As we discussed in Chapter 1, base a theory or a definition on a contradiction, and you're asking for trouble. No matter how you slice it, you can't resolve it. The longer you try, the more likely you'll end up like Norman the android in "I, Mudd" (*TOS:* #41).

Undaunted, Euthyphro comes up with a third definition of piety. Only this time, in order to avoid contradictory logic, he defines it as "what all the gods love." The emphasis is on the word "all," so that only those actions upon which the gods agree are included in this new definition. Yet even with this proviso, there's still a huge philosophical gap between Socrates and Euthyphro. Which brings us to the key ethical question raised in both the dialogue and "Accession": Are "good" and "bad" determined solely by what pleases the gods, or are they concepts that exist even if the gods do not?

If the existence of morality depends entirely on divine approval, that would mean our actions are right or wrong only because a divinity desires us to do them or not to do them. This is the stance taken by Euthyphro in the dialogue, and Akorem in "Accession." Historically, there are those who have held that if God had willed it, two plus two could have easily equaled five, and if God had commanded "Thou shalt kill," killing would be right. That would make our actions arbitrary — or at least subject to interpretation. A divinity could just as easily have wished us to act differently. Had Akorem known a Bajor other than the caste-based society of his native 22nd century, chances are he, too, might have interpreted the message of the Prophets differently.

OR IS THERE SOMETHING ABOUT MORALITY...?

On the other hand, if moral codes are recognized by the divine as right or wrong, it stands to reason that a divinity would want us to do right because it knows what is right. For instance, God recognizes that honesty is better than dishonesty, and so He commands us to be honest. He realizes that killing is wrong, and so He commands us not to kill. In this case, what God (or Buddha, or Allah, or whatever you might call your divinity) commands is *not* arbitrary, but rather the result of knowing what is good. That implies a standard of morality that is somehow independent of God's will. Perhaps that is the reason for His commanding or not commanding a particular action. This is where Socrates stands in the *Euthyphro,* and Sisko in "Accession."

Now, suppose you accept Euthyphro's definition of piety, that what all the gods love is pious and what they all hate is impious. The question remains whether it is this love of the gods that explains why it is good to be pious. If it is, then some behavior is pious simply because it pleases all of the gods. That would mean if the gods (or in the case of "Accession," the Bajoran Prophets) feel a caste system is the best way for us to live, then we should "follow the D'jarras with our heart"—even if we end up killing each other as we implement them.

Clearly, Socrates (and Sisko, for that matter) would say, there's something wrong with this picture.

Unlike Euthyphro, Socrates insists that there are reasons for things being the way they are. There must be something about the pious act itself that accounts for why the gods love it. However, just as Euthyphro reaches the point where he might actually learn something, he abruptly brings the dialogue to an end—just as Kira more or less ends her conversation with Odo after he brings out the contradiction on faith. (Plato may have been a great thinker, but he would have made a lousy dramatist.)

WHERE PLATO FAILS, *STAR TREK* PREVAILS

Fortunately for us, whenever the *Star Trek* writers presented our heroes with an ethical predicament, they always showed us how they resolved it. In the case of "Accession," once Sisko realizes the D'jarras will ultimately cost Bajor membership in the Federation, he knows he has failed the Bajoran people and immediately regrets his decision to abdicate. What's worse, as a Federation officer sworn not to interfere in the normal development of alien life and societies, he knows that, strictly speaking, there's nothing he can do to change it.

Fortunately for Sisko, he also knows that "if a culture is tested and found wanting in the eyes of a starship [commander], he may make changes as he feels necessary." That, as noted *TOS* scriptwriter/historian David Gerrold once put it, is one of *Star Trek*'s primary "subvocal messages."* For an officer in the tradition of James T. Kirk, this means two important things: (1) a Starfleet commander has extraordinarily broad powers over not just the lives of his own crew but the activities of all other peoples he encounters; and (2) even the Prime Directive is open to interpretation.†

In the case of "Accession," when an overzealous monk's adherence to Akorem's teachings results in the murder of an innocent man, Sisko realizes that he must now take action. Just as Socrates had challenged Euthyphro's claim to be a religious expert, Sisko challenges Akorem's claim to be the Emissary. The two men journey inside the wormhole, where they state their respective cases before the Bajoran Prophets themselves. Though Akorem appeals to the ancient texts as proof of his claim, the Prophets, much to his surprise, tell him he got it all wrong. They sent him 200 years into the future to lead them to the true Emissary: Sisko himself. (Talk about *irony*.) What the

---

*David Gerrold, *The World of "Star Trek,"* 2nd ed. (New York: Bluejay Books, 1984), p. 159. Gerrold penned the classic "The Trouble with Tribbles" (*TOS: #42*), and cowrote the original story for "The Cloud Minders" (*TOS: #74*).
†Ibid., pp. 147–48; cf. Stephen Whitfield and Gene Roddenberry, *The Making of "Star Trek,"* (New York: Ballantine Books, 1968), p. 215. Speaking from the perspective of a *Star Trek* writer, Gerrold describes the Prime Directive as a "wise, often troublesome rule" that was to be "more honored in the breach than otherwise . . . . The Prime Directive was a great idea, but it's also a bloody nuisance [because] it keeps the *Enterprise* from being a cosmic meddler, and that's too much of a limitation on the format. It keeps Kirk [and, by extension, Picard, Sisko, and Janeway] from being a moralist because he can no longer say, 'This is right and wrong . . . .' The Prime Directive is a very idealistic rule, but it keeps getting in the way of the story. Therefore, it has to be disregarded [by the writer]. Regularly."

Prophets had foretold long before—that is, the notion that they "will give [the Emissary] back his life"—was now finally fulfilled. Only instead of saving Sisko from death, thus "giving back" his physical life (which is how most of us probably would have interpreted that line of scripture), the Prophets gave Sisko back his "life" as the Emissary to the Bajoran people. This time, Sisko not only accepts his responsibility, he embraces it. As a result of this profound experience, he comes away believing in the Bajoran faith for the first time.

RELIGION AND *STAR TREK*

Both "Accession" and the *Euthyphro* remind us that there may be times in life when matters of faith clash with matters of ethics. If your ethical principles demand that life is sacred, yet your religious leaders enjoin you to fight a holy war, what would you do? If your religion suddenly mandates that your best friend's caste, race, or sex is beneath you, yet you believe we're all created equal, how do you act?

Star Trek would say that if you can work out a resolution that compromises neither your religious nor your ethical beliefs, then by all means do so. By the end of "Accession," we're left with the impression that Sisko, despite his newfound acceptance of Bajoranism, will temper his spiritual leadership with reason. However, if your religious leaders push the issue and demand strict, uncontested allegiance to their teachings, then reason must assert itself—otherwise, as we know from our own experience, the consequences can be tragic. The mass suicides of the People's Temple worshipers in 1978, as well as those of the Heaven's Gate cult in 1997,*

---

*There was an unfortunate link to *Star Trek* in the Heaven's Gate tragedy. One of the cult members was Donald Nichols, the brother of Nichelle Nichols, Lieutenant Uhura on the Original Series.

came about because of unquestioned adherence to one man.

Which goes to show that even if religion (and therefore religious scriptures) alone is the basis for ethics, there's still the problem of interpretation. The Bible, for example, certainly has no shortage of ideas on how we ought to live—so many, in fact, that some flat out contradict each other. Then there's the matter of biblical language, rich in metaphors and hyperbole that reflect the wonderful storytelling techniques of ancient oral tradition. When the Book of Genesis says that Noah was 600 years old at the time he built the Ark, or that it rained for 40 days and 40 nights, those aren't details to be taken literally; rather, they are colorful ways of saying Noah was a really old man, and that it rained for a really long time. The details are dramatized in order to illustrate a greater truth.

Nonetheless, there are those who insist on interpreting the Bible literally. "There will always be fundamentalism and the religious right," observed Gene Roddenberry in 1991. "There will always be people who are so mean-spirited and such limited thinkers [in their religious beliefs]...that nothing else in their limited concept can explain what the existence of a god can."* In light of these comments, one suspects Roddenberry, had he lived to see it, would have particularly liked "Accession." The biggest problem with literal interpretation of scripture, as the episode clearly shows, is that even the most learned of the learned is still capable of getting it wrong.

Moreover, if we go back to the point Socrates makes at the end of the dialogue, we can say divine beings do love morality not because they made it up, but because they recognize some

---

*David Alexander, "Interview with Gene Roddenberry: Writer, Producer, Philosopher, Humanist." Copyright © 1991 and 1998 by David Alexander. All rights reserved. The full text of this 36-page interview, which was originally published in the March/April 1991 issue of *The Humanist,* is available at *www.philosophysphere.com/humanist.html.* The quote referenced herein appears on p. 16 of the on-line version.

essential quality about it that they know to be good. While that may not exactly tell us what morality is (or where it comes from, for that matter), it strongly suggests that the source of morality is not religion itself. In other words, if religion as we know it disappeared entirely from the face of the earth, there would still be ethical principles for us to live by.

The fact is, given Roddenberry's longtime disdain for all kinds of organized religion, it's highly unlikely that religion would be the ethical foundation of *Star Trek* in the first place. "Religion was so full of inconsistencies that I could see no point in arguing each inconsistency out," he told David Alexander in 1991. "I was born into a supernatural world in which my family usually said, 'That is because God willed it,' or gave some other supernatural explanations for what happened. When you confront those statements on their own, they just don't make sense. They are clearly wrong. You need a certain amount of proof to accept anything, and that proof was not forthcoming [from religion alone] to support those statements."*

Still, despite his overall contempt for religious sects and unreasoned adherence to their teachings, one also suspects Roddenberry would have been very saddened by the Heaven's Gate tragedy (which, ironically, occurred only about a year after the day "Accession" was first broadcast). Though by all accounts, the cult members were avid viewers of *Trek*, their final action clearly flew in the face of its creator's underlying message: that only with critical thinking can we solve the problems facing us. For Roddenberry, the only way to prevent fundamentalism and other forms of unreasoned thinking from spreading was education. "Unless we have an educated populace, there's no telling what may come along," he said in 1991. "The pressures of life are so great that a certain percentage of all those uneducated people will come up with strange ideas—strange, violent ideas.

---

*Ibid., p. 5.

They seem to have good answers for all of our problems. I don't think life's problems are such that we have to rely on simplistic answers instead of thinking things through."*

So, if neither culture nor religion would be expected to addresss the ethics we see reflected in *Star Trek*, perhaps we should simply rely on the judgment of our political leaders and lawmakers to guide us in the right direction. But what if our leaders turn out to be morally corrupt? Where do we go from there? Plato had some ideas about that, too. We'll take a look at how he addressed these questions in our next chapter—and along the way, we'll emerge with our first suitable candidate for *Trek*'s ethical foundation.

---

*Ibid., p. 16.

PART TWO

ANCIENT GREEK AND ROMAN MORALITY IN THE STAR TREK FUTURE

"Search your most distant memories, those of the thousands of years that have passed . . . and I am there. Your fathers knew me and your fathers' fathers. I am Apollo."

"Who Mourns for Adonais?"

JUSTICE IN
A SAVAGE ARENA

"The Savage Curtain"
TOS: Episode 77
Stardate: 5906.4
Original Air Date: March 7, 1969

*Wishing to understand the human concepts of good and evil,
Yarnek,* a rock creature from the planet Excalbia, drafts an
unsuspecting Kirk and Spock into participating in a dramatic
experiment. Using a replica of Kirk's longtime personal hero
Abraham Lincoln, the creature lures the officers onto the
surface of the planet. There they encounter a likeness of
Surak (the revered man of peace and logic who founded Vulcan philosophy), as well as four of the wickedest figures in
history: Genghis Khan, Kahless the Klingon, Zora (a nefari-*

---

*According to Michael Okuda and Denise Okuda, *The "Star Trek" Encyclopedia*
2nd ed. (New York: Pocket Books, 1997), p. 570, the final shooting script for
"The Savage Curtain" identifies the rock creature as Yarnek, so I will use this
name for purposes of this chapter. However, as the *Encyclopedia* also indicates,
for some reason when the script was filmed, Yarnek's name was never actually
mentioned—nor was it ever dubbed into the episode that was ultimately broadcast. The syndicated and home video versions of "The Savage Curtain" corrobo-
rate this. Therefore, technically speaking, the talking rock has no name.

ous scientist who conducted cruel experiments on the body chemistries of life-forms on the planet Tiburon), and 21st-century genocidal warmonger Colonel Green. *The Excalbians want Kirk, Spock, Lincoln, and Surak to battle the four villains to demonstrate which, indeed, is mightier: good or evil. To give Kirk cause to fight, the Excalbians rig the* Enterprise *to blow up in four hours if "good" doesn't triumph. Though Kirk is certain his opponents are also illusions, does he dare risk the lives of his crew in order to prove it?*

"Arena"
TOS: Episode 19
Stardate: 3045.6
Original Air Date: January 19, 1967

Kirk wages battle against an alien vessel after it attacks an Earth colony at Cestus III for no apparent reason. The confrontation is cut short by the Metrons—advanced, powerful life-forms who are clearly disgusted by the "inherent violent tendencies" of the two combatants. In order to put an end to the conflict (and protect their space in the process), the Metrons transport Kirk and the commanding officer of the other ship to an artificial planetoid. There, using no other weapons but their own brute strength and ingenuity, the two captains must fight to the death. Though Kirk manages to subdue his opponent (a large, immensely strong reptilian being known as the Gorn), he agonizes over killing him outright upon realizing the Gorn may, indeed, have been justified in attacking Cestus III. But Kirk also knows that, given the rules of the contest, there can be only one survivor—whoever loses will die, along with the entire crew of his ship. Under these circumstances, showing the Gorn mercy might still prove fatal.

All right, I know what you're thinking. How could I put "Arena," one of the most gripping, intensely acted, well-written episodes of the Original Series, in the same league as "The Savage Curtain," admittedly one of the silliest? Other than the similarity in story lines, what on earth could these two shows possibly have in common?

Well, if you look at them strictly in terms of the ethical issues they discuss, quite a bit, as a matter of fact. For one thing, both episodes ask whether virtue, in and of itself, can be recognized among individuals from distinctly different cultures, galaxies, or even periods of time. This, essentially, is the same question Plato raised nearly 30 centuries ago in what is his best-known dialogue, *The Republic*. In fact, forget about the concept of Abraham Lincoln floating about in outer space (not to mention the sight of Captain Kirk splitting his pants while going *mano a mano* with Colonel Green), and you'll find that the premise of "The Savage Curtain" is particularly analogous to that of the debate between Socrates and Thrasymachus in *The Republic*. Granted, the semantics may be different—Socrates and Thrasymachus talked more about justice than goodness.* But when you get right down to it, they're looking for the same thing as the Excalbians: the answer to the eternal question of whether good is better than evil.

---

*It's worth noting, however, that the word "justice" as it appears in *The Republic* is a translation of *dikaiosune*, a Greek word that many scholars believe covers "a wider area than justice, and can be used for right conduct in general. Plato appears to support this idea when [at one point in the dialogue Socrates describes] the search for justice as the search 'for the right way to live.' Hence, it is often suggested that *dikaiosune* should be translated as 'righteousness'...and that it corresponds more closely to 'morality' than 'justice.'" See Julia Annas, *An Introduction to Plato's "Republic"* (Oxford: Oxford University Press, 1981), p. 11.

A CAPTAIN'S MAIN CONCERN

Thrasymachus represents the viewpoint of the Sophists, a group of teachers of rhetoric and philosophy in ancient Greek society renowned for their clever yet often specious reasoning. As the dialogue begins, Thrasymachus tells Socrates that all moral arguments are empty unless they pertain to a struggle for power. While those in political power make up laws that are ostensibly "just" for all concerned, those laws, in his view, are set up only to benefit the lawmakers themselves. The laws are deemed "just" simply to persuade others to obey them. Those who break the laws are called "wrongdoers" and are deemed unjust. Therefore, concludes Thrasymachus, justice is the same everywhere: it serves the interest of the stronger party.

This viewpoint, better known to us as "might makes right," is still widely held today. Many *Star Trek* villains, of course, embody this philosophy, from the four cretins featured in "The Savage Curtain" to the ignominious Khan Noonien Singh ("Space Seed," *TOS: #24*; *Star Trek II: The Wrath of Khan*). Certainly that very impulse is what led the Metrons to devise the contest between Kirk and the Gorn leader in "Arena."

Now, Thrasymachus' idea that a "just" person is one who advances his own interests at the expense of others is probably a teensy bit different from what you and I would think. In fact, most of us would say he's describing the likes of Colonel Green—in other words, a decidedly "unjust" person. And yet, as Thrasymachus points out, an "unjust" person like Green has a considerable advantage over the "just" person precisely because he isn't held back by morality. He wouldn't think twice about exploiting "just" people—to him, anyone nutty enough to put his own self-interests second to those of other people is just asking for it. That would explain why Surak, despite his noble efforts, never had a chance when he tried to negotiate a peace settlement with Green and company halfway through "The Savage Curtain." The poor guy, as Thrasymachus might put it, was headed right for an ambush.

Not surprisingly, Sophists like Thrasymachus held the Colonel Greens of their time in high esteem for their perceived "strength." They also admired criminals, provided they were successful ones. They particularly idolized tyrants, those who so ruthlessly and thoroughly forged their own interests at the expense of others that no one else could challenge them. To wit: Genghis Khan, Khan Noonien Singh, Garth of Izar ("Whom Gods Destroy," *TOS:* #71). To a Sophist, these three men are admirable precisely because they know, better than anyone else, how to put their own good above everyone else's.

Socrates, of course, couldn't agree less. Rather than argue with Thrasymachus outright, though, he decides first to come up with an idea they can both agree on—that government is a skill or craft. From here, Socrates distinguishes between those with a skill (defined as "the stronger") and those served by a skill ("the weaker"). The function of a skill is to make good the defects in those it serves. Looking at this in terms of *Star Trek,* the skill of commanding a ship is simply a trained talent or capacity; Captain Kirk would obviously be the stronger, his officers and crew, the weaker.

The question remains whether the captain practices the skill of command for his own sake or for the sake of the crew. Socrates would say that commanding a ship must be practiced for the benefit of those it was created to serve: the crew. This, without a doubt, also reflects the beliefs of all four *Star Trek* captains. We've seen this demonstrated on countless occasions, including both of our model episodes. Shortly after surveying the damage on Cestus III in the early moments of "Arena," Kirk, Spock, and the rest of the landing party come under fire by the unseen Gorn spacecraft. When Kirk orders Sulu to beam everyone back aboard, the helmsman tells him that can't be done—the *Enterprise* is also being attacked, and the power drawn from the ship's security screens has prevented the transporter from functioning properly. Though Sulu offers to lift the screens, thus enabling Kirk and the others to escape, the captain, realizing that such action would render the *Enterprise* vulnerable, steadfastly refuses. "Keep those screens up until the ship is safe!" he commands. "Don't worry about us until you know the ship is safe." (Like a good captain, Kirk thinks of his "ship" in terms not only of the physical vessel but the lives of all aboard it—a definition with which Socrates would doubtlessly concur.)

As for our other story, the Excalbians in "The Savage Curtain" are shrewd enough to anticipate Kirk's refusal to fight for the sake of fighting. But they also know they can't bribe him with promises of power, prestige, or wealth. So they play the only card they have left—seize the *Enterprise*! Endanger the lives of his entire crew. Threaten to blow the ship to bits unless Kirk capitulates. As Yarnek himself puts it: "Is that cause enough for you, Captain?"

Just as a Starfleet captain should always put his crew's welfare before his own, so should a governor, lawmaker, or political leader in general practice his craft for the benefit of those he serves. Those who wield political power, Socrates would say, should be concerned not with acquiring prestige or wealth but with bettering the welfare of their people. A leader, after all, should provide the leadership skills his constituency lacks. Only if he does this successfully can the city, state, nation, or galaxy he governs be expected to prosper.

That's bunk, Thrasymachus tells Socrates: it's a matter of historical fact that rulers invented the concept of justice for their own prurient purposes. After all, ever since the time of Homer, the ruler has been called the "shepherd" of his people. When a shepherd fattens and tends his sheep or cattle, he's not really concerned with the good of the flock, but rather the eventual shearing and butchering of them for his own profit.

That, in a word, is exploitation. Therefore, says Thrasymachus, the shepherd is really unjust to those he governs. He's only after his own good.

WHAT GOOD IS THERE IN DOING GOOD?

When you think about it, Thrasymachus has a point. Laws are in fact created by those who have the power to create them. If power confers strength, then laws indeed are made by the "stronger" (as Socrates would put it). Moreover, it's not unreasonable to say that those who make laws in our society are guided—at least partly (in some cases, entirely)—either by their own self-interests, or by the interests of those who endorse them. We see this every time a new president, governor, mayor, or other newly elected public official takes office. For the most part, any legislation or policies enacted by these new officials tends to benefit the people who put them in office, rather than the people they're supposed to serve. Therefore, we're really only advancing the interests of those who yield the power when we elect these people in the first place. That, according to Thrasymachus, would account for the influential role the tobacco industry, labor unions, political consultants, and other big-money lobbyists play every year in many elections throughout the United States. Therefore, "justice" (or the law, as we know it) is really nothing more than a set of arbitrary rules imposed on us by people stronger than we are.

But if that's the case, what's the point in being "just," or lawful? Why allow ourselves to be exploited by those with deep pockets, when we could be pursuing our own interests instead?

That's easy, Thrasymachus would say. We're afraid of the consequences. We respect the law not for its own sake, but simply because we don't want to go to jail, pay the fine, or suffer whatever punishment we'd face for breaking it. Deep down, though, we'd rather be unjust, because that's where the money is. In fact, no one in his right mind would want to live a "just" life, because in the long run he'd end up being crushed by those in power. As Thrasymachus might have put it, "Remember what happened to Surak."

How does Socrates respond to this? By again thinking of political rule as a craft. Each craft has a specific benefit: the benefit of captaining a vessel is the safety of the crew, the benefit of medicine is health, and so on. While certainly many of us also earn money while practicing our craft, that money is not the result of our work, but rather a benefit from an additional craft—that of wage-earning itself. It is entirely possible, however, for someone to perform his or her craft well without having any financial incentive. We know that *Star Trek* itself embraces this philosophy because there's no monetary system in the Federation.

Once you separate the skill of wage-earning from the skill of governing, Socrates continues, you can see that no one really wishes to govern. Now, it's certainly true that people who are unjust can be induced into doing just about anything for power or money alone—that, Kirk is told in "The Savage Curtain," is how Yarnek got the four tyrants to participate in his bizarre experiment. But even good, decent, thoroughly just people like Lincoln and Surak would probably avoid the thankless job of government without at least some kind of remuneration.

Think about it. Unless you had the bank account of a Donald Trump or Bill Gates, would you want to take on all the headaches of running an office, a corporation, or an entire country for that matter, if you weren't being paid for it?

In fact, Socrates figures, about the only possible reason a Lincoln or Surak could have for governing merely for the sake of governing is to prevent the election of someone who could do the community harm. In other words, a vote for Lincoln is a vote *not* for Colonel Green (and therefore, not for genocide).

He'd take on the hassles of political office, even without financial compensation, because it's the lesser of two evils.

Which goes to show that good people might simply have different motivations than evil people have.

THE RING OF GYGES

That doesn't really answer our question, though. The reasons good people have for wanting to govern the country or be captain of the Starship *Enterprise* might be different from the reasons bad people have, but that doesn't necessarily make their actions better. Remember that in "The Savage Curtain," Yarnek still couldn't tell the difference between good and evil even after the "good" guys won. To him, both sides "used the same methods to achieve the same results."

Plato* addressed a similar issue in *The Republic*. Just as Socrates seems to have punctured Thrasymachus' balloon, his own brother Glaucon throws a wrench into the works. Glaucon, more or less a silent observer for the first part of the debate, now plays devil's advocate and presents Socrates with an argument most people would support—that in a perfect world, we would all have complete freedom to indulge ourselves. According to this view, justice is desirable because it brings rewards, such as a good reputation (or, in the case of Surak, the legacy of Vulcans embodying his philosophy in peace and friendship for over two thousand years). But if we had our druthers, we'd still rather be unjust, especially if there were no fear of consequences. If we knew we could always get away with serving our own interests, regardless of what it meant to other people, we'd do it in a minute.

---

*I refer to Plato and Socrates interchangeably because Socrates, in fact, wrote nothing; rather, his teachings were expressed through the work of his student, Plato. Occasionally, however, Plato used the figure of Socrates to present his own ideas as well.

The problem is, in a situation where you can stick it to others, there's always the possibility of retaliation. So we play it safe, agreeing not to hurt others, in exchange for not suffering any hurt ourselves. Justice is simply the result of that compromise, with morality, more or less, a matter of looking out for ourselves.

As Glaucon put it:

> They say that to do injustice is, by nature, good, to suffer injustice, evil; but that the evil is greater than the good. And so when men have both done and suffered injustice and have had experience of both...they think that they had better agree among themselves to have neither; hence there arise laws and mutual covenants; and that which is ordained by law is termed by them lawful and just.

Nevertheless, Glaucon also insists that if a just person could get away with it, he'd still exploit his situation, just as much as an unjust person. To illustrate his point, he tells Socrates the story of the ring of Gyges, a ring that enabled its wearer to become invisible. As the story goes, Gyges, a shepherd in the service of the ruler of Lydia, found a gold ring in a chasm, following a violent storm and earthquake. Eventually Gyges noticed that when he turned the setting of the ring so that it faced the inside of his hand, he became invisible to those around him. Realizing the advantages to be gained by his new power, Gyges arranged to become a messenger to the king. He then used the ring to seduce the queen and kill the king in order to take over the kingdom.

WHAT WOULD YOU DO WITH THE POWER OF Q?

From this, Glaucon argues that even a just person, if he got hold of such a ring, would succumb to the temptation and use it exactly as an unjust person would. Therefore, the just person is just only because he's afraid of getting caught in an unjust act. Once that fear is eliminated, though, he's just as likely to be unjust. Certainly that's what happens to Riker in "Hide and Q" (*TNG: #11*), as well as Gary Mitchell in *Star Trek*'s second pilot, "Where No Man Has Gone Before" (*TOS: #2*). In both cases, an ordinarily good man undergoes a dramatic change in personality—not to mention, morality—once he, in effect, puts on the ring of Gyges.

In the *TNG* episode, the mysterious Q, a member of a god-like alien race known as the Continuum, again decides to test the virtue of humanity (in the person of Picard and his crew) by offering "the realization of impossible dreams." This time he plans to seduce First Officer Riker with the lure of superhuman powers. Q, of course, personifies the cynical, Glauconian view that anyone, given the absence of consequences, can be corrupted. Picard, quoting Shakespeare, counters with a defense of mankind's potential that would make Socrates proud: "What Hamlet says with irony, I say with conviction— *What a piece of work is man! How noble in reason, how infinite in faculty! In form and moving, how express and admirable! In action how like an angel, in apprehension how like a god!*" Picard is so confident in Riker's integrity that he stakes his starship command on it.

Q relentlessly goads Riker into using his powers, eventually succeeding when Worf and Wesley Crusher are killed by "animal things" in the Napoleonic setting where Q has transported Picard and the bridge crew. Enraged by the death of his fellow officers, Riker brings them back to life. Uneasy about the effect his powers might have on him, though, Number One assures Picard that he's strong enough to resist using them again—a promise that is immediately tested when Data, unaware of the conversation Riker has just had, asks him to use them to resurrect a young girl who died in a mining disaster. Citing his oath to Picard, Riker refuses, but immediately argues with his captain over the merits of that promise.

Picard assures Riker it was the right move. Perhaps aware of what happened to *Enterprise* officer Gary Mitchell (who became nigh omnipotent after a freak exposure to radiation nearly a century earlier), Picard warns his first officer that "once you become accustomed to that power, when you grow to like it too much," you will lose restraint. (Remember how Mitchell taunted Kirk once he realized just how mighty he'd become in "Where No Man Has Gone Before": "You should have killed me when you had the chance.") While Riker never threatens Picard (as Mitchell did Kirk), he does become increasingly arrogant once he realizes having the power of Q means no fear of consequences. Picard urges Riker to remember Lord Acton's saying "Power corrupts" (to which Riker, completing the maxim, responds, "...and absolute power corrupts absolutely").* Nonetheless, Riker disregards the captain and decides to join Q and the Continuum, but not before bestowing a parting gift to each of his friends: sight for the blind engineer Geordi LaForge; instant adulthood for teenaged Wesley Crusher; a Klingon mate for Worf; humanity for the android Data. Surprisingly, Picard doesn't object to any of this. We soon understand why, though, when one by one, each of the crew members spurn their gifts—a dramatic statement that even Q understands to be a total rejection of him and the omnipotence he offers. When Riker also rejects his "gift," Picard's faith in humanity is completely upheld.

---

*Though apparently a popular adage in the *Star Trek* universe (Kirk also invokes it in "Balance of Terror," *TOS: #9*), that's not quite what Acton said. The correct quote is "Power tends to corrupt. Absolute power tends to corrupt absolutely." This important qualification leaves room for the powerful to choose. Omitting the qualification leaves the powerful without a choice, determined to be corrupt.

KIRK SHOWS MERCY IN THE ARENA

Nonetheless, the fact that both Riker and Mitchell yielded to their own versions of the ring of Gyges raises a concern about human nature, as Glaucon suggests. Mitchell, of course, became so far gone Kirk, indeed, had to kill him to stop him. Maybe Yarnek and the Metrons are right—because of their "inherent violent tendencies," good people are no different from bad people because they often use the same means to achieve their goals. And yet, Socrates would say, the bridge crew's unanimous refusal of whatever gift Q has to offer again suggests that there is something about Q that accounts for why they ultimately reject him.* Perhaps there's also something about good people that enables them not only to know the difference between good and evil, but to show it as well.

For the answer to this, let's turn to "Arena."† Remember what happens once Kirk intuits (along with, almost simultaneously, Spock and McCoy, as they watch the action unfold from the *Enterprise* viewscreen) that the real invader in the matter of Cestus III may have been the Federation itself. "We know very little about that section of the galaxy," concedes Spock.

---

*We see this not just in the final scene of "Hide and Q," but earlier in the episode as well. Though Worf is clearly thirsty after Q transports him to a desert atmosphere, he turns down a goblet of wine from Q on general principle.

†As always, I refer to "Arena" in terms of the broadcast episode. However, because some aspects of James Blish's novelization of the show also reflect the issues raised in *The Republic,* I would be remiss not to mention them. (Blish, of course, based his adaptations not on the telecast version of the episodes but on the original scripts.) For instance, early in Blish's story Kirk, upon realizing the Gorn is more formidable than he'd imagined, attempts a compromise ("Look, Gorn, this is insane! Can't we patch up some kind of truce?"). This sequence was never filmed (or if it was, it didn't make the final cut). Nonetheless, it shows the original script clearly illustrated one of Glaucon's major points: that justice is a matter of compromises we make with each other in order not to get hurt. *See* Blish, "Arena," *Star Trek 2* (New York: Bantam Books, 1968), pp. 5–6.

"Then we may have been wrong," says McCoy. "The Gorns may have been trying to protect themselves."

Once Kirk also comes to this realization, he refuses to kill the Gorn leader. This, frankly, shocks the Metrons. Not only does this "advanced trait of mercy" force them to change the rules of their own game,* it gives them cause to reconsider their assessment of the human race. Perhaps violence isn't the only "inherent tendency" we have.

It's important to emphasize that at the time Kirk decides to spare the Gorn, he does not know what the consequences of his action will bring, nor how the Metrons will react. (You can bet if Socrates were watching this episode with Glaucon, he'd be quick to point that out, too.) For that matter, the Metrons aren't sure how Kirk will react when they offer to destroy the Gorn ship after all. To their further surprise, Kirk proposes that the Federation and the Gorn work out an agreement. Since misunderstanding created the conflict, perhaps communication can resolve it. This resolution pleases the Metrons. "There is hope for you, Kirk," their leader tells him at the end of the episode. "You are still half-savage, but there is hope."

Now, suppose you're given the choice between committing an injustice or suffering an injustice at the hand of another. Those are your only two options. Which would you choose? Socrates recommends suffering the injustice—not because he's a masochist but because, again, it would be the lesser of two evils. This is basically the same decision Kirk has to make in that split-second after he fells the Gorn. Once he realizes the attack on Cestus III was justified, he knows that killing the Gorn leader would be an act of injustice that the Federation, which holds justice and mercy in high esteem, simply would not tolerate.

---

*At this point, the Metrons admit to Kirk they had really intended to destroy not the losing party and his ship, but the winner, precisely because "the stronger, more resourceful race would pose the greatest threat to us."

Granted, this idea would seem to go totally against common sense. None of us ever want to see ourselves, our friends, or our loved ones harmed in any way. A Starfleet commander is supposed to protect the lives of his crew, not leave them open to danger—which, in effect, Kirk is doing by not finishing off the Gorn when he has the chance. Yet Socrates (and Plato, for that matter) believes it is far better to be temporarily oppressed than to be an oppressor at any time. An unjust person, they'd say, is like an alcoholic who is free to satisfy his cravings, and who considers himself happy in satisfying them. Though he may think he's happy, he's really hurting himself by indulging his desires. Consequently, it is a terrible error to say that injustice is all right, or even beneficial, if it is undiscovered. A sensible person, like Kirk, will avoid unjust actions and cultivate those actions that maintain the inner harmony in his soul.

Nonetheless, Kirk tells Spock back on the ship that he won the conflict "by being a sucker."* He is still expressing the Sophist view that justice ultimately is for fools. Even so, his budding reliance on reason instead of violent emotion in a hostile situation leaves the Metrons with plenty of room for optimism for our future. As Kirk himself put it, "We're a promising species, as predators go."

THE RETREAT OF EVIL

Socrates would say that by sparing the Gorn leader, Kirk shows that Glaucon's view of justice is wrong—a just person will act differently than an unjust person acts, regardless of the consequences. True, Yarnek would counter, but that doesn't quite answer the basic question about the relative strength of justice

---

*Blish, "Arena," p. 11. Again, this particular line of dialogue was either never filmed, or ended up on the cutting room floor.

and injustice, good and evil. (After all, despite Yarnek's many advanced capabilities, we're still dealing with a rock.)

So Socrates goes back to Thrasymachus' original claim, that injustice makes people more powerful than justice would. First of all, he observes, injustice can't possibly be a source of strength since the practice of it doesn't bring the community together. In fact, injustice generally divides people:

> [When] a community, or an army, or pirates, or thieves, or any other band which forms for the purpose of wrongdoing attempts to accomplish a goal, they will have a better chance of success if they do not wrong one another.... [Since] immorality makes for mutual conflict, hatred, and antagonism, [it will] make them hate one another and clash with one another and be incapable of doing things together.

We see this point clearly illustrated in "The Savage Curtain," when Genghis Khan and Colonel Green run from the battle in order to save their own lives, without regard for each other or Zora. Their overwhelming self-interest prevents them from working together and accomplishing their desired goal of achieving power. We see this happen in professional sports, as well: oftentimes when a team experiences a losing season, the players become more concerned with beefing up their individual statistics than doing what it takes to help the team win. Similarly, *Star Trek* suggests that evil forces are often defeated not so much by a similar show of violence but by themselves.

"Evil retreats when forcibly confronted," observes Yarnek at the end of the episode. But why is that the case? Because, Socrates would say, it's weaker and less effective than goodness or justice. Whereas justice is a terrific source of strength precisely because it enables people to work more harmoniously in achieving a goal. Like members of a winning team, Surak,

Lincoln, Kirk, and Spock pulled together, no matter what adversity they faced. Surak risked his life for his three friends, Lincoln tried to rescue Surak when he was captured, Kirk helped Spock fight Khan. Their combat was ultimately more effective than that of the "bad" guys because they dealt justly, and harmoniously, with each other.

We see this idea expressed time and again throughout the *Star Trek* series and movies. The crew members constantly overcome enemies and obstacles by working harmoniously. They accomplish their goals as a team, each member performing his or her role without wavering. The crew is synergistic — a whole indeed greater than the sum of its parts.

INJUSTICE ABOARD *VOYAGER*

Socrates then builds on his analysis of group behavior by saying that injustice will have the same effect with any two individuals, setting them "at variance," making them "enemies to each other as well as to everyone who is just." *Star Trek* knows this all too well, as we've seen in episodes such as "Scorpion, Part 2" (*VGR: #69*), wherein Captain Janeway and First Officer Chakotay debate the merits of cooperating with the Borg, the deadly breed of half-machine, half-human creatures first introduced in the *TNG* series. The Borg, as we know, have a highly developed group consciousness (known as the "Borg Collective"), wherein each Borg individual is linked by a sophisticated subspace network that constantly provides each member with supervision and guidance.* Anyone captured by the Borg is automatically assimilated into the Collective. According to "Scorpion," the Borg fears Species 8472, an equally dangerous race of highly technologically developed beings who seek to purge any "contamination" in order to preserve their own genetic purity. The arrogance of Species 8472

---

*Okuda and Okuda, *"Star Trek" Encyclopedia,* p. 51.

threatens the indiscriminate destruction of all other beings. Moreover, they try to impose their will on other societies (shades of ethnocentrism!) without the Borg's motive of creating a more efficient, improved, harmonious Collective through the assimilation of all other societies. Janeway and Chakotay argue over whether to cooperate with the Borg in order to travel through space inhabited by both the Borg Collective and Species 8472.

Contemptuous of human beings, the Borg see the members of the Federation as inferior and fractious, continually encumbered by the clash of ideals and ideas. They condemn the Federation's lack of harmony and all too common inability to cooperate on even the simplest tasks. Observing the dispute between Janeway and Chakotay, Seven of Nine,* the only Borg crew member of *Voyager,* tells the first officer, "You are erratic, conflicted, disorganized. Every decision is debated, every action questioned, every individual entitled to their own small opinion. You lack harmony, cohesion, greatness. It will be your undoing." Not only does Seven of Nine's prediction almost come true as the episode unfolds, her observation that lack of harmony often leads to the undoing of a group of people is, indeed, very Platonic. As we're about to see, Plato also argued in *The Republic* that justice is an inner harmony—and that without inner harmony, a group can accomplish nothing.

KIRK, SPOCK, AND MCCOY: THE THREE PARTS OF THE SOUL

According to Plato, the inner harmony of the soul should be our greatest concern. Plato understood the soul to be a single

---

*Seven of Nine was assigned as Borg liaison to Janeway when the Collective formed an alliance with the captain to defeat Species 8472. When Seven of Nine and her fellow drones attempted to assimilate the *Voyager* crew, she was the only drone from her cube to survive.

stock of psychological energy, which appears as reason, spirit, and the irrational desires. His basic point is that there are various kinds of complexity to be found in human behavior. Our acts rarely come from a single motivational source, but rather are the result of how these three sources of behavior interrelate.

Suppose Kirk became thirsty while fighting the Gorn. Suppose, further, he sees a stream but suspects it might actually be poisoned due to the high concentration of minerals in the surrounding area. His thirst and his disinclination to drink are like two movements in contrary directions. This suggests that our souls contain at least two parts—a reasoning part and an irrational part. But Kirk's actions on the planetoid suggest a third drive, as well. As much as he wants to kill the Gorn, he also seems angry with himself for wanting to perform this action. This anger counteracts his desire to satisfy his "inherent violent tendency" (as the Metrons put it) to kill the Gorn.

Plato believed that anger belongs to the "spirited" part of the soul. This part, sometimes called "willpower," is more a matter of how we feel about things than how we think about them. We often feel our spirit overwhelm us whenever we give in to our irrational desires over our reason. Likewise, whenever we feel disgusted with ourselves, this is a case of our anger overwhelming our spirit. However, spirit is a motivation that can be educated. Just as Kirk's spirit agrees with his reason when he refuses to kill the Gorn, our spirit may cooperate with our reason once it has taken a stand over our irrational desires.

There's no better example of Plato's threefold nature of the soul at work in *Star Trek* than the interaction and interdependence of Kirk, Spock, and McCoy. Kirk, with his ability to make decisions and implement a plan of action, represents spirit; Spock, the logician who has unemotional objectivity, stands for reason; and McCoy (aka "Bones"), the compassionate physician who expresses himself freely, represents the irrational desires. We regularly see the tensions between Spock (as reason) and McCoy (emotion) reconciled by Kirk (spirit).* Indeed, as David Gerrold observes in *The World of "Star Trek,"* the characters of Spock and McCoy are particularly crucial to the Original Series as a whole because they "symbolize Captain Kirk's internal dilemmas. The two of them serve to verbalize the arguments that the captain must consider. Because we cannot get into the captain's head to hear what he is thinking, Spock and McCoy are doubly important to the series' ability to tell its stories well—*it is primarily through them that Kirk's internal conflicts can be dramatized."†*

Corresponding to each part of the soul are three virtues (temperance, courage, and wisdom), each of which we achieve, according to Plato, whenever its respective part (reason, emotion, or spirit) fulfills its particular function. Whenever we keep our irrational desires under control, we arrive at the virtue of temperance. When we keep our spirit in check and avoid rash action, we attain courage. When our reason remains undisturbed by our irrational desires, and continues to adhere to our ideals despite the constant changes we experience in daily life, we acquire wisdom. And when the soul is running on all three cylinders, each fulfilling its special function, a fourth virtue is attained: namely, justice. Justice is therefore the virtue that best describes the well-balanced person, who is temperate, courageous, and wise.

Just as Plato extolled these four virtues, so does *Star Trek* in episode after episode, series after series. Among the examples we've discussed in this chapter, the *Enterprise* crew members

---

*Dorothy Atkins, *"Star Trek:* A Philosophical Interpretation," in *The Intersection of Science Fiction and Philosophy: Critical Studies,* ed. Robert E. Myers, Contributions to the Study of Science Fiction and Fantasy, no. 4 (Westport, Conn.: Greenwood Press, 1983), p. 102.
†David Gerrold, *The World of "Star Trek,"* 2nd ed. (New York: Bluejay Books, 1985), pp. 15–16 (original emphasis).

demonstrate temperance in turning down Riker's gifts in "Hide and Q," Spock and Kirk display courage in "The Savage Curtain," Picard manifests wisdom in "Hide and Q," and Kirk shows justice in "Arena."

THE METRONS REAPPRAISE HUMANKIND

Having equated justice with inner harmony, Socrates now sets about refuting, once and for all, Thrasymachus' claim that injustice pays when it goes unpunished. He compares the image of the soul to a group consisting of a multiheaded beast, a lion, and a person—the beast representing our irrational desires, the lion our spirit, and the person our reason.* Just as temperance, courage, and wisdom are all contained within one soul, so do the beast, lion, and person combine to form one body.

Using this metaphor, Socrates says that an unjust person will yield to his irrational desires and provide the beast with whatever nourishment it requires. By nourishing the beast's irrational desire, he is favoring the enslavement of the best part of the soul, the person, to the worst part. Without self-restraint, the unjust person takes what he wants and does what he pleases. He knows no morality or balance. This means we can now throw Glaucon's view ("an unjust person is happier than a just person") out the window, since such a person is off balance and can never achieve inner harmony.

Let's apply this analogy to the sequence in "Arena" where the Metrons intervene in the conflict between the *Enterprise* and the Gorn ship. "You are one of two ships that have come

---

*As the Greeks defined the human being as "the rational animal," it is quite appropriate to see reason depicted as the person in this odd assemblage. For it is reason alone, according to Plato, that differentiates humans from other animals.

into our space on a mission of violence," the Metrons tell Kirk. "This is not permissible. Our analysis further shows that your violent tendencies are inherent. Hence we will resolve your conflict in the way most suited to your natures." Recognizing the bestial and spirited parts of human nature that served as the driving force behind the chase, the Metrons take this to mean mankind as a whole is off balance, incapable of inner harmony. This would account for their initially dismissive appraisal of our species. When Kirk ultimately shows mercy to the Gorn leader—an act motivated by reason—the Metrons change their minds. Since mercy is a part of justice, Kirk reveals something about the state of his soul when he makes this decision.

Referring to the beast-lion-person metaphor, Socrates says that to favor justice is to make the person the strongest, so that he can keep the beast in check. This, in turn, will promote the tame desires and prevent the savage ones from growing. The person who favors justice will make "the lion his ally, making them friendly to each other and to himself." The act of justice is the maintenance of this harmony. A person will be just when the conflicting elements of reason, irrational desires, and spirit are brought together into a harmonious integration. Only then it is possible for each part of the soul to perform its own function, without taking over functions that belong to another part. By using reason to control his emotions and desires, Kirk in "Arena" shows the Metrons that mankind, in essence, is a spiritually evolving species. It is this evolution of the soul that prompts the Metrons to reevaluate their position.

Which brings us back to the other question we raised at the beginning of this chapter: Can virtue be recognized among individuals from different cultures, galaxies, or times? The answer to that, as both our model episodes show, is a resounding yes. The Metrons acknowledged Kirk's act of mercy to the Gorn; Surak, Lincoln, Kirk and Spock affirmed each other's own inner harmony and joined forces as a team.

As we can see, *Star Trek* clearly disavows the claim that "might makes right." Misused power will be destroyed primarily through the bearer's own actions. Evil forces are defeated not by a similar show of force but by their own lack of harmony. At the same time, the series consistently upholds the Platonic ideals that good is stronger than evil; that we should beware of power, and do what is right regardless of the consequences; that the virtues of courage, temperance, and wisdom are qualities we should foster in ourselves; and that, above all, inner harmony is essential to achieving a good life.

Now that we know that good is better than evil, and that it's recognizable wherever we go, how do we identify what is good so that we can direct our actions accordingly? After all, it's just as possible to be deceived about what is good as it is to be deceived about anything else. Not surprisingly, Plato recognized this problem and proposed an answer for it, as well. Let's see what he had to say about it in the next chapter.

CHAPTER 4

THE CAVE,
THE FORMS, AND
KATHRYN JANEWAY

"Concerning Flight"
VGR: Episode 79
Stardate: 51386.4
Original Air Date: November 26, 1997

A real-life emergency interrupts Captain Janeway's latest excursion with the holographic projection of Leonardo da Vinci. High-tech space pirates infiltrate Voyager's *security shields and use a sophisticated "translocator" device to scan the ship's contents and steal vital computer equipment, including the Doctor's portable emitter. Janeway and Security Officer Tuvok beam aboard the perpetrators' planet to recover the stolen goods. Waiting for them below is the synthetic da Vinci, who was downloaded into the portable emitter and is now living in a workshop owned by Tau, the leader of the techno thieves. Janeway wants da Vinci to lead her to Tau, but soon finds he needs her help even more than she needs his. The confused Maestro doesn't understand that the "new world" in which he finds himself is really a kind of prison.*

When you think about it, the Metron leader's final assessment of humanity pretty much sums up one of the keystone messages of *Star Trek* itself: that we're okay, warts and all. Despite those primitive impulses that sometimes get us into trouble, humanity is a fundamentally decent species guided by nobility and morality. Our true mission, like that of the crew members of each *Star Trek* series, is to learn from one other.

Bright as we are, though, we're also capable of making the same mistakes over and over again. For one thing, as we saw throughout the examples in the previous chapters, we have a really bad habit of jumping to the wrong conclusion. (No wonder the Metrons were annoyed with us.) Kirk assumed the Federation was right in colonizing Cestus III and that the Gorns were wrong in attacking us; Akorem thought the Bajoran Prophets chose him to be the Emissary; Lwaxana nearly compromised her values by marrying Campio because she was desperately afraid of growing old alone. Plato, of course, would say the reason our judgment is so often impeded is that we keep allowing our "beast" or "lion" to overwhelm our reason. When our soul is not in harmony, we tend to see things as they appear to be, instead of how they really are.

In a sense, that's exactly what Captain Janeway has on her hands, in the person (so to speak) of the holographic Leonardo da Vinci, a character we first met in "Scorpion, Part 1" (*VGR*: #68). As the curtain rises in "Concerning Flight," Janeway and the simulated maestro are sopping wet after a malfunction in his flying machine lands them both in the drink. Discouraged by yet another failure to achieve his lifelong goal (namely, conquering flight), da Vinci tells the captain he's about to give up trying altogether and head for France, where he might be "better appreciated." Naturally, this disappoints Janeway; the real Leonardo, after all, was her childhood hero. At the same time, though, this doesn't really surprise her, since the fabricated da Vinci embodies all known aspects of his biographical counterpart, including his unreliability and penchant for abandoning projects. Janeway, not one to give up on a commitment herself, implores da Vinci to push on, only to find her pleas falling on deaf ears. Leonardo blathers on about French bistros and other inconsequential matters rather than face her hard questions about his lack of motivation.

Now, you might wonder why Janeway would bother going to all this trouble. After all, she knows she's not dealing with the real da Vinci, just as Kirk and Spock knew they were never alongside the actual Lincoln and Surak in "The Savage Curtain." Her Leonardo is a holographic projection—he isn't "real." And yet just as Lincoln and Surak "seemed real" to Kirk and Spock (insofar "as they existed in our minds," as Spock observed in that episode), so does da Vinci in Janeway's eyes. Her concern for Leonardo is the same concern we'd show to any friend, particularly one who's about to make a tragic mistake without realizing it.

As a matter of fact, Plato was very big on distinguishing illusion from reality, so he'd probably be the first to applaud Janeway for her efforts. One of his firmest beliefs, as we're about to see, is that if we know someone's in the dark about something, we have an obligation to make that person see the light, no matter how painful that might be for either or both of us.

THE ALLEGORY OF THE CAVE

One of the most famous parts of *The Republic* (indeed, perhaps of all of Plato's writings) is the Allegory of the Cave, a social commentary illustrating "the degrees in which our nature may be enlightened or unenlightened." Socrates suggests that most people live in an underground "cave," having oriented their thoughts around the world of "shadows" (meaning, illusions). The cave dwellers have chains around their legs and necks to show that they're imprisoned; because of their chains, they can only look in one direction, toward a large wall. A fire burns behind them, casting shadows of the people, animals, and images behind the prisoners onto the wall. To the prisoners, the shadow images projected on the wall constitute reality; consequently, they believe those images reflect all of reality. They have no idea what a great big world exists beyond the chains of their cave—that is, their limited perception.

Plato believed that sometimes we're like those prisoners, in that we often see "nothing of [ourselves] or of one another, except the shadows thrown by the firelight on the wall of the cave facing them." Sometimes our perception is distorted because our soul is out of whack, either because of overriding anger (as we saw with Kirk in "Arena") or despair (Lwaxana in "Cost of Living"). Sometimes, though, it's because, like the holographic Leonardo da Vinci, we're only as good as the knowledge instilled in us by our parents, guardians, teachers, and friends.

The problem with holographic figures (not to mention the people in the cave) is that they're incapable of growing. They can't distinguish the shadows of the reality they know from the world beyond the shadows. They not only can't tell the difference, they're not aware that there is any difference in the first place. This, says Socrates, is ignorance—and ignorance, as the Allegory clearly shows, is a form of bondage. The chains on the cave dwellers limit not just their ability to move, but to see, think, and live as well.

I know—nice story, very black and white, but what's it got to do with you and me? There are no jailers of any kind in my life, you may say. Everything's fine. Except that's what the Bajorans thought, too, and we all know what nearly happened to them in "Accession." As Plato (and Gene Roddenberry, for that matter) might put it, whenever we allow someone else to determine our beliefs and values without questioning his or her judgment, the result in effect is sentencing ourselves to a prison of limited perception.

Or suppose you're among the cave dwellers, and Kirk and Spock discover you as they're conducting a geological survey of your planet. They use their phasers to obliterate your chains, and walk you up to the surface. First of all, if you hadn't used your leg muscles in a long time, it would probably hurt like hell to walk. Next, after being ensconced in darkness for so long, you might also be blinded by the sheer brightness of daylight. That's bound to smart, too. Plato suggested that the mind is a muscle that atrophies if it isn't exercised; it's bound to hurt if we put it through a workout after a long period of inactivity.

Finally, once you've adjusted yourself to all these changes, our heroes tell you there's a lot more to life than the shadow images. How you respond to this key moment of truth, Plato would say, will have a critical effect on the rest of your life. For example, how many of us have resolved to exercise in order to lose weight, only to quit after a day or two once we discover how hard it is? Similarly, the newly liberated cave dweller in the Allegory is overwhelmed not just by the sunlight and the pain in his leg muscles but also by the staggering realization that reality, as he once saw it, was wrong. At first, he tries to turn back to the cave and the shadows of his limited perception; though he now knows that his perception is an illusion, at least it's an illusion that's familiar and comfortable.

None of us really likes change, even if we know it might be good for us. Remember how Kira struggled with the return of the D'jarras in "Accession." Like many of us, she felt pulled by the desire to follow her principles and the comfortable alternative of conforming. Sometimes we'll "cave in" to peer pressure, just as Kira did after Vedek Porta insinuated that not "following your D'jarra with all your heart" was a sign of disloyalty. We'll go with the majority because, again, we don't want to cause any pain—to ourselves, or to others.

NO PAIN, NO GAIN

Granted, Socrates would say, escaping bondage, or learning the truth for the first time, can hurt. Remember how devastated Natira became after her bubble was burst in "For the World Is Hollow and I Have Touched the Sky" (*TOS:* #65). Confronting the truth forces you to recognize you were wrong, and often challenges you to change the way you live in accordance with these new beliefs and values. But whether you're serious about toning your body or developing your mind, the same four words apply: No pain, no gain. (Plato would have made a terrific personal trainer in his time.)

Besides, the Allegory continues, once he gets past that initial burst of pain, the newly liberated cave dweller eventually finds himself adjusting to the light. Sunlight, for Plato, represents the enlightenment of knowing all that is supremely good. Only after we see the light is it truly possible to live a good life. The journey to enlightenment is often slow and painful, but ultimately worthwhile.

There's just one catch. Speaking of our newly liberated friend, Socrates observes, "Now he would begin to draw the conclusion that it is the Sun that produces the seasons and . . . controls everything in the visible world, and moreover is in a way the cause of all that he and his companions used to see." Once he's been exposed to the sun, and therefore enlightened as to what is truly good, the former cave dweller realizes he must return to the cave and share his epiphany with those who are not enlightened. He does this knowing full well his friends might ridicule him, and perhaps even kill him out of ignorance—an idea we see neatly illustrated in "This Side of Paradise" (*TOS:* #25). Remember what Kirk goes through when he tries to enlighten his crew about the dangerous side effects of the Omicron Ceti III spores? The entire crew, having already succumbed to the powers of the pleasure-inducing spores, not only mock him relentlessly, they mutiny against him! Then, once the captain finally discovers the antidote to the spores later in the episode, he nearly loses his life trying to get Spock to help him implement it.

Though rescuing the crew from the effects of the spores was hardly easy for Kirk (indeed, as he says to Spock at the end of their struggle, "It was painful... in more ways than one"), Socrates would undoubtably remind the captain that the reward of knowing he helped liberate his crew from the chain of ignorance is well worth any pain he endured along the way.

JANEWAY TEACHES THE MAESTRO

We also see the lessons of the Allegory applied throughout "Concerning Flight," only with an added twist.* Like the newly liberated cave dweller, the holographic Leonardo has his bearings shaken once he is transported into the "new world" of Tau, whom he considers his new master. In the case of da Vinci, the reality he must face is the fact that he is, quite literally, not the man he thinks he is.

Janeway was clearly the enthusiastic apprentice to the maestro during the holographic flight experience that begins the

---

*While it's unclear whether the episode was deliberately intended as a modern rendition of Plato's story, "Concerning Flight" certainly incorporates several of the allegory's key images: da Vinci describes his workshop in Florence as a "cave of ignorance" compared to the digs in his new surroundings, and later uses the positions of "the sun and the shadows" to help Janeway locate Tau's fortress. In addition, the Doctor, rendered immobile following the theft of his mobile emitter, laments aloud that he is "a prisoner," while the episode closes by zooming in on a sketch of a caged bird.

episode. However, by this point in the story, she's now the teacher who, as Socrates would say, must help her student see the light. (As if trying to recover *Voyager*'s stolen equipment on an alien planet wasn't enough for her to do.) Only Janeway knows that her befuddled friend, like the cave dwellers in Plato's allegory, is not free, but rather at the mercy of whoever controls his projected image. "Your new world is a prison," she says as she implores da Vinci to escape with her. "You're under [Tau's] control." Not unlike the figures of Glaucon and Thrasymachus in *The Republic,* the holographic Leonardo argues with his "teacher," insisting to Janeway that we are all prisoners on some level ("When are our lives free from the influence of those who have more power than us?"). Leonardo finally agrees to go with the captain, but not before encountering a painful surprise: armed guards shoot him from behind with a phaser. Not aware that he's a holodeck projection (and thus, has no "back" in the physical sense), da Vinci doesn't understand how he could have survived such a blast unscathed. After escaping from the thugs with the help of a site-to-site transporter, Janeway uses da Vinci's own words to enlighten her pupil on another reality of his new world: "Leonardo, you've always said that it's a poor apprentice who can't surpass her master. There are things in this world that I understand, and you don't." Practically speaking, as well as philosophically, Janeway knows the reality of da Vinci's "new world" far better than her holographic friend does.

As they flee up a steep and rugged ascent (a parallel to the cave dweller's ascent out of the darkness and into the light) the befuddled Leonardo again questions the nature of his existence and his perception of reality. "My mind cannot accept the evidence of my eyes," he tells Janeway. "To see objects disappear into thin air, to see lightning pass through my body..." Like a good teacher, Janeway patiently guides Leonardo along the path to enlightenment, using simple analogies he can understand: If you were a sparrow in a tree, how might that impact how you understand the world? Were that the case, da Vinci realizes, his mind would be so small, he couldn't possibly understand the world even if "Aristotle himself were to perch on my branch and lectured till he fell off from exhaustion." Janeway then drives the point home: "And as a man, can you admit that there may be certain realities beyond the limits of your comprehension?" Only a fool would deny that, the holograph admits. Just as the liberated cave dweller looks back on what he formerly called reality and recognizes it as illusion, da Vinci, too, knows there's more to reality than he previously thought. Only now is he truly able to "escape" the chains of ignorance.

Of course, action follows enlightenment. "Concerning Flight" punctuates this final point of Plato's allegory in a clever, exciting way. Remember how despondent da Vinci once was over his failure to conquer flight. Perhaps, he relates to Janeway near the end of the story, constant failure has caused his heart "to remain in flight." That, he now realizes, might account for his restless nature, his tendency to leap from project to project without ever completing anything. "But now," he says in a moment of insight, "who knows what I cannot accomplish?" It's therefore fitting that da Vinci finally accomplishes his lifelong goal shortly after he has "seen the light." Near the edge of a cliff, Janeway and Leonardo happen upon a newly constructed version of the maestro's flying machine and use it to flee Tau's men. For da Vinci, the "escape" is not only a physical flight from danger, but indeed a symbolic flight from the shackles that bound him and the ignorance that clouded him. Like the newly liberated cave dweller in the allegory, he, too, wishes to share his gift of enlightenment. Back aboard *Voyager*, da Vinci tells Janeway he's still headed for France—only this time, he's motivated not by self-pity but by a desire to share his knowledge of the "new world" with the king.

In both Plato's Allegory of the Cave and "Concerning Flight," we see examples of people imprisoned, whether by illusions, the induced will of a computerized or human leader, or some other means. These "chains" impair the ability of these characters to think for themselves and to act accordingly. While escape is possible, the process is often painful; nevertheless, it's worth the effort, because the end result has a healthy effect on the rest of our lives. For Plato, the ascent from the depths of the cave into the upper world represents the upward journey of the soul. This journey culminates in understanding the cause of "whatever is right and good." Such an understanding of what makes something right or good will certainly change what a person believes and values, as well as how he or she acts in the world.

PLATO'S FORM WORLD

All right, now that we know it's better to live in the light than dwell in the dark, what do we do to recognize the light? Is "good" something we can actually physically see? Like our friends in *Star Trek*, Plato certainly knew that we live in a physical world dominated by time and space. Yet he also believed in a second world—the world of Forms, an immaterial realm that exists beyond the limits of time and space. These Forms are unlike anything we've seen in *Star Trek* (or anywhere else, for that matter); they are changeless, eternal, nonmaterial patterns whose basic nature is beyond our perception.* Though they may occasionally become visible to the naked eye, the objects we see are not the Forms themselves, but rather

---

*While the Wormhole Aliens of *Deep Space Nine* are indeed immaterial and not in time, they do exist in a certain region of space. Likewise, though the aliens in "Return to Tomorrow" (*TOS:* #51) are described as beings of "pure energy without matter," they do experience time.

copies of them. Particular things, such as space stations or anti-matter, are real only to the extent that they copy a Form. In short, the Forms are essentially ideals; they exist somewhere beyond the human mind.

Look at it another way. To think or communicate requires the use of concepts. A statement such as "A spacecraft can fly to other planets" uses the concept known as "spacecraft." When we utter this statement, we're not referring to a particular spacecraft (such as the *Enterprise* or *Voyager*), but rather the class of spacecraft in general. The general term "spacecraft" does not refer to any particular thing that we can perceive with our five senses. That would mean one of two things: either there's no such thing as a concept known as "spacecraft" (in which case, any talk of spacecraft, warp drives, inertial dampers, replicators, and the like would be pointless), or indeed there is. If there is such a thing, Plato argued, it must exist among the immaterial realities—namely, the Forms. In fact, were it not for the Form of Spacecraft, we'd never be able to think about and discuss spacecraft of any kind in the first place.

One function of the Forms, according to Plato, is to provide universal standards for conduct, the concepts we know as "good," "evil," "justice," and "injustice." Therefore, they are more real than anything else we know. Not surprisingly, the Forms are the foundation of Plato's entire theory of morality.

We've already established that doing good is better than causing evil, and that it's easier to differentiate between the two once you've seen the light. But exactly how does one grasp an ideal? How can we possibly recognize that which is "good" if we can neither see, feel, nor touch it? Simple, according to Plato—through deep reasoning. The differences between good and evil, right and wrong are absolute. As we've seen in the previous three chapters, they're not relative to the customs, tastes, or desires of individuals or social groups, nor they do not change from place to place or vary from time to time.

When you think about it, we often speak of goodness and justice to define ideal people, actions, or institutions in terms of how we criticize existing ones. We make qualified judgments about them, describing them as "more or less" good, "more or less" decent. That implies a standard of goodness and justice that's somehow different from the person who does the judging and separate from whatever we judge. In other words, the people we judge, measured against our ideal of justice, oftentimes fall short of it. We never think in terms of a perfectly just society—though we can surely conceive of one. In fact, this concept of an "ideal justice" enables us to evaluate which societies are closest to it, and which are furthest. For example, the justice of Q, the Federation, and the Borg may be judged by the objective and eternally true Form of "Justice." Odo in fact expresses this essential Platonic notion in "A Man Alone" (*DS9:* #3): "Laws change, depending on who's making them...Cardassians one day, Federation the next...but justice...is justice..."

For Plato, ethical thought is based not on culture, religion, or power, but rather on the development of the soul (that is, the mind). Only through the soul can we possibly contemplate such eternal realities as the Forms. Knowing these timeless ideals, we can then understand what it means to build a good society, become good individuals, and live our lives accordingly.

SEVEN OF NINE'S HOLY GRAIL

As much as *Star Trek* borrows from Platonic thought, we've never seen anything quite like the Forms in any of the series or movies. *Trek* has, however, frequently advocated a desire for perfection quite similar to Plato's esteem for the Forms, as evidenced in such episodes as "The Omega Directive" (*VGR:* #89), wherein Janeway and Seven of Nine lock horns over what to do with an unstable, highly dangerous molecule known as Omega. Janeway is bound by a highly classified Starfleet order mandating the destruction of the substance whenever it's encountered. Seven, on the other hand, embodies the Borg belief that Omega can be captured and therefore neutralized for study.

Now, I realize this isn't a perfect parallel. After all, Plato's Forms are immaterial, while a molecule, microscopic though it is, obviously is not. They're also indestructible, which Omega clearly isn't. However, the Borg's reverence for Omega is very similar to Plato's esteem for the Forms, insofar as both represent perfection. "The molecules exist in a flawless state, infinite parts functioning as one," explains Seven to Chakotay in the episode. "I am no longer Borg, but I still need to understand that perfection. Without it, my existence will never be complete." Like Plato's Forms, Omega stands for an ideal; understanding this ideal is a quest of the highest calling. Indeed, Janeway likens the Borg's desire to understand Omega to King Arthur's search for the Holy Grail. The same could probably be said for Plato and the Forms.

Seven dismisses the "Omega Directive" as yet another example of our tendency to destroy whatever we don't understand simply out of ignorance and fear. "I can alleviate your ignorance," she says to Janeway. "As for your fear..." The key lessons of the Allegory of the Cave are that moral failings are the result of ignorance, and those who are "more enlightened" have a duty to "alleviate" the ignorance of others. In this particular sequence of the episode, Seven is taking on the role of Socrates.

Seven does acquiesce to her commanding officer, though, and begins constructing a harmonic resonance chamber, which may "contain and stabilize the molecule." Janeway assists her, but is soon called away when she learns the explosion that had rocked *Voyager* earlier in the story originated from a wrecked moon outpost with a prewarp civilization. Upon beaming down onto the surface, she discovers a test chamber where scientists from the colony had been experimenting with the Omega molecules. Here the captain faces one of those classic *Star Trek* dilemmas: Does she confiscate the molecules in order to destroy them (thus implementing the Omega Directive), or does she follow the Prime Directive and leave them be? Of course, as we know from David Gerrold's observation in Chapter 2 ("If you really want the story to work, pay no attention to the Prime Directive"), there can only be one answer: "For the duration of this mission," she says to Tuvok, "the Prime Directive is rescinded."

Though Seven again debates the merits of destroying the molecules, her commitment to her new collective (namely, *Voyager*) ultimately wins out. Together, she works with Janeway on neutralizing Omega in the test chamber when suddenly the molecules begin to spontaneously stabilize. For Seven, the moment amounts to witnessing utter perfection; in fact, she's so transfixed by the sight, she doesn't realize she has only ten seconds to get out of the decompression chamber before Omega is jettisoned into space! (Janeway, of course, pulls her out in the nick of time.)

As the story concludes, we see that Seven's fleeting encounter with the essence of Omega continues to have a profound impact on her normally phlegmatic self. While running the Leonardo da Vinci simulation inside the holodeck, she keenly observes the program's many religious components, including a crucifix, to help her "understand what I saw in Cargo Bay Two." Though the Borg have assimilated many species with mythologies to explain such moments of clarity, Seven admits to Janeway that she'd dismissed them as trivial. "Perhaps," she now recognizes, "I was wrong." Not unlike the newly liberated cave dweller in Plato's allegory, she is momentarily stupefied upon seeing how mistaken she was about reality—in this case, spiritual reality. Indeed, Janeway suggests, as Socrates might, it is perhaps only now that Seven experienced spirituality for the first time.*

Both "Concerning Flight" and "The Omega Directive" embody the Platonic notion that we achieve enlightenment only after confronting ignorance and embracing certain (often painful) truths about ourselves. "Enlightenment" stands for knowing all that is good—or, as the ancient Greek philosopher himself might put it, the Form of the Good. Though sometimes we might need someone else to lead us out of darkness (as Janeway guided Leonardo and Seven), how we proceed from there is ultimately up to us. Furthermore, once we've seen the light, we have an obligation to share it with others who haven't, no matter what the cost.

Clearly, both episodes show that the essence of Platonic thought is alive and well in the world of *Voyager*. Can the same be said for the other three series, too? Have we finally found our own Holy Grail, the ethical foundation of *Star Trek* itself? Assuming that's the case, what would that mean on a practical, everyday basis? As we'll see in Chapter 5, the Original Series addressed not only these questions but other critical aspects of Plato's philosophy as well.

You might want to brace yourself, though. Some of the answers are a little surprising.

_____

*Janeway's exact line to Seven: "If I didn't know you better, I'd say you just had your first spiritual experience." Perhaps the captain is drawing on the spiritual insight she experienced in "Sacred Ground" (*VGR*: #43), an episode we'll discuss in Chapter 15.

PLATO'S STEPCHILDREN AND BEYOND

"Plato's Stepchildren"
TOS: Episode 67
Stardate: 5784.0
Original Air Date: November 22, 1968

The Platonians are a society of 38 humanoids from the Sahndara star system who patterned their "tiny republic" after the philosophy of Plato. When Sahndara exploded over two millennia ago, the survivors eventually settled on a planet they named Platonius. There they discovered kironide, a rare and powerful chemical component that, when ingested, endows them with extraordinary telekinetic abilities. To ensure the secrecy of their strength, however, the Platonians have remained unknown to the rest of the galaxy—until the sudden illness of their "philosopher-king" Parmen prompts them to send out a distress signal, which the Enterprise *answers. McCoy finds that the Platonians have no resistance to physical injury, prompting Parmen to recruit him as their permanent physician. When McCoy refuses to stay behind, Parmen tries changing the doctor's*

*mind by subjecting Kirk and Spock to acts of cruelty that
are "Platonic" in name only.*

Remember the question we posed in the middle of Chapter 3:
Which is the lesser of two evils, suffering pain at the hands of
another, or hurting someone else? Since Plato believed inflicting injustice on others causes more disharmony to our souls
than any indignity we might experience ourselves, we agreed
that it's far better to endure the abuse of an unjust act than to
commit it.

Having said that, we also know that everyone has limits.
Perhaps even Plato himself would have reconsidered his own
advice had he been made to slap himself in the face repeatedly,
coerced into singing nonsense songs ("I'm Tweedledee, he's
Tweedledum, two spacemen marching to a different drum"),
forced into hysterical fits of laughter and tears, and nearly
trampled to death—all in the same hour! These, of course, are
among the many humiliations Kirk and Spock withstand, to the
delight of the Platonians, over the course of "Plato's Stepchildren," also known in the annals of *Star Trek* as the show in
which Kirk and Uhura team up for TV's first interracial kiss.
Given the sadistic nature of Parmen and his people, Plato
would have been ashamed had he known his name would be
linked with this or any society that clearly enjoyed acting so
horribly. To say this is not what he had in mind when he first
conceived his ethical theory probably qualifies as the under-
statement of the year.

But let's give the Platonians the benefit of the doubt. We
know from the episode that after their original planet novaed,
they briefly settled on Earth during the time of Plato. Let's say
they were serious about implementing the ideals of *The Republic* when they set about creating a new society. If they truly
aspired to promote virtue in the state, they couldn't have
picked a better model.

The problem is what happens once you allow yourself to lose sight of your original goals. As Parmen and friends are about to illustrate for us, you not only run the risk of doing Platonism injustice, you might become unjust yourself.

PLATO'S NATURAL DIVISION OF LABOR ABOARD THE *ENTERPRISE*

Before we talk about the episode, though, let's take one last look at Plato's theory of justice and the soul in order to understand exactly where the Platonians went wrong. As we know from Chapter 3, Plato held that each individual has a soul comprised of three parts (reason, emotion, and spirit), with each part assigned a corresponding virtue (temperance, courage, and wisdom). When the tripartite parts are working in harmony, each fulfilling its special function, we acquire a fourth virtue, justice itself. Given these beliefs about the individual, it shouldn't surprise us to discover that Plato had similar beliefs about the structure of a collective body, be it a city, state, community, or starship crew. To him, a state was nothing more than an individual "writ large."

Plato taught that the ultimate purpose of the ideal community was to ensure a way of life in which all citizens may attain happiness through virtue. To make this possible, the community should be organized under the principle of the natural division of labor—meaning, each member of the community should perform the task for which he or she is best naturally suited. For instance, a person who displays artistic talent should be an artist, one who indicates scientific aptitude should be a scientist, whoever has a "green thumb" should be a gardener or farmer. Think along the lines of the old Bajoran D'jarras, with one major exception: in Plato's ideal society, there is no caste discrimination. Each member of each class does what he or she does best, with complete respect for the occupations of the others.

Just as an individual soul has three parts, so does the collective body: the Guardians (representing reason), the Warriors (standing for spirit), and the working population (corresponding to our physical desires). Were he to explain this in terms of *Star Trek*, Plato would say Kirk, Picard, Sisko, and Janeway belong to the Guardians, as they all possess sufficient reason in their souls to become incorruptible and wise rulers. Worf, Kira, and B'Elanna Torres are among the Warriors, as each has the stuff of which courageous soldiers are made. (Presumably, the "red shirts" from the Original Series would fall under this category, too, since they're always getting killed in the line of duty.) Lastly, the various engineers, communications and security officers, counselors, bartenders, and shopkeepers in the *Trek* universe comprise the working population.

Just as the parts of the individual lead to the corresponding virtues of wisdom, courage, and temperance, the same goes for those of the community. Plato believed a community owes its wisdom to the Guardians, its smallest group of people; a community is wise not so much because of the presence of wise people but because it's structured so that wise people govern. Likewise, the communities aboard the *Enterprise, Voyager,* and Deep Space Nine are wise precisely because the likes of Kirk, Picard, Janeway, and Sisko are the captains—it's their sound judgment as Guardians that makes their respective communities wise. Plato equates wisdom not merely with good judgment but also with the ability to plan and deliberate in accordance with policies that are framed for the good of the community, in a way that goes beyond self-interest. Only the Guardians have the education and the temperament to reason on behalf of the community as a whole, rather than just some part or group within it.

Courage, which Plato defined as the ability to preserve correct belief about what is to be feared, can be found in the society's Warrior class. Courage is more than having the right beliefs as to what should and should not be feared; it also means "sticking to your guns," so to speak, in the face of force and temptations. A state will be courageous when its Warriors defend the good of the community.

Temperance in Plato's ideal society differs slightly from the other two virtues, in that it resides not just in one part of the community, but indeed all three. Temperance consists of an agreement as to who should govern and who should be governed. Recall that temperance in the individual sense involves controlling our desires. The Warriors and productive classes have strong and uncoordinated impulses, whereas the actions of the Guardians are controlled by knowledge. Therefore, if people who are wise govern a community, it would also be right for people who lack that ability to defer to their judgment.

Not surprisingly, this view of temperance paves the way for justice, since justice is also a virtue that concerns the whole society in relation to its parts. Justice, for Plato, results when each member of the community performs that one task for which he or she is naturally suited. Unlike temperance, which requires a recognition of our duties and place in society, justice behooves us to know our natural talents and to develop them as best we can for the good of the community. It consists in the three classes having just the right amount of power in proportion to their roles.

Building on the principle of the natural division of labor, justice in the ideal society requires all citizens to recognize that, by virtue of performing the role for which they are best suited, each is contributing in some way to the common good. That's certainly an idea expressed a lot on *Star Trek*, particularly with regard to the crew of the *Enterprise*. As we touched on briefly in Chapter 3, the various crew members recognize and are content with their given roles on the team: Dr. McCoy isn't interested in displacing Spock as science officer, and vice versa, nor do engineer Scotty, communications officer Uhura, or helmsman/weapons officer Sulu covet each other's positions. Each knows where his or her particular talents and weaknesses lie; each has sufficient humility to step aside when someone else can perform a task more competently. The common good in this case is the overall mission of the *Enterprise.*

Accordingly, all aboard the ship accept and agree that only Kirk is best suited to be captain. The inverse of that, of course, is the situation we see in "Mirror, Mirror" (*TOS:* #39), wherein an ion storm causes a malfunction in the transporter, zapping Kirk, Uhura, McCoy, and Scott into a barbaric parallel universe where *everyone* wants to be captain—everyone, that is, except the goateed Spock ("I do not desire the Captain's seat...I much prefer my scientific duties"). While this sentiment may *seem* to epitomize the Platonic ideal of doing what one is best suited to do, consider that the Spock who says this comes from an alternate reality in which captains are routinely assassinated by those who wish to move up in rank. This reciprocal Spock declines to be captain simply because he wishes to "remain a lesser target." In other words, he's not looking after the good of the crew, but rather his own.

Star Trek also expresses the notion that collective harmony is a goal to which all should aspire in the person of *Voyager's* Seven of Nine. Recall Seven's prediction in "Scorpion, Part 2" (*VGR:* #69) that the lack of harmony between Chakotay and Janeway over how to deal with Species 8472 "will be [their] undoing." Like other Borg drones, Seven believes that the individual should be subordinate to the collective good (a point on which she sometimes clashes with her commanding officer, as we'll see in another example a few pages hence). She takes this thinking one step further in "The Omega Directive" (*VGR:* #89), wherein she assembles her engineering charges into a Borg-like hive collective, to the point where she even assigns them Borg denominations (Harry Kim, much to his chagrin, becomes known as "Six of Ten"). As she explains to Chakotay, "The crew can be quite efficient when properly organized." Clearly, Plato would applaud Seven for applying his concept so enthusiastically.

PHILOSOPHER-KINGS AND PHILOSOPHER-QUEENS IN THE *STAR TREK* UNIVERSE

Plato held that in the ideal state political power and the love of wisdom* should be united in the same people. A wise Guardian is a philosopher invested with supreme political authority—in a word, a "philosopher-king."† The leader of the community should have not only good judgment, but also the ability to plan and deliberate in accordance with policies that are framed for the common good. Accordingly, it would be wise for those in the community who have not developed these virtues to defer to their leader's judgment for the good of the whole.

The title "philosopher-king" aptly describes not only how Sisko performs his role as Emissary on *Deep Space Nine,* but also how Janeway governs her ship on *Voyager.* Indeed, whether she's deleting the memories of the holographic Doctor without his permission ("Latent Image," *VGR:* #105), killing Tuvix to save the lives of Tuvok and Neelix ("Tuvix," *VGR:* #40), stripping Seven of Nine for parts despite her strong protestations ("The Gift," *VGR:* #70), or ordering that B'Elanna be operated on against the chief engineer's express wishes ("Nothing Human," *VGR:* #102), Janeway has shown, more so than any other *Star Trek* commander, that she's not afraid to occasionally override the personal rights of individual crew members for the

---

*Etymologically, the term "philosophy" in ancient Greek means "love of wisdom."

†Or, for that matter, "philosopher-queen." Plato believed women could be equally as wise rulers as men.

good of the entire team. In order to make these decisions in good conscience—and we know from episodes such as "Night" (*VGR: #95*) that the captain is indeed very sensitive to her conscience—the philosopher-queen must believe she has greater wisdom than those whose decisions she has overridden.

Granted, as a decision maker, Janeway might sometimes strike you as a little brusque. When it comes to dealing with personnel, she doesn't always demonstrate the élan of Kirk or the charm of Picard; indeed, sometimes she ends up chafing people's feelings.

What would Plato say to this? In a word (well, three words): *"You go, girl!"*

The fact is, Plato was a staunch advocate for subordinating the will of the individual for the collective good. If you belong to the working population, if you lack the skills to govern, you must be content to let others think for you—namely, the Guardians or the philosopher-king or philosopher-queen. It is the Guardians or the philosopher-kings or -queens who achieve harmony in the community by keeping the rest of the population under control.

Why do most people need to be controlled? Because, Plato believed, we're basically weak-willed. (Certainly Seven of Nine would agree with that. Just look at the way she treats Ensign Kim.) Left to our own devices, we're likely to become easily distracted by material things—whereas only the Guardians or the philosopher-kings or philosopher-queens have the proper training and temperament to reason on behalf of the entire community. Therefore, since most of us can't be trusted to govern ourselves, it's up to the Guardians or the philosopher-kings to infuse us with as much reason as possible. We need this infusion to ensure not just our own inner harmony, but that of the state as well. Only in this way can a state (or nation, or starship crew) truly become a harmonious collective.

Again, we see this illustrated by way of Seven of Nine. The Borg mentality of controlling the individual drones for the good of the Collective is very much Platonic in nature. The Borg Queen, Seven would say, is the equivalent of Plato's philosopher-queen. Though Seven no longer considers the Borg Collective as her home, she still keeps much of its philosophy close to heart. Like Plato, Seven certainly would agree that most people can't be trusted to govern themselves; they must rely on the wisdom of their leaders for the sake of harmony. Despite how often she clashes with Janeway, it's nonetheless natural for Seven to ultimately accede to her captain as she would the Borg Queen.

Now, let's see how Plato's ideas play out in the world of "Plato's Stepchildren." When the diminutive Alexander—the lone Platonian without telekinetic ability on account of the pituitary hormone deficiency that has also caused his short stature—first encounters Kirk, Spock, and McCoy, he refers to Parmen* as "our present philosopher-king." That certainly seems appropriate, given how much "our [original] leader liked Plato's ideas," as Alexander also elucidates. Later on, Parmen himself describes the planet as a "tiny Republic," and appears to embody Plato's views on Republican behavior by refusing to be addressed as "Your Excellency" ("Philosopher-kings have no need of titles," he explains to Kirk).

The problem is, the way Parmen and the other Platonians mistreat Alexander—not to mention, Kirk, Spock, and McCoy— could hardly be called wise, especially considering what Plato himself had to say about such matters in *The Republic*. (Remember how, just prior to the story of the ring of Gyges, he had Glaucon point out that the problem with treating others unjustly

---

*The name "Parmen" is similar to that of Parmenides, a pre-Socratic philosopher who held that the concept of change was logically neither thinkable nor expressible. Perhaps Meyer Dolinsky, who wrote the script for "Plato's Stepchildren," had this in mind when he named the characters for this episode.

is that it leaves you vulnerable to retaliation.) Furthermore, Plato believed that the wisdom and education of the Guardians should teach them to control their desires. That clearly isn't the case with the Platonians, who delight in indulging their every psychokinetic whim, at the expense of those who do not have their powers.

In fact, the only truly "wise" member of the "republic" (insofar as controlling one's desires is concerned) turns out to be Alexander himself, who refuses to be injected with kironide once the *Enterprise* three determine how to use it. "You think the power is what I want—to be one of them?" he asks Kirk. "To just lie there and have things done for me, a blob of nothing? You're welcome to the power!" Alexander knows too well how corrosive the chemical can be to one's soul. Not wishing to give in to "the beast" (and thus, cause disharmony inside himself), all he wants is for Kirk to take him "someplace where they never heard of kironide or Platonius."

PLATO'S RULES FOR A PHILOSOPHER-KING OR PHILOSOPHER-QUEEN TO LIVE BY... OR, HOW TO AVOID CORRUPTION IN FOUR EASY LESSONS

Given how strongly he believed that power tends to corrupt most people, Plato would have likely applauded Alexander for wisely exercising such temperance. Not only that, he held that most philosopher-kings, fully aware of how often power changes a person for the worse, were wise enough not to crave it in the first place. Which goes back to another point we talked about in Chapter 3: namely, that just people such as Lincoln and Surak would ordinarily shrink from the responsibility of governing. About the only possible motivation they could have for seeking office would be preventing someone worse from being in power.

Plato felt that given the choice, anyone who came to know the Forms would much rather spend his or her time contemplating them than return to the Cave, thus becoming reentangled with the prisoners and their reward system. Yet, as we know, he also maintained that those fortunate enough to experience such bliss (that is, the Guardians and the philosopher-kings or philosopher-queens) have an obligation to enlighten those who are not. Therefore, Plato insisted, the leaders of the ideal society should exercise as much precaution as possible to prevent themselves from becoming tempted by the narcotic of power. With that in mind, he made the following recommendations:

1. They should possess only a few personal items;
2. They should dine not in luxury, but at a common table;
3. They should not be permitted to own, or even touch, silver or gold; and
4. They should live together as a family in one house.

We've seen these rules espoused time and again by the various *Star Trek* commanders throughout each series. The Federation, of course, has no money system to speak of; Picard frequents the Ten-Forward lounge, just as anyone else would; luxuries such as the holodeck are available to captain and crew alike; and, indeed, everyone aboard resides under one roof, be it called the *Enterprise, Voyager,* or Deep Space Nine.

For that matter, even the Platonians are orthodox when it comes to these rules. They enjoy meditation and cultural pursuits equally, which certainly conforms with the program of education Plato recommended for the Guardian class. In addition, Parmen's wife, Philana, tells McCoy that they have eliminated "overemotionality and concern for family" from their society. While this statement may seem to conflict with Plato's fourth prescription for a utopian society, it's actually quite consistent. Plato emphasized the importance of living together as a family, but he was not thinking of blood relations or a nuclear family. Philosopher-kings or philosopher-queens should not have exclusive relationships with spouses or children; sexual intercourse should therefore be strictly controlled by eugenic rules. In other words, he believed in genetic engineering. Application of this particular rule on Platonius is contradictory at best. According to Philana, the Platonians "instituted a mass eugenics program" back when they were still on Sahndara. Even so, her apparently monogamous relationship with Parmen flies in the face of this very same rule.

Given how cruel, unjust, and power-hungry the Platonians have become (not to mention their penchant for exclusive marriages), it's obvious that strict adherence to Plato's ideals broke down for them somewhere along the line. Kirk says so himself to Parmen: "And you consider yourself Plato's disciple!"

Ah, but we are, insists Parmen. "We've managed to be in peace and harmony for centuries, my dear Captain."

"Whose harmony—yours?" asks Spock. "Plato wanted beauty, truth, and, above all, justice."

This time the Vulcan's remarks strike a nerve in the philosopher-king. "Circumstances have forced us to make a few adaptations of Plato," he concedes. "But ours is the most democratic society conceivable! Anyone at any moment can be and do just as he wishes, even [become] ruler of Platonius, *if* his mind is strong enough."

Of course, you can bet if Plato heard these lines, he'd be spinning in his grave. A republic, strictly speaking, is not a democracy; if Plato really had "a democratic society" in mind, one suspects he would have called *The Republic* something else. The reason he wanted power limited to one person, or one faction, in the ideal society in the first place is precisely because of what happened to the Platonians. Once they succumbed to the powerful, telekinesis-inducing, and thereby self-indulgent capabilities of kironide, they let their desires overwhelm them. Consequently, they completely lost sight of what his philosophy was all about. Therefore, Plato would tell Parmen, any resemblance between the practices I prescribed and the Platonism you have carried out is purely coincidental.

KIRK TO PARMEN: A SOUND MIND BEATS A STRONG MIND EVERY TIME

Obviously, what happened to the Platonians underscores the basic point of the "ring of Gyges" story: absolute power has a tendency to corrupt people. Take away fear of consequences, and an ordinarily good person can just as easily turn into a bad person. We saw that happen to Riker in "Hide and Q," and Gary Mitchell in *TOS*'s second pilot.

Still, let's go back to the question we raised a few pages back. Plato asserted that most philosopher-kings would never crave power precisely because it's so seductive. Even Alexander, the so-called fool of Parmen's society, spurned the opportunity to acquire telekinetic powers like those of the other Platonians for fear of becoming "just like them." But is Plato absolutely right on this point? Are we that weak-willed overall? Is it possible some of us might willingly "put on the ring of Gyges," for the good of the community, and still maintain harmony in our souls?

Once Kirk discovers the secret of kironide, he orders McCoy to inject him (along with Spock) with an infusion that is double the concentration found in Parmen's blood. Not only would the dosage make the captain twice as strong as the Platonian leader, it also runs the risk (if the lesson of the ring of Gyges holds true) of making him twice as bad. Yet Kirk maintains temperance throughout his showdown with Parmen, in the heat of the moment, as well as afterward. When Alexander loses his cool and tries to stab Parmen, the philosopher-king forces the dwarf to turn the knife on himself. Kirk uses his newly acquired psychokinetic powers to save Alexander, and eventually proves that he is, indeed, stronger than Parmen. He causes the dwarf to wield the knife at Parmen's throat; after a brief struggle, Parmen yields. Kirk's victory is so decisive, the other Platonians literally shrivel into nothing at the sight of their fallen leader.

But it isn't over yet. Alexander, realizing he now has the upper hand on Parmen after centuries of abuse, begs Kirk to allow him to kill his onetime tormentor. Perhaps bearing in mind that courage ultimately means standing behind one's convictions no matter what, Kirk tells his little friend to remember what he'd said not long before when he refused to be injected with kironide: "Do you want to be like him?" Realizing the captain is right, Alexander shakes his head, and drops the knife.

Of course, that doesn't stop Kirk from blasting the Platonians as only he knows how: "Listen to me, Parmen—I could have had the power, but I didn't want it! I could have been in your place right here and now. But the sight of you and your Academicians sickens me. Because, with all your brains, you're dirtier than anything that ever walked or crawled in the whole universe!"*

Which goes to show maybe Plato was right all along. Perhaps most people wouldn't want to wear the ring of Gyges, even if it were forced on them.

Then again, even though it "sickens" him to stoop (or better yet, raise) himself to Parmen's level, Kirk keeps himself in bal-

---

*At least, that's what Kirk was *supposed* to say. While it's true that Alexander utters these words on camera, in James Blish's novelization of "Plato's Stepchildren" (*Star Trek 11;* New York: Bantam Books, 1975, p. 187), the "you sicken me" speech actually belongs to Kirk. Blish, as we know, based his adaptations on the original scripts. Obviously a change was made in this important scene by the time the episode was filmed, though the reason why is unclear.

ance by displaying wisdom and mercy, just as he'd done against the Gorn leader in "Arena." Though the captain proves his mind is stronger than Parmen's after all, the source of his strength had nothing to do with kironide, and everything to do with inner harmony. That would explain why neither he nor Spock became "twice as bad" after ingesting the chemical, as the "ring of Gyges" story would have us believe.

Think back to what Parmen says to Kirk in the wake of defeat. The deposed leader knows that once Kirk files his report to Starfleet Command, the secret of kironide will become public; thus, the Platonians will no longer have exclusive control of their native power source. But at this point, he realizes Kirk is right. "None of us can be trusted," he says. "Uncontrolled power turns even saints into savages. We can all be counted on to live down to our lowest impulses."

At first blush, this appears to be *Star Trek's* way of advocating one of the basic points of *The Republic*—that mankind must be controlled because we're essentially irresolute. After all, Kirk puts the Platonians under the command of Starfleet because they're incapable of keeping themselves.

But couldn't you say that Kirk's behavior in the heat of battle shows once again there's hope for us all, that we're not as weak-willed as Plato believes? Wouldn't that poke a hole in the proverbial balloon?

Not so fast, Plato would say, his finger wagging with each syllable. I never said *all* of us were weak-willed, but rather *most* of us.

He'd be right, you know. That's why he believed we needed the Guardians in our society—people like Kirk. Only they have the temperament to govern without letting power corrupt them. Only they are capable of keeping their power under control. Therefore, it wouldn't surprise Plato a bit to watch Kirk pull off that nifty little hat trick at the end of the episode (dispensing wisdom to Parmen, imploring courage from

Alexander, and displaying temperance within himself). After all, he'd add, that's the way a Guardian's supposed to act.

COULD PLATO'S *REPUBLIC* LEAD TO ANOTHER PLATONIUS?

Perhaps the key lesson from "Plato's Stepchildren" is that no matter how lofty or admirable your goal is, once you lose sight of your original objective, you're bound to fail. Once the Platonians yielded to the pursuit of their own desires, they lost not just their virtue but their unity of purpose as well. From that point on, their development as a people was permanently stunted.

Of course, times change, and occasionally it becomes necessary to make "a few adaptations" to ensure the growth of an institution or nation. Plato founded his school of thought, the Academy, with the intention of leading others to absolute truth. Over the years, however, future Academicians came to believe that "knowing the truth" was in fact impossible. In other words, like their counterparts in *Star Trek*, Plato's actual disciples also veered from the original path.

Nonetheless, one question remains. If the Platonians followed *The Republic* to the letter, the kironide factor notwithstanding, would they have turned out any different? After all, Plato had some pretty extreme ideas. For one, he rejected individualism, arguing instead for the Borg-like subordination of the masses to the power and supremacy of the state. While his idea of a sovereign philosopher-king looks good on paper, in practice it's precariously close to a dictatorship. Even so, he'd say, that beats democracy, which bestows power on the majority (regardless of whether they're right). He saw democracy as a rule by the mob. So, in a sense, you could say Parmen's denial of the individual rights of Alexander, Kirk, Spock, and McCoy could indeed reflect Plato's teachings, and that the mind-control the Platonians had over objects was not unlike the mind-control Plato advocated over the citizenry by way of propaganda.

Even so, Plato justified all this by claiming his theory was based on the eternally true Form of Justice. He held that the Guardians in his utopian society are entitled to absolute power because only they possess knowledge of the Forms and the nature of a just society—a knowledge which they have an obligation to apply. To know the Good, Plato would say, is to do the good.

So, where does this leave us as we continue our search for the ethics of *Star Trek*? On the one hand, the series as a whole clearly embodies many key components of Platonism: justice exists within the individual; it's possible for all of us to realize a higher level of moral consciousness; good is stronger than evil; evil tends to destroy itself; and finally, the virtues of courage, wisdom, temperance, and justice lead to the good life. Yet, as we've seen in "Plato's Stepchildren," "Accession," and other episodes we've discussed, *Star Trek* also consistently champions our individual human freedom—which clearly goes against many of Plato's rigid societal recommendations. In addition, there's nothing quite like Plato's doctrine of Forms in any of the *Trek* series and films.

Is there an ethical theory that emphasizes justice and the other virtues, but without the objectionable or irrelevant aspects of Platonic thought? Perhaps we'll find the answer in the work of Plato's own disciples. After all, as Janeway reminded the holographic da Vinci, "It's a poor apprentice who can't surpass her master." With that in mind, let's see in our next chapter what Plato's most illustrious student had to say.

KIRK FINDS
THE GOLDEN MEAN

"The Enemy Within"
TOS: Episode 5
Stardate: 1672.1
Original Air Date: October 6, 1966

A routine geological survey of the planet Alpha 177 turns treacherous when magnetic ore from the surface causes the transporter to malfunction. When Kirk returns from the landing party woozy and shaken, the engineering team escorts him to his quarters—unaware that a second Kirk is about to materialize on the platform! Scott discovers the problem with the transporter when a doglike creature beamed up from the planet is split into two beings—one tame, one vicious. Not yet aware that the same thing has happened to the captain, the chief engineer advises that the landing party remain on the surface until he can repair the transporter. Meanwhile, though the benign half of Kirk remains calm yet impassive, his animalistic double runs amok, committing violent, impulsive acts (including sexually assaulting Yeoman Rand). Though the manic Kirk is eventually held at bay, the rational Kirk finds himself utterly incapable of making command decisions so long as he remains separated from his emotional self—a crisis that could have deadly ramifications for the crew members stranded on Alpha 177. Nighttime temperatures on the planet can drop as far as 120° below zero.

Given the ethereal nature of the Forms, many ethicists believe that Plato's theory of virtue is way too abstract to provide a practical guide for human behavior. After all, the Forms are not just ideals, they're immaterial. As we said before, it's awfully hard for us to grasp something we can neither see, feel, nor touch.

Nonetheless, some of Plato's disciples maintained that virtue ethics has its merits, provided the theory can be reformulated in a concrete and understandable way. Among them was Aristotle (384–322 B.C.), Plato's most notable student of all. For Aristotle, virtuous action comes down to one thing: rational control of the irrational part of the mind. Problems of morality arise whenever our emotions override the rational part of our minds, leading us to one extreme action or another. Virtue in the Aristotelian sense comes about by avoiding extremes and letting our reason lead us to what he called "the mean."

This concept is easily understood in terms of *Star Trek*— just think of the relationship between Kirk, Spock, and McCoy. As we mentioned in Chapter 3, Spock and McCoy symbolize the rational and emotional factors that Kirk has to weigh with each decision of command. The two characters literally verbalize the internal arguments the captain must make for the sake of the crew (not to mention those of us watching him on TV). Kirk realizes he tends to be rash and impetuous; he even cops to it in *Star Trek VI: The Undiscovered Country.* "You're a great one for logic," he says to Spock. "I'm a great one for... rushing in where angels fear to tread. We're both extremists. Reality is probably somewhere in between." Knowing this about himself accounts for why Kirk relies so heavily on both Spock (who personifies reason to its extreme) and McCoy (likewise, extreme emotion) in order to decide what to do at critical junctures. As Aristotle would put it, he's simply trying to modify his actions by the mean between extremes.

But let's say one of those faculties were suddenly taken away from Kirk. Would that impair his ability to command? Could he still come to the right decision at crunch time? "The Enemy Within" suggests the answers to these questions are yes and no, respectively. As it happens, Aristotle said the same thing. In fact, had he lived to see *Star Trek,* he'd love this particular episode simply because it captures the essence of his virtue ethics philosophy in a nutshell.*

ARISTOTLE'S THREE KEYS TO VIRTUE

Kirk is certainly beside himself in this one, isn't he? Not only must he account for the lives of Sulu and the other crew members who are freezing to death on Alpha 177, he has to pull himself together in order to do it! Since this certainly qualifies as a moral dilemma, it's appropriate for us to pose the question: what should the virtuous person do?

A strict Platonist would say, "Use your head, man! Reason it out—contemplate the Forms! Therein lies the answer." After all, that's what Guardians are supposed to do; it's a behavior that's practically ingrained. And that advice would be fine, provided it isn't one of those times when you can barely contemplate your navel because your manic half is literally running around assaulting female officers, beating up technicians, and generally wreaking havoc aboard your ship.

---

*Then again, Aristotle might also like this episode for less lofty reasons—such as the fact that Kirk keeps a clay bust that looks suspiciously like the ancient Greek philosopher on a shelf near his bed. Look for it yourself in the sequence in which rational Kirk retires to his quarters shortly after returning from Alpha 177.

Aristotle would also advise Kirk to reason it out—only he'd say there's more to it than that. How we respond to a given situation is not determined simply from momentary impulses, long-held mechanical reactions, or even how we've acted in similar spots before. In other words, it's not automatic. Though Aristotle believed a virtuous person is one whose actions are guided by reason, he felt our emotions also play a key role in determining in how we ultimately should act. And that, plus the fact that virtue is not ingrained, is what differentiates Aristotelian ethics from Platonic virtue theory.

According to Aristotle, for an act to be truly virtuous, the following three conditions must always be met:

1. *The person must know the quality of the act he or she performs. He must know what he is doing and know that it is a good thing to do.* Put another way, a good act is not one that accidentally has good consequences, nor one that you do only because someone told you to do it. That lottery ticket you slipped inside your mom's birthday card just might net her ten million dollars tomorrow night. But if it does, that's no act of virtue on your part; that's just luck. Or say you won the money yourself and donated it all to the church on the advice of your tax consultant—that wouldn't be a virtuous act, either, unless your heart was in it.

So long as Kirk is split in two, he cannot possibly be virtuous under this first condition. Even if one of his halves ordered Scotty to beam up the landing party from Alpha 177—and the crew members came away with no ill effects from either the malfunctioning transporter or the subzero temperatures—that still wouldn't count as a virtuous act. After all, the purely emotional Kirk is incapable of knowing what he is doing, while the waffling Kirk is incapable of making up his mind. Because the captain flunks both requirements of this condition, Aristotle would say that any virtuous result he achieves in his divided state that seems virtuous is not truly virtuous.

2. *The action must be the result of choice and be chosen for itself. An act can hardly be called good if the person is forced to do it, or if he or she does not decide to do it.* To be virtuous you must do what is right just because it is the right thing to do. The divided Kirk flunks this prerequisite, too. As we just pointed out, without his irrational part, the captain is apprehensive and cannot make a choice. Although "emotional Kirk" makes choices, he clearly does so for reasons other than virtue. For example, when he acts friendly to Transporter Technician Wilson, he couldn't care less about Wilson's well-being; he just wants his phaser. Whereas, a person who has the virtue of friendliness in mind is pleasant to others with no ulterior motives.

3. *A truly good action must reflect a firm and settled character.* Ebenezer Scrooge is not suddenly virtuous just because he bought the Cratchit family Christmas dinner after three ghosts nearly scared him to death the night before. Rather, Aristotle would say, he becomes virtuous only if he continues to do such actions on a regular basis, as a measure of the person he wishes to be. (Which, of course, was Dickens' point, too.) People of virtue must not be easily put off by temptations, difficulties, or the persuasion of others. They remain committed to their actions, regardless of the circumstances.

Clearly, the divided Kirk does not have a firm and settled character. Therefore, it's impossible for him to perform a truly virtuous act until he gets his own act together.

IS HALF A KIRK BETTER THAN NONE?

The *Enterprise* crew consider the manic half of Kirk an "evil" imposter, while regarding the rational half of the captain as his normal, beloved self. If that's the case, perhaps they should have just wasted "bad Kirk" with their phasers and let his "good" half survive. That would certainly seem logical, right?

Yes, except that rational Kirk finds that both his strength of will and his determination reside in his emotional half. Without these faculties, he cannot make the choices necessary for ethical action to happen. Indeed, the rational Kirk realizes that emotion is a necessary part of a psychologically healthy human being. "I have to take him back—inside myself," he says to McCoy. "I can't survive without him. I don't want to take him back. He's like an animal—a thoughtless, brutal animal. *And yet it's me.*" Reason and emotion may be entirely separate functions, yet they're critically interdependent. To sever one from the other leads to psychological death—that is, insanity. Again, this accounts for why the rational Kirk routinely relies on both Spock and McCoy in moments of decision. It also explains why he says that he "can't survive" without his emotional part in "The Enemy Within." Neither half of Kirk is complete without the other.

In contrast, there's no such debate going on inside the irrational Kirk. Extremely paranoid of losing his power as a starship captain—indeed, to the point where reasoning is not possible—he sees no alternative but to kill his double. "But you can't kill me," the rational Kirk tries to explain to his manic half. "You can't, don't you understand? I'm part of you. You need me. I need you." Problem is, the irrational Kirk *can't* understand—he's so far gone, he's incapable of listening to reason. So he fires his phaser at his rational counterpart (though, fortunately for Kirk, he hits a control panel instead).

The interaction between the two Kirks dramatizes an important principle of Aristotelian ethics: the more volatile the emotion, the more likely we are to reach a wrong moral judgment. Likewise, the less emotionally agitated we are, the greater the chances that we will weigh alternative courses of action and reach a sound moral judgment.

Generally, when we become dispassionate, we're so meek or hesitant that we can no longer form independent judgments. When that happens, we tend to rely on the judgments of others. This is what's going on with Kirk in this episode. Once he discovers his irrational double is running amok, the rational Kirk wants to inform the entire crew what has happened—to him, that's the sensible, honorable thing to do. "They're a good crew," he reasons. "They deserve to know."

Spock, however, tells him that's a bad idea. "No disrespect intended," says the first officer. "But you're the captain of the ship. You haven't the right to be vulnerable in the eyes of your crew. You can't afford the luxury of being anything less than perfect. If you do, they lose faith—and you lose command!"

Spock isn't simply appealing to Kirk's ego. When it comes to politics (be it those of leading a nation, or commanding a starship), image is everything. One reason why we have the 25th Amendment* in place today is simply because we always want our leader to "look presidential." The same goes for Starfleet captains. Deep down, of course, Kirk realizes that—in fact, it was probably one of the first things he learned as a cadet. "What I don't know," he says to Spock, "is why I forgot that just now."

The reason Kirk forgot is that without his emotional side, he's simply not himself. Shaken by his own lack of judgment, he now defers to Spock: "If you see me slipping again, your orders are to tell me." This is as close as Kirk gets to making a decision while in his divided state. Were Aristotle watching this sequence, he might well use it as a classic example of how a

---

*Interestingly enough, this particular constitutional amendment, which calls for the vice president to assume the office of chief executive immediately should the president ever be incapacitated, was ratified in 1967, not long after "The Enemy Within" first aired.

suppressed emotional life can hinder us from forming sound judgments, as well as acting on the basis of those judgments.

KIRK'S VIRTUOUS PAIN

Every ship needs someone at the helm. It's a lonely position, encompassing an extraordinarily broad range of responsibilities; not everyone, Plato would remind us, is capable of taking on that kind of burden. What makes Kirk such a great captain is that he's essentially a decider—indeed, "a man of decision and decisive action." As much as he "solicits information and estimates from his principal division officers, in the final analysis, Kirk will [always] make the decision."*

That's why it's so painful to watch him in "The Enemy Within," particularly in the moments after Spock and Scott apparently repair the transporter. To run a test, the chief engineer beams down both halves of the doglike creature to Alpha 177, then reenergizes it onto the *Enterprise*. Though the furry animal returns in one piece, it doesn't appear to be moving. McCoy examines the dog, then looks up and says, "He's dead, Jim." (As many of us know, that's the first time Bones utters his trademark line in the series.)†

Could the same thing happen to the two Kirks? Spock thinks not, reasoning that the shock of splitting and then rejoining was too much for the animal's system to take. As a human being, Kirk has the intelligence to control his fear with reason, and thereby prevent the same shock from occurring—a capability the little dog simply does not have. McCoy, however, believes it's possible the dog's death had nothing to do with

---

* Stephen Whitfield and Gene Roddenberry, *The Making of "Star Trek"* (New York: Ballantine Books, 1968), pp. 215–16.
† "The Enemy Within" also marks the first time we see Spock's patented Vulcan nerve pinch.

shock; he wants to perform an autopsy before further action is taken. But there isn't time for that—the longer they debate the issue, the greater the chances Sulu and the rest of the landing party will die on the now subzero freezing planet. *Kirk must do something now.*

Only he can't make up his mind. Wracked with pain over his inability to decide, he pathetically cries out, "Help me...somebody make the decision!"

Again, speaking from the perspective of a Trekker or an admirer of Captain Kirk, it just plain hurts to see our hero in such anguish. Yet Aristotle would say, "This is a good thing"— not because he's a sadist or a proponent of vacillation, but because he believed the truest measure of our character is the pleasure or pain we feel in performing good or bad actions. A virtuous person feels pleasure in doing a virtuous act, and pain when he or she is unable to do good. Therefore, Aristotle would conclude, the agony Kirk suffers over his inability to decide what to do, especially at a time when the lives of the landing party lie in the balance, is the mark of a virtuous man.

KIRK'S EXCESS AND DEFICIENCY

Aristotelian virtue is a moral state involving choice in the matter of pleasures and pains. Virtue is the disposition to feel pleasure and pain appropriately because these feelings are often directly at issue in action. The key word here is *appropriately.* Had Kirk felt pleasure over the plight of Sulu and the other crew members freezing their buns off on Alpha 177, that would have been totally inappropriate.

Why is virtue concerned with pleasure and pain? Well, because some people actually find pleasure in doing bad things, or causing other people pain. For instance, the first thing the manic Kirk does after he's beamed aboard is head for sickbay, where he orders McCoy to pour him a shot of Saurian brandy.

When Bones doesn't respond quickly enough, Kirk grabs him by the arm and again demands the brandy. He then snatches the entire bottle and strides purposefully to Yeoman Janice Rand's cabin, where he makes unwanted (and uncharacteristic) sexual advances toward her. When Rand resists him, the irrational Kirk throws her to the floor; however, when she cries out for help, he flees, but not before punching out Technician Fisher, the crewman who happened to be first on the scene.

If Aristotle were watching this episode, he'd say that the tremendous pleasure the irrational Kirk felt over the way he mistreated McCoy, Rand, and Fisher (not to mention his corresponding failure to feel pain over the harm he'd done them) tells us as much about his character — or lack thereof — as his actions do. To him, the unruliness of the emotions is what causes the most trouble for Kirk, as well as for human beings in general. Unlike reason, our emotions lack an internal system of controls; thus, they can become a destructive force within us if we allow them to run rampant. An excessive amount of uncontrolled emotional energy can indeed transform a person into a tyrant, a madman, a rapist, or worse.

The draining effect that uncontrolled emotions can have on us is neatly illustrated in "The Enemy Within." Manic Kirk is the very picture of excess, Aristotle would say, in terms of both anger and fear; therefore, he is incapable of moral reasoning. Our emotions enable us to see only certain aspects of the choices available to us — namely, whether those choices are more desirable to us, or less. Manic Kirk really has only two options: cooperate with his rational half, or seize control of the ship. Does he weigh them both? Of course not. Rejoining his rational counterpart never crosses his mind. This Kirk's emotions cause him to focus only on the pure power of the position, without taking anything else into consideration — such as the fact that a captain needs the respect and trust of the crew in order to be a truly effective leader.

When strong emotions overwhelm us, our reasoning ability becomes so constricted that we often can't consider any other course of action. To avoid that, Aristotle recommends following what he called the "Golden Mean." To him, all virtues and vices, like all feelings and actions, can be measured by a scale of excess, intermediate, and deficiency. Virtue, or "the mean," is the intermediate between the two extremes—it's a rule of choice between two extremes of emotion or action. The mean is an appropriate action or feeling responding to a particular situation at the right time, in relation to the right people, with the right motive, and in the right way.* In other words, what is excessive anger for this particular situation might have been too little for a different situation.

The following chart lists Aristotle's virtues, showing where they fit in relation to the extremes of emotion or action.

DEFICIT [VICE]	MEAN [VIRTUE]	EXCESS [VICE]
Cowardice	Courage	Foolhardiness
Inhibition	Temperance	Intemperance
Miserliness	Liberality	Extravagance
Shabbiness	Magnificence	Vulgarity
Poor-spiritedness	Gentleness	Irascibility
Maliciousness	Righteous indignation	Envy
Sarcasm	Truthfulness	Boastfulness
Boorishness	Wittiness	Buffoonery
Shamelessness	Modesty	Shamefacedness
Lack of ambition	Proper pride	Ambitiousness
Peevishness	Friendliness	Obsequiousness

Now, let's see how the extremes of feeling or action result in vice in the case of the divided Kirk. The rational Kirk dis-

---

*Aristotle's understanding of the mean of virtue must not be confused with the common mathematical or statistical concepts of mean. They have nothing in common except existing between extremes.

plays poor-spiritedness, while the irrational one exhibits irascibility. They must clearly come together before he can achieve the mean of gentleness. Rational Kirk walks around the *Enterprise* shamefacedly (especially after Spock chews him out), while his bug-eyed counterpart has no shame at all. To restore his pride, the captain will need to reconcile his rational side's lack of ambition with his irrational side's blatant ambitiousness.

Spock certainly appreciates the concept of balance that Aristotle's Golden Mean represents. As his previous remarks indicate, he holds Kirk's ability to make lucid, effective decisions in high regard. Though he'd rather not see the captain in this divided condition, he nonetheless finds the predicament fascinating. "We have an unusual opportunity to appraise the human mind—or to examine, in Earth terms, the roles of good and evil in a man," he observes to Kirk and McCoy. "His negative side, which you call hostility, lust, violence; and his positive side, which Earth people express as compassion, love, tenderness. We see here indications that it is his negative side that makes him strong—that his 'evil' side, if you will, if properly controlled and disciplined, is vital to his strength. Your negative side removed from you, the power of command begins to elude you."

In other words, command is a balance between positive and negative energies—an equilibrium of the forces generated by each of these energies. In Aristotelian terms, we need to find a mean between our positive and negative energies in order to act in the right way. Spock knows this as well as anyone else on the *Enterprise*. "Being split in two halves is no theory with me," he reminds McCoy. "I have a human half, as well as an alien half, submerged, constantly at war with other. [I speak from] personal experience, Doctor. I survive it because my intelligence wins out over both, makes them live together." As we know, Spock's Vulcan ancestors, like the irrational Kirk in this episode, spent much of their time fighting among each other.

They solved this problem by suppressing their emotions through strict training and adherence to the rules of logic.

Of course, while Aristotle would likely applaud the Vulcans for striving to find a mean, he'd also be the first to say they went a bit too far. Consider Spock's noble yet completely inappropriate attempt to comfort Kirk in his moment of pain: "If I seem insensitive to what you're going through, Captain, understand—it's just the way I am." Aristotle would say that the Vulcan in Spock makes him deficient in emotional sensitivity. That accounts for why he's such a good number two man, though not necessarily a good number one.*

WHAT MAKES KIRK BRAVE?

Aristotelian ethics also teaches that the mean is acquired through imitation, practice, and habit. The habits that we develop result in states of character; these states of character are virtuous if they produce acts that are appropriate to the mean. With that in mind, Aristotle argued that young people particularly need moral paradigms (what we would call "role models," or personal heroes) to guide their actions in situations that are unfamiliar to them. Of course, because the many individual situations we encounter every day can vary so much from day to day, time to time, and place to place, no single, impersonal standard can possibly determine how each of us should act in every circumstance of life. Since persons of virtue characteristically know how one should act, that makes them invaluable standards for the inexperienced person. Nonetheless, none of us is truly virtuous, according to Aristotle, until we've become experienced and wise in our own right, such

---

*Spock's lack of emotional sensitivity causes friction among several crew members when the shuttlecraft mission he commands goes awry in "The *Galileo* Seven" (*TOS:* #14), an episode we'll examine in Chapters 8 and 14.

that we can judge for ourselves how best to achieve the mean regardless of the circumstances.

It's interesting to note that Kirk's personal hero is not an adventurer or a military leader, as one might expect, but rather President Abraham Lincoln. Remember how the captain praised Lincoln in "The Savage Curtain" for his virtuous nature, particularly his attempt to bring about equality and brotherhood. Aristotle would say that young Kirk used Honest Abe as his measure of virtue until he could achieve sufficient experience and wisdom to be his own judge of what is morally right in each particular situation.* Clearly, Kirk has Lincoln's compassion, as we've seen in the likes of "The Mark of Gideon" (TOS: #72), "All Our Yesterdays" (TOS: #78), and of course, "The Enemy Within." He manifests wisdom on many occasions, including "The Cloud Minders" (TOS: #74) and "Plato's Stepchildren." Certainly time and again he's shown courage that would make the Great Emancipator proud, in episodes such as "Arena," "Amok Time" (TOS: #34), "The Devil in the Dark" (TOS: #26), "The City on the Edge of Forever" (TOS: #28), "Bread and Circuses" (TOS: #43), and again in "The Enemy Within."

But even persons of virtue have their fears. Bear in mind the sequence in our model episode in which manic Kirk is brought into sickbay, his body dramatically weakened as a result of the duplication process. As he lies on the examination

---

*Likewise, each of the three other *Star Trek* captains also uses role models to help them achieve their individual standards of excellence. Besides inventor Leonardo da Vinci, Janeway's personal heroes include pioneer female aviatrix Amelia Earhart ("The 37's," VGR: #20). Ballplayer Buck Bukai, the man who broke Joe DiMaggio's 56-game hitting streak in 2026 ("The Storyteller," DS9: #14; "If Wishes Were Horses," DS9: #16), has long been a hero to 24th-century baseball fan Sisko, presumably for the same reason many real-life fans admire the work ethic of Cal Ripken, who broke the record for consecutive games played in 1995. Picard, of course, invokes Shakespeare as a paradigm of sorts while defending mankind's integrity in "Hide and Q" (TNG: #11).

table, he cries out, "Help me!" Rational Kirk takes his hand and urges him to hold on—indeed, to use his mind so that he won't be afraid. This reiterates the point Spock had made moments before in the debate following the death of the regenerated dog—that unlike animals, we can quell any fear we might have by using our reasoning capabilities.

Now, just exactly how does reason quell our fears? Aristotle believed we can either fear something too much, or too little—meaning, fear can be disproportionate to the value of what we fear. Therefore, we can talk ourselves out of fearing something too much by convincing ourselves that what we fear isn't so bad after all. How many times have you awakened screaming (or shuddering, or both) because of a nightmare brought on by that scary movie you rented the night before? Chances are, either you or your partner (assuming you also managed to awaken him or her) calmed you down by assuring you "It's okay, honey, it's not real, it's just a dream, it's just a movie." Once we acknowledge that what we fear is not as bad as we thought, our fear is receptive to reason. Reason can then either compensate for the deficiency in our fear, or remove the excess. Again, rational Kirk shows us how it's done. Knowing his irrational half is afraid of dying, he coaxes his double into removing his excess fear by helping him see that death is not inevitable—at least, not right away.

"The Enemy Within" drives this point home later in the sequence, this time in the person of McCoy. Though rational Kirk knows he needs to bring his other half "back inside himself" in order to survive, the experience of seeing his most animalistic excesses literally brought to life still leaves him a little shaken. Bones reassures the captain that he's no different from anyone else: "We all have our darker side—we need it! It's half of what we are. It's not really ugly—it's *human*." As much as he hates to admit it, McCoy knows Spock is right. "Without the negative side," he continues, "you couldn't be the captain, and you know it! Your strength of command lies mostly in him." In his own way, the doctor is reiterating the fundamental Aristotelian point that we need both our emotion and our reason to function in order to respond correctly to the various situations we encounter in life.

Having heard plenty about his deficiencies at this point, the rational side of Kirk despondently asks what he has going for him. "You have the goodness, the intelligence, the logic," says McCoy. "Perhaps that's where man's essential courage comes from. For you see, [your irrational half] was afraid. You weren't."

McCoy's insight into human nature also echoes the teachings of Aristotle, who wrote a great deal about the important role reason plays in bringing about courage in his *Nichomachean Ethics:*

> The person who faces and who fears the right things and from the right motive, in the right way and at the right time, and who feels confidence under the corresponding conditions, is brave, for the brave person feels and acts according to the merits of the case in whatever way reason directs.

Like McCoy, Aristotle believed the courageous person needs intelligence and logic to know how to identify which things are the right things to fear, and to determine how he should act according to the "merits of the case." Moreover, said Aristotle, the courageous person needs goodness to act for a noble purpose.

HOW EMOTIONS FACILITATE VIRTUE

Now, what about the climactic moment when irrational Kirk takes on both his rational double and the entire bridge crew in a last-gasp effort to seize control of the ship—is that an act of courage on his part, or is he just being foolhardy once again? Indeed, it's easy to see how these actions could be interpreted as brave. As Aristotle put it, "Those who act on emotion also seem to be brave—as wild beasts seem to be when they attack those who have wounded them." Nonetheless, he thought it a mistake to regard such people as brave, since they fight "[only on account of] their feelings, not because of honor or as reason prescribes." To him, the act of confronting danger out of pure emotion becomes courageous if, and only if, decision and a noble goal both enter into the picture. If we think about it in those terms, it's impossible to consider irrational Kirk anything but foolhardy. After all, being excessively impulsive, he's incapable of deliberation; therefore, he cannot possibly come to any decision or be guided by reason. Rational Kirk, on the other hand, is truly courageous under these conditions—with the safety of his crew foremost in mind, he calmly talks his counterpart into dropping his phaser and surrendering.

Precisely how do we control our fear in order to act bravely? Again, by using our reason. As the dramatic dichotomy of Captain Kirk reminds us, as much as we need emotional energy in order to command, we must also harness that energy. Our emotions enable us to perform actions more promptly and easily than rationality alone; if controlled by reason, our emotions can actually intensify our moral life. For instance, courage is a virtue necessary for command. While courage and fear may seem to be mutually exclusive, they're actually compatible. The truly brave person not only fears what he should when there is a reasonable basis for fear, he or she can also stand up to this fear and confront danger.

Similarly, courage is also compatible with anger, provided it conforms to the guidance of reason. Even anger can result in justice, as Deanna Troi reminds us in "Descent, Part 1" (*TNG:* #152). "Feelings aren't positive or negative, they simply exist," she says to Data. "It's what we do with those feelings that becomes good or bad. For example, feeling angry about an injustice could lead someone to take a positive action to correct it." Sometimes the increased adrenaline brought on by a person's anger can give her the physical boost she needs to deal more effectively with a difficult situation. Uttering this sage advice, Counselor Troi couldn't have been more Aristotelian.

THREE PRACTICAL RULES WHEN YOU'RE SPLIT IN TWO

Don't get me wrong—achieving the mean isn't as easy as it sounds. For every right way to act in a given situation, there are hundreds more where we can go wrong. Fortunately, Aristotle had the foresight to take that into consideration. Knowing how difficult it is to do what is "rare and praiseworthy and noble," he gave us three practical guidelines to help us achieve the mean:

1. *Avoid the extreme that is more opposed to the mean.* For instance, cowardice and rashness are the extremes of courage. Since cowardice is more opposed to courage than rashness is, we should try to avoid being cowardly more than we should try to avoid being rash. In other words, choose the lesser of two evils. The *Enterprise* crew does just this throughout Kirk's divided state. Knowing that the rational Kirk more closely resembles their captain than his savage, uncontrolled counterpart, they side with him all through the episode.
2. *Stay within yourself. Consider your natural inclinations and act accordingly, bearing in mind your strengths and weaknesses.* Suppose you have a hard time controlling your temper, and you'd like to change that. Using this piece of advice, you should strive to become so calm that nothing makes you

angry. Since you're such a hothead, your attempt may result in a response that is neither too placid nor too angry. Again, though his strength of will is clearly diminished during his divided state, rational Kirk stays within himself, drawing on his innate "goodness, intelligence, and logic" as he works toward his goal: putting himself back together. (Of course, all he really needs is a properly working transporter. If only it were that easy for the rest of us. . . .)

3. *Be careful of immoderate pleasure, "for we can scarce judge her impartially."* When we yield to pleasure (in whatever form it happens to be), the last thing we want to do is debate the finer points of ethics. Indeed, what does irrational Kirk want foremost after he first materializes? Instant gratification (first he wants a drink, then he wants sex). Aristotle doesn't oppose the pursuit of pleasure for its own sake; he'd just like to remind us that excess pleasure—at inappropriate times, and under inappropriate circumstances — is a strong inducement to vice. Partying is fine, he'd say; just don't overdo it. Being under the influence, by definition, means not having control of our own faculties. When that happens, as the incident in Yeoman Rand's cabin reminds us, we're capable of doing harm to others, as well as ourselves.

JANEWAY, SEVEN, AND THE IMPORTANCE OF CONTEXT

For Aristotle, exact rules of action are not possible. Not even the wisest ethicist can firmly establish hard-and-fast rules for right action—every situation is different, and what would be done in one situation should not be done in another situation. In addition, Aristotle recognized that there are innumerable outside factors affecting an action; thus, it's also impossible to form exact rules without knowing all the facts of a particular situation. Therefore, when faced with a decision, we should determine to act "at the right time, on the right occasion, toward the right people, for the right purpose, and in the right manner." A person of virtue knows that the right thing to do in one situation may not always be appropriate for another. Indeed, the entire tenor of Aristotle's virtue ethics is that no one type of response is right for all situations. With that in mind, we need to develop moral sensitivity to weigh and take into account the importance of the various factors in each situation.

In other words, for every mean, there's a context. Finding the appropriate mean for a particular context is often a matter of trial and error. What was right before may not be right next time.

Star Trek has illustrated this principle on a number of occasions, though perhaps never as clearly as the situation depicted in *Voyager*'s "Latent Image" (*VGR:* #105). The holographic Doctor accompanies Harry Kim and Ensign Jetal on a shuttlecraft mission, but things go awry when their craft is invaded by an alien species. Kim and Jetal suffer critical spinal and neurological damage as a result of the attack. However, by the time they're beamed to *Voyager*'s sickbay, the Doctor discovers he has time to save only one of their lives. For a holograph normally programmed to follow orders based on the calculation of variables in each circumstance (meaning that the concept of "choice," as most of us know it, has been basically eliminated), this is a most extraordinary situation. Since the variables in this case are the same—the extent of the damage in both victims is identical—the Doctor finds he has to make an arbitrary choice (save Kim, or save Jetal) or risk losing them both. He chooses Kim, simply on the basis that he knows him better. However, this action soon causes a "feedback logic" error between the Doctor's cognitive and ethical programming that replays the event continually, to the point where the holograph becomes destructively obsessive about the memory. (Presumably the formal principle of justice, which states that justice is the similar and injustice the dissimilar treatment of individuals, was built into his program.) To resolve the problem, "for [his] benefit and the welfare of the entire crew," Janeway deletes all memory of this event from the Doctor's programming.

Eighteen months later, with the help of Seven of Nine, the Doctor discovers what Janeway did to his memory. (Seven had not yet joined the crew at the time of the original incident.) When Seven challenges her, the captain poses the question: "If one of my crew chose to put a phaser to his own head, should I let him?"

"It would depend on the situation," replies Seven.

Anticipating this response, Janeway emphasizes, "It always depends on the situation, Seven—but we can debate philosophy another time." Like an Aristotelian ethicist, Janeway knows that the right thing to do depends on the context of the situation—the right time, the right occasion, the right purpose, and so forth.

But if finding the appropriate mean always depends on the context, does this mean that "the mean" is relative? Let's think about that one. Remember that relativism claims there are no universal ethical standards; what's right and wrong depends on the individual beliefs of a person or culture. In other words, matters of ethics are arbitrary. Though Aristotle believed no one course of action is applicable to every situation, he also held there is indeed a right course for every situation. Not only that, once we take all relevant factors into consideration, such as the time, occasion, intention, and the people we're dealing with, we'll find that anyone else in our shoes would assuredly act the same way. That's not arbitrary at all.

Do Janeway and Seven agree that for every situation there's one right thing to do? Of course, they do; they just don't always agree as to what that course of action happens to be. Still, it's important to remember that they often disagree for the same reasons most of us do: because they have different perceptions of one or more factors of the particular situation. In the case of "Latent Image," they differ on the nature of individuality versus that of a holograph; once they resolve their difference, they do agree on the right action.

Nonetheless, should any of these factors vary, the situation may very well call for a different response. In other words, we have to be willing to bend with the wind. Janeway occasionally forgets this; sometimes, she seems excessively confident about her decisions to the point of being stubborn. When Seven challenges her on the matter of deleting the Doctor's memory without considering his preferences, Janeway staunchly defends her decision. Though the Doctor has been allowed to evolve as a human would, she argues, in essence he's no different from a starship replicator—though he seems to have a mind of his own, he really doesn't.

But as Aristotle also said, "There are many ways of going wrong, but only one way of going right, so that the one is easy and the other hard—easy to miss the mark and hard to hit." Therefore, if a virtuous person realizes she might have missed the mark, she should take action to correct the mistake.

To her credit, that's exactly what Janeway does in "Latent Image," after the Doctor again shows symptoms of the same "feedback logic" error that led to the problem of 18 months before. When the captain second-guesses the fairness of allowing the holographic Doctor to have a "soul," only to take it away from him "at the first sign of trouble," she approaches Seven for advice. Like the Doctor, the former Borg was allowed to evolve as a human would, once she was reassimilated from the Collective. Bearing that in mind, Janeway asks, "If you had the chance to change or erase what we did to you—would you?" When Seven says "No," the captain has her answer. Due to Seven's response, Janeway now realizes that the right course of action is to allow the Doctor to rehabilitate himself—indeed, as a thinking, feeling human being would—but with the help of his friends.*

Which brings us back to "The Enemy Within." Though Kirk ultimately had to face his demonic side head on, he could not have mustered the strength to do so without the support of Spock and McCoy. The epilogue of the story also addresses the concept of context. Spock asks Kirk whether he should inform the crew as to the whereabouts of his "double." Perhaps remembering the Vulcan's original comments about how a captain ought to be perceived, Kirk tells him this time that won't be necessary. "The imposter is back where he belongs," he says. "Let's leave it at that."

Certainly many facets of the Aristotelian notion of courage can be applied to *Star Trek*. But the *Nichomachean Ethics* also discusses numerous other virtues in great detail—two of which are also integral to the ethics of the series. We'll take a close look at these in our next chapter.

---

*We'll revisit "Latent Image" in our discussion of existentialism in Chapter 15.

EQUITY AND FRIENDSHIP IN STAR TREK

"Justice"
TNG: Episode 9
Stardate: 41255.6
Original Air Date: Week of November 9, 1987

Upon establishing a Federation colony in the Strnad Solar System, the Enterprise *orbits Rubicam III, whose idyllic society is a curious mixture of hedonistic sexuality and near-puritanical adherence to the law. Riker, Troi, Yar, Worf, and Wesley Crusher become enchanted by the planet after meeting its friendly inhabitants, the Edo. What better place for a long-overdue shore leave? Unbeknownst to the away team, however, an undercurrent of fear also pervades this veritable Eden. Edo society is regulated by a small number of law enforcement officials ("mediators") who monitor randomly selected "punishment zones." Anyone caught breaking a law in these areas is executed, without exception. Because the designated punishment areas always vary, and only the mediators know which zones will be watched, the system provides an absolute deterrent against any transgressions of the law. When young Wesley is marked for death after he unwittingly commits a breach in a punishment zone, Captain Picard must choose between honoring the Prime Directive (thereby not interfering with the customs of Rubicam III)—or violating it to save Wesley's life.*

"The Menagerie" (two-parter)
TOS: Episode 16
Stardates: 3012.4, 3013.1
Original Air Dates: November 17 and 24, 1966

Before Kirk assumed command of the Enterprise, *Spock served under Captain Christopher Pike for more than 11 years. One of their earliest missions took them to Talos IV, a planet of highly advanced telepathic humanoids who used their extraordinary powers of illusion to entrap Pike as part of a desperate effort to repopulate their dying species. As a result of this incident, Starfleet issued General Order No. 7, prohibiting further contact with Talos IV due to the addictive nature of the Talosians' illusion-creating technology. When Pike becomes permanently crippled and mute after suffering severe radiation burns, Spock abducts him aboard the* Enterprise, *then locks the ship on a course for Talos IV so that Pike can live out the illusion of a life unencumbered by his disabled body. But Spock's equitable actions could cost him everything. Violation of General Order No. 7 is a court-martialable offense punishable by death.*

In a sense, "Justice" and "The Menagerie" are variations on the same theme we talked about in the last chapter: that when it comes to ethics, there are no hard and fast guidelines. Doing what's right is not simply a matter of following rules, but a process of always taking everything into consideration.

Of course, there's a little more to these episodes than that. Before we delve into them, though, let's take a moment and recap the basic difference in philosophy between Aristotle and Plato. Aristotelian virtue ethics holds that while reason alone must prevail for ethical action to result, reason doesn't necessarily work alone—the emotions play a vitally important role in determining what we ultimately should do. Whereas Plato believed our bodies and our emotions hindered our ability to live a truly good life (which, to him, could be achieved only by way of contemplating the Forms), Aristotle taught that how we feel is indeed the driving force behind how we act. As we saw in Chapter 6, Captain Kirk's strength of command resides in his emotions; though they must also be channeled by reason, without them he cannot lead. While Plato wrote as if we should barely tolerate our spirit and appetite (because they interfere with the contemplation of the Forms, which he felt is so essential to ethics), Aristotle felt we should embrace them because they have *everything* to do with ethics—we need body, soul, and reason to live a fulfilled, virtuous life.

Plato's virtue philosophy is also pretty rigid in some places, and certainly doesn't take individual circumstances into consideration. Granted, Aristotle had his rubric, too, but he took something else into account that Plato apparently didn't: namely, that everyday living is an inexact science. While Aristotle maintained there's a proper course of action for every situation we face, what we ultimately should do, as Janeway showed us, always depends on the individual nature of each situation. What's right in one instance may not necessarily be appropriate in another.

Both "Justice" and "The Menagerie" address the Aristotelian idea of context, only they take it a step further. Sometimes there are extraordinary circumstances that go beyond the original precepts of the law. To not even take these into account would indeed be criminal.

Aristotle called the principle of justice that takes extraordinary circumstances into account "equity." Equity plays an important role in the world of *Star Trek.* Not only does it explain why Kirk and his successors keep breaking the Prime Directive (without ever being punished), it underscores another Aristotelian concept that's also central to the ethics of the series—namely, the very nature of friendship.

EQUITY AND THE PRIME DIRECTIVE

"Justice" shows us one surefire way in which law enforcement can lead to absolute justice. The problem is, Edo society went from one extreme to another. Once lawless and dangerously violent, it eventually adopted the "punishment zone" system, wherein anyone caught breaking a law in an arbitrarily chosen area is automatically put to death. Because only the mediators know where the punishment zones are at any given time, it's no wonder the rest of the population is so gosh-darned friendly. They're afraid to do each other wrong!

But the episode also shows us the problem inherent in any legal system: because the law can only be structured in general terms, it frequently cannot deal with the particular needs of an individual case. Consider Starfleet General Order No. 1—or, as it's more commonly known in the *Star Trek* universe, the Prime Directive. First introduced in "The Return of the Archons" (*TOS:* #22), this mandate prohibits Starfleet personnel and spacecraft from interfering in the normal development of any society.* To ensure compliance, the rule adds that any Starfleet

---

*David Gerrold, *The World of "Star Trek,"* 2nd ed. (New York: Bluejay Books, 1984) p. 147.

vessel or crew member who violates the Prime Directive is "expendable."*

We've already discussed how the Prime Directive is basically *Star Trek*'s version of Catch-22: while it's central to the philosophy of seeking out new life and new civilizations, it essentially prevents our heroes from taking ethical action in cases where ethical action clearly must be taken. From a practical point of view, the show's writers have wisely disregarded it (or at least found clever ways around it) to avoid painting themselves into the proverbial corner.

Philosophically speaking, Aristotle would say that *Star Trek*'s consistent handling of the Prime Directive reflects a keen understanding of the principle of equity. "Equity" refers to the sort of justice that goes beyond the written law; it provides a way for relaxing the rigor of the legal system from outside that system itself. In other words, it asks us to read between the lines. As *Star Trek* has shown us time and again, even Starfleet General Orders may be overridden in a particular situation by other directives or ethical principles that are clearly more compelling.†

Aristotle held that sometimes the law requires correction simply because written law, by its very nature, cannot possibly account for the almost infinite variety of situations of daily life. The people who founded the United States may have been the brightest men of their time, but even they

---

*Michael Okuda and Denise Okuda, The *"Star Trek" Encyclopedia,* 2nd ed. (New York: Pocket Books, 1997), p. 385.
†The Prime Directive has been violated consistently throughout each *Star Trek* series. In addition to "Justice," it was breached in such episodes as "A Taste of Armageddon" (*TOS: #23*), "The Apple" (*TOS: #38*), "A Private Little War" (*TOS: #45*), "Patterns of Force" (*TOS: #52*), "Pen Pals" (*TNG: #41*), "Who Watches the Watchers?" (*TNG: #52*), "Devil's Due" (*TNG: #87*), "Captive Pursuit" (*DS9: #6*), "Accession" (*DS9: #89*), "Let He Who Is Without Sin" (*DS9: #105*, an episode we'll discuss in Chapter 8), "The Darkling" (*VGR: #61*), and "The Omega Directive" (*VGR: #89*). Cf. Okuda and Okuda, *"Star Trek" Encyclopedia,* p. 385.

couldn't think of everything. That's why the U.S. Constitution has been amended so many times. After all, human thinking has its limits; there are bound to be circumstances beyond the parameters of the law as it was originally conceived. If existing law doesn't take this into consideration, Aristotle would say, perhaps it should.

Equity, therefore, is a virtue for realizing what is actually just in a real situation. That which is legally just is determined by the legislator (the Edo god, in the case of "Justice"), who frames laws that regulate the ordinary course of events. But, as Aristotle would remind us, the very ordinariness that underlies laws also makes them potentially defective precisely because it doesn't account for extraordinary situations. It's unreasonable for Rubicam III to sentence young Wesley Crusher (or, for that matter, anyone else who's just set foot on the planet) for breaking the law, especially given the arbitrary nature of the punishment zones. Ignorance of the law, in this case, must clearly be considered before justice can be rendered. "There can be no justice so long as laws are absolute," Picard pleads before the Edo god. "Life itself is an exercise in exceptions." Riker seconds the thought: "Bravo! Since when has justice been as simple as a rule book?" The Edo god eventually comes to see the wisdom in equity, and allows the *Enterprise* to go its way—with Wesley in tow.

Nonetheless, while the principle of equity may justify the constant violation of the Prime Directive, it doesn't necessarily warrant it. Equity, like all virtues, involves a choice guided by reason. Picard clearly weighed all options carefully before choosing a course of action that delivered justice while still keeping interference with the "normal development" of Edo society to an absolute minimum. You can bet that when Kirk, Janeway, and Sisko breach the Prime Directive, they do so only after likewise choosing compromises that minimize the Federation's impact on the galaxy.

Since Aristotle believed that achieving the mean is always a matter of trial and error, it shouldn't surprise us that the notion of equity plays an essential role in his virtue ethics. A truly just person, ever mindful that everyday life is "an exercise in exceptions," will know that the moral force of equity exerts a stronger claim on us than mere compliance with the law. Like his fellow *Star Trek* captains, Picard realizes that some instances call for a level of justice that transcends what's on the books; though he respects General Order No. 1, he also knows that he sometimes must break it so that justice can truly prevail. "Now I have sworn to uphold [the Prime Directive]," he says in "A Matter of Time" (*TNG:* #109). "Nevertheless I have disregarded that directive on more than one occasion...because I thought it was the right thing to do."* So while equity is a kind of justice, it is also a virtue that operates when the law cannot account for extraordinary situations.

SPOCK, THE EQUITABLE KIDNAPPER

Clearly, *Star Trek* is willing to violate its own rules when it comes to dealing with the laws of other cultures. But the Prime Directive is not the only Starfleet order scrutinized by the laws of equity. The Aristotelian virtue figures prominently throughout "The Menagerie," the two-part episode that cleverly incorporates footage from "The Cage," the first pilot of the Original Series.

No matter how much the Vulcan in Spock dominates his personality, he's still half-human. He's still capable of expressing, if not warmth, then certainly strong feelings of loyalty and friendship. Friendship is also an integral part of Aristotelian thinking—and we'll get into that a little later. For now, though, let's look at Spock's loyalty to his first commanding officer,

---

*He has disregarded it at least nine times, if we're to believe Admiral Satie's accusations in "The Drumhead" (*TNG:* #95).

Captain Pike. *The "Star Trek" Encyclopedia* speculates that Spock was a cadet his first year on the *Enterprise;* if that's the case, he may very well have seen Pike as a mentor. That kind of relationship almost unfailingly engenders strong feelings of devotion, particularly on the part of the student over the course of his or her career.* Plus, spend a decade of your life with someone (be it in marriage, work, or outer space), and you're bound to learn a thing or two about him. Perhaps Spock knew Pike was proud of his virile condition, or that he never really got over Vina (the Earth woman he fell in love with while imprisoned on Talos IV, 13 years before). Or maybe he simply couldn't bear to see his former captain now mute and immobile as a result of the radiation burns.

Of course, Spock would never admit to seeing it that way. "There's no need to insult me," he says to Kirk at the end of the episode, after the captain playfully chides him for showing such "flagrant emotionalism." Indeed, the Vulcan insists that he's "been completely logical about the whole affair."

Naturally, he's right. Though Spock still risks the death penalty (not to mention a mutiny conviction), the court-martial proceedings aboard the *Enterprise* are part of an elaborate fiction he arranged with the Talosian keeper once the vessel was in orbit over Talos IV. Mindful of his present captain's strength of will, Spock knew Kirk would be too preoccupied with regaining control of his ship to consider his extraordinary request. Creating a situation in which he has to be court-martialed therefore enables Spock to argue his case—which he does, with the help of images of the *Enterprise*'s original mission on Talos IV that are being beamed up from the planet. Once these images are also transmitted to Starbase 11, even

---

*Apparently Spock wasn't the only one who held Pike in high regard. Mendez tells Kirk that in the aftermath of Pike's tragic accident, no one in Starfleet "had the heart" to remove him from the active duty list.

Commodore Mendez realizes the tremendous gift the Talosians could offer Pike—the opportunity to live the rest of his life "unfettered by his physical body." Taking into consideration Pike's important contributions to space exploration, the commodore informs Kirk that General Order No. 7 is suspended on this occasion, and that all charges of mutiny against Spock have been dropped. Clearly, the circumstances in this situation demanded an equitable response.*

The matter of granting Spock's request, however, resides with Kirk alone. The captain clearly agrees that, all things considered, allowing Pike to live on Talos IV is the equitable thing. Nevertheless, he can't help wondering why his friend went to such great lengths when all he really had to do was ask. "Even if regulations arc explicit," he says to Spock, "you could have come to me and explained."

Spock knows Kirk isn't just blowing smoke when he says that. The captain is not above bending the rules on behalf of his friend; he certainly did everything he could to defend the Vulcan throughout the "court-martial." Logically speaking, however, it didn't make sense to Spock to ask Kirk to risk the death penalty—even out of friendship. "One of us was enough," he explains. Indeed, one could say it was the only equitable thing to do.

Both "Justice" and "The Menagerie" show us *Star Trek*'s stance on capital punishment. This form of punishment has been abolished, at least in the 23rd century; though General Order No. 7 remains "on the books," it has never since been applied. Could it be that *Star Trek* finds capital punishment inequitable?

---

*We also see the concept of equity illustrated in "Time's Orphan" (*DS9:* #148), wherein the normally rule-conscious Odo allows the O'Briens to steal a runabout in order to help Molly, their daughter. He may reason that in this situation, it is the only equitable thing to do.

THREE KINDS OF FRIENDSHIP

Much of the success of *Star Trek* has been attributed to the bonds of friendship among the characters in each series. So it would show Aristotelian prudence on my part to discuss the virtue of friendship in *Star Trek.*

Before we begin, I should point out that "friendship" is not the same as "friendliness," one of the virtues listed in our chart in Chapter 6. Remember that the person who is pleasant in the right way is "friendly," with the mean being "friendliness"— while the person who is excessively friendly is obsequious. "Friendship," on the other hand, is a virtue involving affection for one's associates. For Aristotle, two people are friends only if their mutual affectionate feelings are acknowledged and known to each other.

But why are two people drawn to each other? What is it that makes a friendship strong enough to last? To answer these questions, Aristotle distinguishes between three kinds of friendships, based on the various factors that draw and connect us to one another. Sometimes, we're connected to people for utilitarian reasons; in other cases, purely for pleasure; still other times, because we recognize the sheer goodness of another person.

We all need "friendships of utility" because none of us is economically self-sufficient. We need other people to provide us with certain skills and products, since we have neither the time nor the aptitude to fill all our needs. That's why we're usually nice to our mail carrier, paperboy, or neighborhood merchants—it's the old notion of taking care of those who take care of us.

On a higher level, there are "friendships of pleasure." These are friendships we form with someone because we take a natural delight in their company. Lwaxana Troi has a lot of friendships of pleasure (though not necessarily with any of the *Enterprise* crew members).

On yet a higher plane is the "friendship of goodness," where one friend strives to help the other live the best life, no matter what—even if it means violating General Order No. 7.

According to Aristotle, we always wish our friends well for their own sake (regardless of the nature of the friendship), and vice versa. In friendships of utility, we wish them well because we'll benefit from their good service, whereas with friendships of pleasure, it's because they're fun to be with. Granted, our well-wishing in these cases might be a little self-serving. Then again, we tend to base these relationships on what we get from them, be it a decent haircut or a drinking companion. That's not the case with friendships of goodness. Here, we wish our friends well simply because they're good people. We do so regardless of whether we receive anything in return (except, perhaps, their goodness).

How can we tell which category our various relationships fall into? That's simple, according to Aristotle: just examine the state of mind that binds you and your friends together. If I go to ball games with Jim because we both love to talk baseball more than anything else, that's a friendship of pleasure. If I go to ball games with Jim because I don't like to sit alone and he's the only other person I know who likes baseball, that's a friendship most likely forged out of utility. If I go to ball games (or spend any time, for that matter) with Jim simply because I care about him and admire the sort of person he is, that's clearly a friendship of goodness. Regardless of the degree of friendship, each type of relationship is based on a shared goal. In each case, Jim and I have some agreement as to our likes, dislikes, interests, and most importantly, basic values and ideals. As Sisko's son, Jake, says to his young Ferengi friend Nog, "We spend so much time together...and we seem so much alike...I sometimes forget we're different" ("Life Support," *DS9*: #59).

FRIENDSHIP IN *STAR TREK*

In the lower rungs of friendship, we care for our friends not so much because they're good people, but because they're useful or entertaining. These relationships tend not to last much beyond the point at which they've served their purpose. Think of Quark, the Ferengi barkeeper in *Deep Space Nine,* and the nature of his friendship with Dr. Julian Bashir and Chief Engineer Miles O'Brien. They're his two most popular customers, so naturally he wants to keep them happy—the more they drink, the more they spend. Without question, that's your basic friendship of utility. But it doesn't always stay on that level. After all, Quark personally likes Bashir and O'Brien; he seems genuinely interested in them both whenever he listens to their problems. So long as his relationship remains profitable, he continues to wish them well. Quark might refuse them a particular service sometimes because it would eat into his profits, but if he does, he'll compensate by offering them another drink on the house. He'll even go so far as help them out now and then, regardless of whether the favor benefits him in return—though he couldn't care less about baseball, he agrees to play on the team after O'Brien gets hurt in "Take Me Out to the Holosuite" (*DS9:* #154).

Friendships of pleasure aren't characterized entirely by self-interest, either. Strictly speaking, the friendship of O'Brien and Bashir would be considered one of pleasure in the Aristotelian sense. Whether it's having a drink, playing darts, or sharing various adventures in the holosuite, they mostly get together for reasons of entertainment. Nonetheless, they clearly care for each other, and have done things for one another that go beyond the surface level of pleasure. Similarly, when Lwaxana took young Alexander Rozhenko under her wing in "Cost of Living," she wanted to teach the boy how to enjoy life, and have some fun in the process. But their relationship became much deeper than that, to the point where she learned more from Alexander than she'd ever imagined.

The friendship of the good—wherein two persons, having spent enough time together to know each other's essential character and to trust one another, grow to love one another because of their good qualities—is the kind of friendship that achieves "the mean." Since Aristotle devotes a good chunk of the *Nicomachean Ethics* to discussing this ultimate degree in human relationships, we'll do the same here. We certainly see this level of friendship embodied throughout all four *Star Trek* series, including the episode "Justice." Though Picard seems aloof at times, he genuinely cares for the well-being of his crew members—he has compassion for Dr. Crusher as she agonizes over her son's fate. He also apologizes to Data after calling him a "babbler" in the heat of the moment, reminding the android that he often sees things "in a way that we do not—but as they are."

Perhaps the best example, though, of "friendship of the good" in *Star Trek* is the relationship between Kirk and Spock. We've seen how much Kirk needs Spock, especially when it comes to decisions of command. But as we saw in "The Menagerie," he clearly cares for his first officer; indeed, he considers the disciplinary proceedings against Spock to be "the most painful moment I've ever faced." Spock, in turn, cares for Kirk, so much that he wouldn't allow the captain to risk the death penalty by asking him to breach General Order No. 7 (though he knows Kirk would have done so in a minute). Theirs is a friendship based on mutual recognition of each other's individual goodness—even in parallel universes (as we see in "Mirror, Mirror," when Kirk recognizes that Spock's essential integrity also resides in the Vulcan's mirror counterpart). Each have qualities that attract the other; indeed, in many ways they complete one another. Aristotle believed this kind of relationship is very powerful, because it encourages a growth in virtue that would be far more difficult to attain outside the relationship.

Once formed, friendships of the good tend to be permanent because they're based on reciprocal love for each other's good characteristics—characteristics that, once formed in a person, tend to last forever. This idea is explicitly expressed in *Star Trek II: The Wrath of Khan*, when Spock tells Kirk, "You are my superior officer—you are also my friend. I have been and always shall be yours." Later in the film, just prior to Spock's death scene, the Vulcan says it again for emphasis: "I have been, and always shall be, your friend." Such a deep abiding friendship, Aristotle would say, is very rare because there are few such people as Kirk and Spock. Not only that, friendships of the good need a lot of time and familiarity in order to truly nurture and grow.

Kirk and Spock love each other for who they are, not merely for what they can derive from their relationship. Though they may derive both advantage and pleasure from their relationship, that's not an essential feature of the friendship itself. They have been and always will be friends, because they're focused on the good of each other. Though they might expect their relationship to be advantageous, that's not its characteristic feature—they'd expect the same from anyone else aboard the *Enterprise*. Their friendship certainly never would have lasted were it based on pleasure alone—as much as he likes Spock's company, Kirk could surely find someone better to share a good laugh with. Even when the Vulcan tries to be funny (or, as was the case in *Star Trek IV: The Voyage Home,* uses "colorful metaphors"), the captain usually discourages him because he hasn't "quite got the knack of it."

Indeed, Kirk and Spock think of each other as another self, such that what's good for one is good for the other. Consider the sequence near the end of "Amok Time" (*TOS:* #34) when Spock is about to turn himself in to Starfleet authorities, believing he has just killed Kirk on the planet Vulcan moments before.* He doesn't realize that McCoy had injected Kirk with a neural paralyzer that caused the captain's heartbeat and breathing to stop long enough to create the appearance of death; that way, Spock could win his fight with the captain without actually killing him. When he sees that Kirk is indeed alive, Spock is so ecstatic to see his friend alive that he momentarily breaks form, embracing the captain with utter joy and relief: "Jim!"

Of course, once Spock realizes what he's done, he becomes embarrassed by his outburst: he immediately puts the brakes on his emotions and resumes his normally placid countenance. Though Kirk understands this completely, Bones can't resist teasing Spock for "showing genuine human feeling," if only for a moment. Though we know Kirk isn't averse to poking fun at the Vulcan himself (such as when he tweaked him for his "flagrant emotionalism" on behalf of Captain Pike), he always does so gently, and never at the expense of Spock's dignity. Sensing that Bones might be going a bit too far on this occasion, the captain diffuses the matter by changing the subject: "Come on, Mr. Spock. Let's go mind the store."

Aristotle reminds us that in friendships of the good, we take pleasure from our friends simply because they're in our lives. We always want to be near them, because we can never get enough of such pure bliss. We need them "to live with and share in discussion and thought with—for this is what living together would seem to mean for [rational] beings." Kirk and Spock regularly discuss their thoughts with one another, whereas the friendship of Bashir and O'Brien is based on shared activities. What makes the Kirk and Spock relationship

---

*In this episode, Spock found himself pitted against Kirk in a battle to the death when his intended Vulcan mate T'Pring announced she wanted the captain instead. "Amok Time" is also the episode that introduced the Vulcan hand salute, as well as the phrases "Live long and prosper" and "Peace and long life," into the *Star Trek* lexicon.

a friendship of the good is not simply the fact that they share discussion and thought with each other, but rather the binding force of their characters. They are both good people—or "just individuals," as Aristotle would put it—who recognize the goodness in each other.

IS *STAR TREK* MORE COMPATIBLE WITH PLATONIC OR ARISTOTELIAN VIRTUE ETHICS?

Both Plato and Aristotle emphasized the importance of reason to the moral life—a notion that *Star Trek* creator Gene Rodden-berry firmly upheld, as we've previously discussed. Both philosophers believed that our reason should guide our emotional responses to help us determine the right thing to do in any particular situation. From what we've seen thus far, does *Star Trek* lean more toward one school of though than the other—or does it somehow embrace both?

To answer that, let's first go back to the Allegory of the Cave. Remember that Plato believed once we've seen the light, we have an obligation to enlighten others. We can't retreat into our cave of illusions. We must face reality as it truly is, and lead others out of the darkness—no matter how painful that proves to be. Now, compare that with Kirk's decision to return Pike to Talos IV at the conclusion of "The Menagerie." Though Vina may appear to be beautiful, and Pike likewise "unfettered by his physical body," those are still illusions. The reality is, they're both horribly deformed.

Plato would absolutely freak at the idea of encouraging Pike and Vina to live out the rest of their lives in illusion. He would insist they accept the pain of reality and embrace the Forms. Aristotle, on the other hand, would commend Kirk for his sound judgment. He'd say the captain took all factors, extraordinary and otherwise, into consideration and decided an exception in this case was the equitable thing to do.

Aristotle's ethics clearly provides us with an account of virtue that can be more readily applied to *Star Trek*—not to mention everyday living. Many of the characters on each series seem to value the wisdom of finding the mean. Also, Aristotle's philosophy is much more down to earth than Plato's; it doesn't rely on such highly abstract notions as a "world of Forms." More importantly, it takes into account the important role our feelings play in determining moral action (unlike Plato, who believed our emotions are more hindrance to virtue than help). Further, the Aristotelian notions of context and equity celebrate our individualism by asking us to consider the circumstances of each particular situation we face, and to allow room for exceptions whenever necessary. Compare that to the rigid, absolute nature of Plato's ideal society, which would stifle many of the individual freedoms that *Star Trek* (as well as humanity in general) holds dear.

Now, I realize all this talk about how we should let reason alone guide our actions can be awfully cumbersome—and yes, even boring. Did any of these people have fun? Is it possible for something to be right just because it feels good? As a matter of fact, there is a school of ethical thought that suggests pleasure indeed should be our guide. Let's consider this rather appealing point of view in our next section.

CHAPTER 8

WHEN WORLDS COLLIDE: HEDONISM VERSUS STOICISM

[OR, JADZIA AND WORF CLASH IN PARADISE]

"Let He Who Is Without Sin..."
DS9: Episode 105
Stardate: Unknown
Original Air Date: Week of November 11, 1996

The planet Risa is the Club Med of the 24th century. With its tropical climate, beautiful beaches, and hedonistic lifestyle, it's the hottest ticket in the galaxy—and the perfect spot for a romantic getaway. Certainly that's what Jadzia Dax had in mind when she and Worf go there on holiday. Only Worf wants to spend the time discussing their relationship, while Jadzia simply wants her Klingon lover to relax and indulge himself. While the couple argue over each other's values, doomsday prognosticator Pascal Fullerton continues his crusade to "restore the moral dignity and cultural traditions of the Federation." Fullerton's propa-

ganda falls entirely on deaf ears—until he meets Worf. Convinced that Jadzia and the other patrons of Risa are "soft" and have no self-control, the stoic Klingon helps Fullerton rain on everyone's parade by tampering with the planet's weather control system. But when the fanatical evangelist goes too far—to the point where the vacationers' lives are endangered—Worf realizes he must stop Fullerton before it's too late.

Aristotle wasn't the only disciple of Plato who went off in his own direction. Consider Aristippus (435–366 B.C.), the father of ethical hedonism, who maintained that all good is based on pleasure alone—particularly, the immediate gratification of all our sensual desires. In fact, Aristippus and his followers (known as "Cyrenaic hedonists," after Cyrene, Aristippus' native city in North Africa) firmly believed we should strive for as many pleasurable moments as we can possibly experience. While these folks may not have originated the saying "Eat, drink and be merry," they certainly took it to heart!*

Hedonism takes pleasure seriously. Not only does it implore us to seek pleasure as many times (and in as many ways) as possible, it insists that we settle for nothing less than the maximum level of intensity in all our pleasurable activities. The more intense the experience, the more pleasurable it is for the individual. Physical enjoyments are far more desirable to the Cyrenaic hedonist than those of the mind precisely because bodily pleasures are more intense. While moments of epiphany often bring about a shudder of excitement, that *frisson* we feel

---

*Though this time-honored maxim is often accredited to Benjamin Franklin, it actually goes back to the Old Testament: "A man hath no better thing under the sun than to eat, and to drink, and to be merry" (Ecclesiastes 8:15). Ecclesiastes is a book of proverbs attributed to Solomon, the legendary king of Israel, who predated Aristippus by approximately 600 years. Source: *Compton's Interactive Encyclopedia,* 1998 edition.

is not quite the same as the sheer ecstasy of enjoying a gourmet meal, a fine wine, a walk in the sun (or the rain, if that's your fancy), or plain old good sex. Doubtlessly, Aristippus would have loved the planet Risa: from its lush climate and fabulous beaches, to its nubile-bodied patrons and their frequent rites of *jamaharan*, it truly is a "pleasure planet."

While all hedonists believe that pleasure alone is intrinsically good, some of them have had different ideas on how pleasure, and the good that comes from it, should be achieved. Epicurus (341–270 B.C.), for example, would be considered a "moderate hedonist" by Aristotelian standards. Though Epicurus agreed that all pleasure, even the most licentious, is good, he felt we should not seek every pleasure indiscriminately, or avoid every pain. At the very least, he believed, we should consider the consequences of overindulging. Before we help ourselves to a second or third helping of I'danian spice pudding or Thalian chocolate mousse, he would remind us that gorging on rich, highly caloric desserts can make us ill, perhaps even obese. That would be a bad thing. After all, if we're sick, we can't partake in any more pleasurable activities until we're well again. Since the aim of the hedonist is to experience as much pleasure as possible, we should therefore carefully consider anything that might curtail the number of pleasurable experiences we can possibly have before deciding how to act.

Ironically, when Worf warns Jadzia not to have any icoberry torte because it makes her spots itch, for the time being, at least, he is speaking like a Epicurean hedonist— unwittingly of course. Worf opposes hedonism on general principle, for reasons we'll get into later on.

Just as we should avoid overindulging in some pleasures, Epicurus also advised shunning certain other forms of immediate gratification because they, too, can lead to considerable pain. For example, let's say Captain Kirk takes a weekend shore leave in Las Vegas, and the Federation showers him with tickets for unlimited free food and booze. Knowing the captain's rash nature, it's a pretty sure bet he won't be able to resist stuffing himself at every all-you-can-eat buffet in town, or downing all the Saurian brandy he can get his hands on. Perhaps he also takes a liking to some lovely young thing whom he invites upstairs to "check out my captain's log."

Now, let's say Kirk's body has its own pleasure and pain sensors, and that we could chart them on a graph such as the one below. The horizontal line would represent an equilibrium (that is, a state in which Kirk feels neither pleasure nor pain), with his "pleasure" readings appearing above the line, and his "pain" below. With that in mind, the chart for his weekend would look something like this:

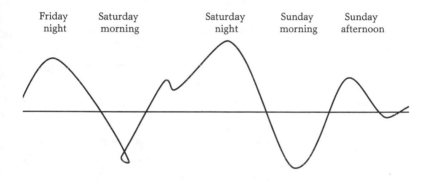

| Friday night | Saturday morning | Saturday night | Sunday morning | Sunday afternoon |

Notice how for every pleasure Kirk experiences, the corresponding pains that follow tend to run deeper and last much longer. The pains could be due to the killer hangover he's got from all that drinking; the severe nausea from overeating; the sudden onrush of fear and anxiety because he can't remember exactly what happened the night before (let alone whether he used a condom); or perhaps all of the above. It'll take a day or two before his body recovers from all that revelry, perhaps even longer to clear up the anxiety.

It's not that Epicurus was a party pooper. Rather, he just wanted us to remember that too much of a good thing tonight can bring on pain and misery tomorrow—a point not unlike Aristotle's third guideline for achieving the mean ("Be careful of immoderate pleasure"). Since the goal of hedonism is to enjoy life to its fullest, a wise hedonist ought to take pains to avoid anything that might impede that goal.

THREE KINDS OF DESIRES, ONE KIND OF TRANQUILLITY

Epicurus also held that certain physical desires could never be fully satisfied. Consequently, if we give in to these cravings, we're only asking for pain, discomfort, or disappointment precisely because they might never be fulfilled. Think of an alcoholic, a drug addict, or even a smoker, for that matter, whose insatiable desire requires constant indulgence. Since he cannot imbibe or partake continually, he's likely to experience great physical pain (be it severe shaking, chills, or worse) during those periods of withdrawal when he's without his addictive beverage or substance.

We can avoid this kind of discomfort, of course, by devoting ourselves to pursuing only the right kinds of desires. To help us choose the right path, Epicurus distinguished between three kinds of desires: (1) "natural and necessary," which are the things we absolutely need to survive as physical beings (such as food, drink, and sleep); (2) "natural and unnecessary," the things which, while not necessary physiologically speaking, are nonetheless natural (such as sex, love, and respect); and (3) "unnatural and unnecessary," the things in life we could do without and still be happy (such as fame, power, wealth, and luxuries). Accordingly, he believed we should pursue the first kind of pleasure (as well as, albeit in a more limited way, the second kind), but forgo those of the third.

I see you scratched your head as you read that last sentence. Surely all of us have had champagne wishes and caviar dreams we'd like to have come true. Why on earth, then, would any self-respecting hedonist advise us to do without them?

The answer, when you think about it, is quite logical. Since we're not born with the unnatural and unnecessary desires, Epicurus argued, they're not essential to us. Second, while true love may indeed be hard to find, it's certainly far more attainable for most of us than fame, wealth, and power. Though some are born into money and prestige, many others have to work hard for them. Acquiring such riches requires certain kinds of sacrifice not all of us are willing to make. Finally, even after we attain these luxuries, there's still a price—no matter how much power or money we have, it's in our nature to want more. No matter how large a market share our company controls, there's always going to be competition; we can't afford to ease up, lest some other company overtakes us. All of this stuff can cause stress, ulcers, migraines, and other kinds of headaches—which in turn impedes our ability to enjoy life's pleasures. Look at it that way, and you can understand why a moderate hedonist would recommend not bothering with "unnatural and unnecessary things."

Clearly, for Epicurus, the pursuit of pleasure is not simply a matter of "checking your brains at the door," but rather an exercise that should be practiced with the wisdom that comes from a discriminating mind. In other words, just as reason prevails in Platonic and Aristotelian philosophy, so it does in Epicurean thought. In the case of moderate hedonism, wisdom comes from the ability to weigh the long-term effects of pleasure and pain through intelligence, foresight, and reasoning. Our reason enables us to assess all pleasures in terms of their corresponding pains, and to discriminate those pains which are worth enduring for the sake of pleasure from those which are not.

Since rational control is central to Epicurus' philosophy, the fact that he valued the pleasures of the mind (such as art, literature, music, and philosophy) over the physical pleasures (rampant eating and drinking, and sexual intemperance) should come as no surprise. Reason is critical, because it is the means both for controlling our pleasurable activities and for allowing us to enjoy them.

Now, let's imagine Kirk on a totally different type of weekend—the kind Epicurus would recommend, involving healthy food, diverse aesthetic pleasures (perhaps engaging Spock in a game of three-dimensional chess), and long enjoyable conversations with McCoy. Using the same type of chart as before, our readings for the weekend might look like this:

| Friday night | Saturday morning | Saturday night | Sunday morning | Sunday afternoon |

Granted, Kirk probably didn't find this weekend as exciting as his romp in Las Vegas. Nonetheless, as we can see from the chart, the pleasures he came away with lasted much longer, while the pains he felt were nowhere near as severe. In fact, once he balances the pleasures against the pain, the captain would probably agree that the second weekend was a far more pleasant experience than the first.

Which brings us to another key aspect of Epicureanism. By using reason to weigh the consequences of overindulging, as well as to avoid those pleasures that cause more pain than others, the wise hedonist comes to experience the greatest pleasure of all—tranquillity.

For Epicurus, a truly good life consists of having a tranquil mind sustained by simple pleasures, a sensible diet, and good friends. The good life is obtained by kindness and friendship with those around you. The wise person will avoid both the temptations of immediate pleasures and the temptations of choosing the intense experience over the more tranquil one.

Finally, there is one other important distinction between Epicurus and the other ethical philosophers we've studied. Unlike Plato and Aristotle (both of whom were concerned with our individual actions, as well as those of society), the ethical theory Epicurus fashioned was entirely egocentric. The sole criterion for rejecting pleasures is whether they bring *us* more pain than pleasure; whether our pursuit of pleasure causes others pain is not addressed. Likewise, he taught only that we should consider the long-term consequences our actions could have on ourselves, without necessarily considering how they might impact society as a whole.

STAR TREK IN PARADISE

So what role does hedonism play in the ethics of *Star Trek*? Certainly "Let He Who Is Without Sin..." incorporates several key components of Epicureanism. We saw earlier how Worf implores Jadzia to consider the consequences of eating icoberry torte. In addition, consider how thoroughly the inhabitants of Risa reject the ideology of Pascal Fullerton,* which focuses on "restoring the moral dignity of the Federation." Everyone (except Worf) is too engrossed in pursuing their own pleasures to take him seriously, let alone his concerns about

---

*Presumably Pascal Fullerton was named after Blaise Pascal, the French philosopher who conducted scientific research on atmospheric pressure before devoting himself to studying the spiritual problems of human beings. While Fullerton similarly appears concerned with the welfare of the Federation, the key difference is that he changes the atmosphere of the planet Risa to put pressure on the vacationers to accept his philosophy.

society as a whole. In fact, the only reason they attend Fullerton's crusades is because they find him, as Arandis put it, "entertaining."

While the Risans tend to lean more toward the blatant hedonism of Aristippus, Jadzia, as we mentioned before, certainly appears to be more Epicurean. Unlike Leeta and Bashir, she's not interested in pursuing indiscriminate sexual trysts (though, of course, Worf jealously misinterprets her friendship with Arandis as just that kind of thing). All she wants is to enhance her pleasure in her monogamous relationship with her Klingon lover. Though she does have some Cyrenaic tendencies (she does want that icoberry torte, consequences be damned), Jadzia would probably agree with Epicurus that the good life (at least when it comes to one's vacation or shore leave) is found not in service to others, but rather in the pleasant company of a good friend and a wonderful lover.

In fact, you could say the very concept of shore leave is *Star Trek*'s way of saying that a little hedonism is good for the soul. As we see in both "Let He Who Is Without Sin..." and "Cost of Living,") even someone like Worf is capable of loosening up once in a while.

Still, how we act on vacation is just that—how we act on vacation. In other words, it's a time in which we "vacate" ourselves from our normal routine, whereas how we act in our daily lives is often quite different. Similarly, *Star Trek*'s attitude toward what constitutes "normal" human behavior centers around two concepts that clearly go against the principles of hedonism—namely, duty and responsibility to others. For instance, consider the side effect the spores have on Kirk's crew in "This Side of Paradise" (*TOS:* #25): they bestow such complete feelings of contentment on everyone that nobody wants to leave the planet! The spores, of course, have a particularly dramatic effect on Spock, whose capacity for happiness, joy, and love is unlocked for the first time. Thus, when Kirk gives him an order, the normally obedient Vulcan declines, simply because "he doesn't want to."

A hedonist watching this episode would point out that under these conditions, Spock has everything a man can ever need—including the love of a woman who happens to look like Jill Ireland! Why would Kirk want to take that away from him? Because, as the captain later explains to Dr. McCoy, somehow it isn't natural for us to have it so easy: "Maybe we don't belong in Paradise, Bones. Maybe we're meant to fight our way through. Struggle. Claw our way up, fighting every inch of the way. Maybe we can't stroll to the music of lutes; we must march to the sound of drums [instead]."

Star Trek echoes this sentiment in another episode, "The Apple" (*TOS:* #38), wherein Kirk destroys Vaal, the sophisticated master computer that controlled the humanoids of Gamma Trianguli VI. Vaal had kept the people who worshiped it in a garden where there is no disease, no death, and ultimately no growth. Though Spock argues that sabotaging the computer would be a direct violation of the Prime Directive, Kirk and McCoy hold that humanoids (which the inhabitants of the planet essentially are) need to grow in order to thrive as a culture. Under Vaal's leadership, they argue, the people of Gamma Trianguli VI have stagnated—no humanoid culture that is allowed to remain that way could ever be considered viable or "normal." Therefore, the Prime Directive doesn't really apply in this instance.

Both "This Side of Paradise" and "The Apple" clearly suggest that pleasure alone does not make us complete—we have other needs, as well. Contrary to hedonistic principles, one of those needs is the need to work. After you've stopped laughing, consider this: even those who can afford to play golf all the time usually don't. They always want to make another movie, start up another company, or launch some other project—not simply to make more money, but also out of a fundamental desire *to be productive*. That would also account for those people we've all read about who continue working even though they've won enough money from the lottery to buy the company. Like it or not (as Kirk implies), that's part of who we are. In fact, most of us would agree that when we genuinely like what we're doing, we often find great pleasure in our work.

Even when the *Star Trek* characters find themselves ensconced in paradise (or environments where dreams come true), it never seems to be of their own choosing. If they're not under the influence of Omicron Ceti III spores, they're either hallucinating ("Shore Leave," *TOS: #17*), have been kidnapped ("The Cage," *TOS: #1*; "I, Mudd," *TOS: #41*), or have lost their memory and don't know any better. The latter instance happens to Kirk in "The Paradise Syndrome" (*TOS: #58*), after he, Spock, and McCoy investigate a veritable Atlantis or Shangri-la inhabited by descendants of native American Indians. When the captain becomes separated from them, Spock and McCoy are forced to leave him behind to divert an asteroid headed directly toward the planet. Due to complications, Kirk lives on the planet for over two months, during which time he is mistaken for a god after he saves the life of a young boy by using basic CPR. Totally liberated from his duties as a starship captain, he falls in love, marries, and impregnates the beautiful priestess Miramanee, all the while embracing the joys of his newfound innocence. "All I can tell you," he says to his young bride, "is that I'm happy and peaceful here. I'm not sure, but I think I've never felt that way before." It doesn't last, of course. A jealous Salish, the tribal chief whom Kirk displaced, unmasks our hero as a false god, causing an uprising that eventually claims the life of Miramanee and their unborn child. Though Kirk finally regains his memory (with the help of Spock and the Vulcan mind-meld), he must also bear the pain of a paradise truly lost.

The "paradise is not for us" motif also appears in "The Way to Eden" (*TOS: #75*), in which "space hippies" hijack the *Enterprise* and force the crew to search for the mythological planet of Eden. Using the ship's computer, Spock locates a radiantly sunny garden, teeming with colorful flowers and bountiful fruit trees. It is truly an Eden. But when Chekov touches a flower and is severely burned by its acid, McCoy discovers there's something wrong with this picture. Indeed, all the plant life on Eden contains acid. The message is clear: despite its abundant beauty, no one can possibly survive on this planet.

Even the *Star Trek* movies take up this theme. In *Star Trek V: The Final Frontier,* Spock's half brother, Sybok, commandeers the *Enterprise* to seek Sha Ka Ree* (the Vulcan name for Eden); not surprisingly, the mythical planet is exposed as a trap once it is found. Meanwhile, in *Star Trek: Generations,* Picard and Kirk must overcome the overwhelming attraction of the Nexus, a timeless zone of pure pleasure that the nefarious Dr. Soran is seeking. The Nexus is yet another hedonistic fantasyland. There, Picard experiences the blissful family life he never had, while Kirk, who was apparently killed by Soran 78 years before, is alive and well, enjoying an idyllic farm life in his native Iowa. The two legendary starship captains join forces and eventually defeat Soran and save the world—though not before Kirk really does lose his life for good.

In film after film, episode after episode, *Star Trek* spurns the notion of paradise as a permanent lifestyle. Instead, it consistently champions such principles as self-development and responsibility to others. Indeed, Picard brings Kirk out of the Nexus by ultimately appealing to the captain's taste for adven-

---

*According to Michael Okuda and Denise Okuda, *The "Star Trek" Encyclopedia,* 2nd ed. (New York: Pocket Books, 1997), p. 439, the name Sha Ka Ree is a pun based on the name of the actor originally considered for the role of Sybok: Sean Connery.

ture, duty, and desire "to make a difference." Though the series frequently depicts paradisiacal societies, these civilizations are ultimately revealed to be unnatural, illusory, or hampered by some other flaw (such as the rigid Edo judicial system in "Justice"). Therefore, it's safe to say that hedonism, despite its many appealing qualities, is not part of the ethics of *Star Trek*.

ALL RIGHT, THEN . . . HOW ABOUT STOICISM?

Around the time Epicurus developed his philosophy, another school of ethical thought took shape—Stoicism, the principle that self-control is of utmost importance. The three foremost Stoics were Marcus Aurelius, a Roman emperor; Epictetus, a slave who earned his freedom; and Seneca, a dramatist and high-ranking government official. The Stoics believed that love of pleasure is a trap to be resisted precisely because it robs us of our control. Stoicism is often contrasted with Epicureanism because they developed so closely together in time. Perhaps the producers of *Deep Space Nine* had that idea in mind as well when they set about planning "Let He Who Is Without Sin . . ."

We've already established how Jadzia embodies hedonistic thought the moment she sets foot in Risa. Worf, on the other hand, is the epitome of Stoicism when he accuses his *par'-machkai* of having no self-control: "At times you are too impulsive. You act without thinking." Because everything Jadzia does reflects on him, Worf needs to know that she's as serious about their relationship as he is. Though Jadzia does indeed take the relationship seriously, she also believes there's a time and place for everything; she urges her lover to relax and enjoy their vacation together.

The next morning, she laments to her friend Arandis that Worf has such a "tough time" enjoying himself. Apparently Worf takes to heart the old Stoic admonition: "Do not laugh much, nor at many things." Whereas Jadzia clearly wants to indulge in the many amusements Risa has to offer (she laughs and clearly enjoys herself as she and Arandis mold clay together), Worf shuns the island's merriments (not to mention the notions of smiling and acting pleasant in general) as though they were deadly. The Klingon warrior seems to live by this Stoic proverb, too: "Avoid entertainment given by outsiders... but if an appropriate occasion arises for you to attend, be on the alert to avoid lapsing into the behavior of such laymen." Having set pleasure aside, the Stoics claim that the only good is virtue—which in turn is attainable only through reason.

All right, you might ask, if the Stoics are so unconcerned about pleasure, are they equally indifferent to pain? Not exactly. First of all, it's impossible in their view to experience pain, fear, or sorrow as negative states unless we consider bodily suffering as an evil. According to Stoic philosophy, however, the notion that bodily suffering is an evil is a mistake in judgment. Like Plato, the Stoics insisted the only evil, or the only vice, that exists is the result of ignorance. Physical pleasure and our desire for it come from mistaken judgments (that is, judgments made out of ignorance) as to what is good. Pleasures tempt the virtuous and reward the vicious, while pains torment them both; but virtue makes people superior to both pleasure and pain. The Stoic in Worf, accordingly, sees the pleasures of Risa as a temptation to be overcome. And, of course, we know from other episodes that he doesn't regard bodily suffering as an evil.

Now, there is one aspect of Stoicism that most of us would probably agree with: personal qualities such as honor and courage are held to be considerably more important than any pleasurable or painful experience. The Stoics believed there are four personal qualities essential to living a good life: simplicity of habits, endurance, self-restraint, and dedication to the community. Worf embodies them all throughout "Let He Who Is Without Sin..." Whereas Jadzia, Leeta, Bashir, and Quark all wear swimsuits throughout their stay on Risa, Worf chooses to remain in his Starfleet uniform ("they're designed for comfort even in the most extreme environments"). Though the others tease him relentlessly for his utter lack of fun, he endures their comments all the same. The sight of Bashir and Leeta "cheating" on each other during their "separation ritual" naturally upsets Worf, as it would any other Stoic who values self-restraint. He believes in monogamy, which explains why he wants to marry Jadzia (and eventually does, later in the series). Finally, Worf sides with Pascal Fullerton and his New Essentialists out of a genuine concern for the welfare of the Federation. When he realizes Fullerton's movement is misguided, he cuts his ties with them for the very same reason.

Worf and Jadzia are at odds with each other throughout the entire episode—she prefers pleasure over politics, he prefers politics over pleasure. We should expect nothing less when a Stoic and a hedonist become lovers. After all, the original Stoics stressed patriotism and civic responsibilities. They believed because we are naturally social, we should always fulfill our social duties—even while we're on vacation. Certainly that's what initially attracted Worf to Fullerton and his movement. The New Essentialist notion that the Risans' self-indulgent revelry and "pampered, spoiled disposition" is "eroding the foundation of the Federation society" also reflects a Stoic attitude. When Worf finds Fullerton's analysis of recent Federation history both "insightful and disturbing," he agrees that shutting down the party planet is the right thing to do.

In contrast to the aggressive social activism of the Stoics, the hedonists completely withdrew from politics. Jadzia doesn't wish to engage in a heated political discussion in the middle of her vacation; she just wants to have fun. Though she realizes the tropical climes of Risa are "artificially created," and that the planet relies on the most elaborate weather control system in the Federation to mask its naturally rain-soaked, geographically unstable condition, she also feels none of that really concerns her. The paradise is there for their enjoyment, regardless of how it came to be.

All Jadzia wants is to spend time with Worf—why else would she go with him to hear Fullerton's speech? Like the other vacationers, she doesn't really take Fullerton seriously; like Arandis, she doubts that one man, "no matter how determined" can change the minds of the planet's many visitors. Worf, ever the Stoic, disagrees: "Kahless fought off an entire army at Three-Turn Bridge. And he was only one man." Just as the Klingons revere Kahless as one who bravely confronted death, so the Stoics admired Socrates for facing death with courage and tranquillity.[*] This paradigm of superb control over the emotions provided the Stoics with a model after which to pattern their lives. To them, Socrates was the ultimate example of a person who did his duty against selfish inclinations, who focused on the good of the soul rather than bodily things. Similarly, Worf, ever mindful of the threat the Dominion poses to the Federation and its citizenry, believes the vacationers of Risa should put aside their self-indulgent inclinations and concentrate on duty—a good of the soul.

Like Socrates, the Stoics compared moral improvement to medical treatment—though the process of healing involves

---

[*] According to Okuda and Okuda, The "Star Trek" Encyclopedia, p. 228, Kahless the Unforgettable is the renowned warrior who united the Klingon Empire 1,500 years ago. Though clearly a great man in Worf's eyes (his legend is central to Klingon mythology and religion), whether other cultures would also consider Kahless a heroic figure is open to debate. This is, after all, the same Kahless whom the Excalbians cited as one of the four wickedest figures in history in "The Savage Curtain." Of course, whereas in the days of the Original Series the Klingons were sworn enemies of the Federation, that condition no longer applies in the era of TNG, DS9, and VGR. Nonetheless, given this ambiguity, one suspects the Stoics, had they known about Star Trek, would insist that Kahless was not quite in Socrates' league.

pain, that very pain strengthens our wills. The Stoics believed if that we're unable to handle the minor adversities in life, there's no way we can be expected to tackle the major ones. As a remedy, they proposed starting an "exercise program" for the spirit with easy "weights" or problems, then gradually building up to larger ones. The objective is to make our spirit so strong, we can withstand anything. Similarly, Worf feels the best way to cure the vacationers of their moral ills and apathy toward Federation threats is to give them a somewhat painful experience; like the Stoics, he starts them off with a minor inconvenience (he rigs a tricorder to sabotage the weather grid, causing rain to fall on the planet).

Naturally, Jadzia is upset—after all, her vacation (not to mention those of a few hundred thousand other people) has been ruined. "You must be feeling pretty good right now," she says to Worf, her hands on her hips. "The weather is terrible, the guests are miserable, and more and more people are leaving every day." Bashir's criticism, meanwhile, is even more pointed: "With all due respect, Commander, I think you're out of your mind!"

Worf, of course, endures their barbs—he takes satisfaction in the sudden mass exodus ("Their response only proves my point"), while insisting he's been quite rational about the whole affair. "If Federation citizens cannot handle a little bad weather," he reasons to Bashir, "how will they handle a Dominion invasion?"

Worf really does have everyone's best interests at heart (though Jadzia and Bashir probably don't see it that way); after all, he believes in dedication to the community at large, as a good Stoic should. The Stoics believed all rational beings are citizens of the same community. Rational beings all bear the divine spark, the one element that connects us to God and, therefore, to each other. Similarly, Worf is looking after not just his friends' needs, but the good of the entire Federation, too.

WORF'S CONTROL PROBLEM

As well as he personifies simplicity of habits, endurance, self-restraint, and dedication to the community, there's one personal quality Worf hasn't quite achieved—wisdom. The wise person, according to Stoic teachings, picks his battles; that is, he restricts his desires to what he can do, so that his desires are always satisfied. To lead a good life, we must know what is and what is not under our control. Everything pertaining to our emotions, our mind, and our choices is under our control, while everything the external world does to us is out of our control. While we cannot control the circumstances of our daily lives, we can control our reaction to them. That guy seated at the table next to you jabbering into his cell phone can't annoy you unless you let him. As much as you'd like to toss his phone through the window, you can't really do that. What you can do, a Stoic would recommend, is change your attitude about him. Rather than be annoyed, either think of him as adding another "dimension" to your total dining experience or block him out of your mind. (Of course, if that doesn't work, you could always leave.)

Worf, however, is not clear on the Stoic concept of control. Indeed, he spends far too much time worrying about matters that are beyond his control: Jadzia's cravings for icoberry torte, her friendship with Arandis, her political indifference (or at least her unwillingness to talk politics while she's on vacation). The Klingon wants to control every aspect of his life, including Jadzia herself. But as Jadzia reminds him, "You have to realize there are some things in life you can't control. One of them is me." Worf still must learn that a wise Stoic—indeed, a wise *person*—should never try to control his lover's friendships and activities or anyone else's, for that matter.

It's worth noting that while Klingons certainly value honor and discipline, generally speaking, they're also an exuberant people, who have tremendous passion for life and enjoyment of the moment. Thus, Worf's adherence to Stoic principles makes him an anomaly among his own kind. As he explains to Jadzia, the reason he "holds back" from having fun stems from his childhood. When he was first adopted by the Rozhenko family, he found it difficult to fit into the world of humans, and consequently became a bit of a hell-raiser. One day while playing soccer, he inadvertently caused the death of a human boy when their heads collided in the heat of competition. Though the boy's death was clearly an accident, Worf felt responsible nonetheless; ever since he has practiced extreme self-control whenever dealing with humans. The tragedy forced him to reflect on his way of life, and eventually led him to adopt a lifestyle resembling Stoic ethical teachings.

Unlike most debates between classical hedonists and Stoics, the conflict between Jadzia and Worf is eventually resolved when the two lovers find a middle ground on which to coexist. In fact, by the time they kiss and make up at the end of the episode, the big fella shows he's beginning to get the hang of "being on vacation."

STAR TREK'S FOREMOST STOIC

There is one other aspect of Stoicism we haven't covered. Like Socrates, the Stoics believed the emotions were something of a hindrance because they often prevent us from achieving order and tranquillity in our lives. For that reason, a true Stoic should suppress his or her emotions at all times. Though Worf consistently demonstrates Stoic characteristics throughout *The Next Generation* and *Deep Space Nine*, technically speaking, we can't really consider him a true Stoic because he does tend to be very emotional.

However, there is another *Star Trek* character who not only practices the four personal qualities of Stoicism, he grasped the

Stoic concept of wisdom long before Worf ever did. On top of that, he comes from a planet that overcame its violent ways by rejecting emotionalism and embracing a philosophy based on pure logic.

Indeed, the real "poster boy" of Stoicism in the *Star Trek* universe is none other than Mr. Spock. Time and again, the Vulcan first officer puts into practice the principle of emotional objectivity. He urges Kirk to use reason to control his fear in "The Enemy Within." He also uses it to ward off the affections of Droxine, the high advisor's daughter in "The Cloud Minders" (*TOS*: #74), by informing her that "Vulcans pride ourselves on our logic." When Droxine flirtatiously asks if he's always in complete control of his emotions, Spock drives the point home—"Emotions interfere with logic"—with a firmness that would make Marcus Aurelius proud.

Spock's appreciation of reason and control over his emotions is also apparent in "Amok Time" (*TOS*: #34), in the scene in which he learns T'Pring has chosen Kirk over him (thus forcing Spock to fight for her, per Vulcan tradition) simply because she wants another man, Stonn, who (unlike Spock) is "simple and easily controlled." When Spock "sees no logic" in T'Pring's answer, she calculates three possibilities, all of which would result in her getting what she wanted: "If your Captain were victor, he would not want me, and so I would have Stonn. If you were victor, you would free me because I dared to challenge, and again I would have Stonn. But if you did not free me, it would be the same—for you would be gone again, and I would have your name and your property, and Stonn would still be there."

If we were in Spock's shoes, of course, we'd become outraged, angry, or otherwise upset to hear such obvious, scheming duplicity. Our model Stoic, however, reacts in the best Vulcan tradition: he doesn't let it bother him. In fact, he even admires T'Pring for her "flawlessly logical" reasoning.

"Amok Time" also shows how Spock embodies the Stoic notion of acceptance. Unaware that McCoy injected Kirk with a neural paralyzer, thus creating the illusion of death, Spock believes he has actually killed his captain and is prepared to surrender himself to Starfleet authorities. Similarly, when our Vulcan friend kidnaps Pike and hijacks the *Enterprise* in "The Menagerie," he is willing to face the consequences of his actions, to the point of insisting on a formal court-martial.

Like Worf, Spock occasionally rubs people the wrong way (most notably Dr. McCoy) if they simply don't understand the Stoic outlook on life—or death. As we mentioned before, Stoicism teaches that we must distinguish between the things in life we can control and those we can't. Though death itself, of course, is one of those things beyond our control, how we *perceive* death is not. As Epictetus, one of the earliest Stoics, once observed: "It is not the things themselves that disturb men, but their judgments about these things. For example, death is nothing dreadful...but the judgment that death is dreadful, this is the dreadful thing."

Bearing this in mind, we can now make sense of Spock's peculiar reactions to human tragedy in episodes such as "The *Galileo* Seven" (*TOS: #14*) and "Journey to Babel" (*TOS: #44*). In the first example, the seven-member mission led by Spock turns disastrous when their shuttlecraft loses fuel and is forced to land on Taurus II. Three crewmen are attacked and killed by the vicious, spear-carrying aborigines that inhabit the planet. Lieutenant Boma asks Spock to perform a burial rite to honor the victims. Most would agree that Boma's request is not unreasonable, given our need to grieve the loss of friends, colleagues, and loved ones; indeed, that's part of what makes us human. When the Vulcan refuses ("A few words on behalf of the dead will not bring them back to life"), Boma becomes angry and accuses Spock of being insensitive. Without necessarily excusing Spock, remember that his value system is...

well, different, given his Stoic temperament. The way he sees it, he can't do anything about the dead men; he can, however, try to get the surviving crew members off the planet before they're also killed. Because that's something he can control, he believes that should be his primary focus.

Similarly, when Spock appears indifferent after his father, Sarek, collapses after his heart valve malfunctions in "Journey to Babel," he's simply accepting of what has happened—and what might happen. Though McCoy performs an emergency transfusion that saves Sarek's life, Spock knows that, logically speaking, death itself is nothing to fear.

In episode after episode, Spock exemplifies Stoic principles. He controls his emotions, accepts the things he cannot change, and thoroughly advocates reason. Perhaps if Kirk, McCoy, and the other members of the *Enterprise* had boned up more on their Stoic philosophy, they would have understood their Vulcan friend better. Then again, their relationship with the first officer would not be quite as "fascinating."

Yet another philosophical movement came into being around the time when Stoicism was at its most influential: Christianity, which in fact embraced some principles from Stoic doctrine, helping it to gain acceptance. Among the concepts common to both ideologies are accepting the things we cannot change, conforming to the will of the divine, and disdaining bodily pleasures. Of course, the title of our model episode on Stoicism is derived from the New Testament. The full passage reads "Let he who is without sin cast the first stone."

Does this mean that Spock and Worf also embrace Christianity? And if not, what does it tell us about the ethics of *Star Trek*? Let's take a look at these and other questions in our next chapter.

PART THREE

CHRISTIANITY AND CONTRACTS

"Faith moves mountains... of inventory."
Ferengi Rules of Acquisition,
Rule 104

CHAPTER 9

KIRK AND KIRA
BATTLE EVIL:
CHRISTIAN ETHICS

"And the Children Shall Lead"
TOS: Episode 60
Stardate: 5029.1
Original Air Date: October 11, 1968

Responding to a science colony's distress call on the planet Triacus, Kirk, Spock, and McCoy arrive to find all adult members of the party dead, apparently the result of a mass suicide. The surviving children, meanwhile, are remarkably unaffected by the loss of their families. Kirk's only clues to these bizarre events are the increasingly paranoid log records of the expedition leader, Professor Starnes—and the strange legend of the planet itself. Triacus was once home to a band of marauders who terrorized the inhabitants of the Epsilon Indi system. Though the malefactors were eventually destroyed, legend has it that the evil within them will rise again and spread throughout the galaxy. Indeed, it has, in the form of an angelic-looking spirit who is using the children as pawns in his plan to take over the universe. Shortly after they're brought aboard the Enterprise, *the "friendly angel" orders the unwitting youngsters to cause fearful hallucinations to consume Kirk and his crew in an effort to take over the ship. Though Kirk and Spock somehow manage to squelch their individual "beasts," they must still find a way to save the children and defeat the fast-spreading evil before it's too late.*

"The Reckoning"
DS9: Episode 145
Stardate: Unknown
Original Air Date: Week of April 29, 1998

Sisko's faith in the Bajoran Prophets is tested following the discovery of an ancient archaeological artifact. Upon examining the relic, Sisko encounters the Prophets in a vision and learns he must help them bring about "the Reckoning," an event that will result in either "the beginning" or "the end." Hoping the inscription on the old stone might clarify the cryptic message, Sisko transports the artifact to Deep Space Nine for translation—a move that upsets Kai Winn, the spiritual leader of the Bajorans. While the captain insists the Prophets somehow wanted the tablet removed, the Kai believes the hurricanes and tornadoes that have beset Bajor since the tablet's removal can only mean that the Prophets are angry. The Kai obtains an order demanding the return of the artifact to Bajor. However, upon examining the relic one last time, Sisko finds himself strangely compelled to smash the stone to pieces, unleashing a violent vortex of energy that causes a power drain on Deep Space Nine. The captain's only explanation is that he has again acted according to the will of the Prophets. Sisko's conviction is affirmed when a Prophet released by the energy takes over Kira's body and announces that the Reckoning is at hand. The Reckoning is a violent confrontation between the Prophet and the evil Pah-wraith Costomachin that could yield a "Golden Age" for Bajor—or bring about the end of their entire civilization. Though the spirit can be removed from Kira through the emission of chroniton particles, Sisko insists that the showdown must proceed without interference. The captain's faith in the Prophets is then put to the ultimate test when the Pah-wraith chooses its own vessel: his son, Jake Sisko!

Remember the basic question we examined in Chapter 3, whether good is better than evil? With the help of Plato and "The Savage Curtain," we made our case for good's superiority so clear even a rock could understand. We then touched on the same idea in our look at "The Enemy Within," insofar as Kirk's irrational half (which the episode characterizes as his "evil" side) ultimately could not survive without the strength of his rational (or "good") qualities. Because good is stronger, the notion that evil needs some sort of catalyst to battle good therefore makes sense. That same idea, of course, is one of the themes that ties this chapter's two model episodes together. Just as Gorgan requires the help of his unsuspecting young charges to carry out his plan, the Pah-wraith needs a host of its own (in this case Jake) in its face-off against the Prophet.

But is that always the case? We know that Gorgan's spirit lives in the cave on Triacus, and that Kirk is certainly spooked when he goes inside the cave at the beginning of the episode. Is Gorgan somehow strong enough to make himself known to Kirk without the help of the children? If that's possible, why then does he disintegrate when he loses control of the youngsters at the end of the show? For the answers to these and other questions on the nature of evil, let's turn our attention to the Christian philosopher Saint Augustine of Hippo (A.D. 354–430).

EVIL IS THE ABSENCE OF GOOD

Augustine, one might add, wasn't always a saint; in fact, once upon a time he would have died for a place like Risa and its freewheeling sexual mores. As a young man, he was lured by the licentious port city of Carthage in North Africa, where he took a mistress and soon fathered a son. However, upon discovering the works of the Stoic philosopher Cicero, Augustine decided that achieving philosophical wisdom was even more important than fulfilling his own sexual urges, to the point where his hedonistic indulgences became a source of self-reproach. Seeking an answer to his inner turmoil, he turned to the Manichaeans, who held that there are two basic principles in the universe: light (meaning, "goodness") and darkness ("evil"). These two principles are in constant conflict with each other—a conflict that is reflected in human life as a battle between the soul (composed of light) and the body (darkness). Though Augustine first attributed his uncontrolled sexual urges to the power of darkness, he somehow knew there was more to it than that. To say that some external force alone caused his moral unrest wasn't a satisfactory enough answer.

Borrowing a page from Platonic thought, Augustine developed an ethical theory that teaches evil is the absence of good. This particular philosophy, as we're about to see, answers many of the key questions raised in our first episode.

Of course, in any Platonic type of philosophy, the concepts of "being," "truth," and "goodness" are all considered different aspects of the same reality. Accordingly, that which is greatest in being is also greatest in truth and goodness.

BEING = TRUTH = GOODNESS

Augustine, however, reasoned that some things are better—or have more goodness, truth, or being—than others. If that's the case, it implies there are various degrees of goodness, truth, and being. Yet if goodness, truth, and being are all one and the same, then the degrees of the one must correspond exactly to the degrees of the others.

Now, we can easily understand the concept of goodness having degrees, or that some people are morally "better" than others—we see this in action just about every time a *Star Trek* captain violates the Prime Directive. But how exactly can some things have more "being" than others? After all, a thing either exists or it doesn't—right? What Augustine meant is that one thing can have more "reality" than another, insofar as a horse can have more reality than his shadow, or a tree can have more reality than its reflection in the water. Take away the shadow and the reflection, and the horse and tree would both still exist. Take away the horse and tree, on the other hand, and the images disappear, too. The horse and tree, therefore, have more "being" because, unlike the shadow and the reflection, they don't require the presence of something else to trigger their existence. Since the degrees of goodness correspond to the degrees of being, the horse is also better than his shadow, and the tree better than its reflection.

Being Christian, Augustine took the story of Moses from the Book of Exodus and grafted it onto this basic Platonic assumption. God tells Moses to order Pharaoh to liberate the Israelites, and to mention he was sent by "The God of your father." When Moses asks what he should say if Pharaoh asks for the name of God, God replies, "I am who I am."* Now, a Christian Platonist such as Augustine would reason that since

---

*Not only does this sound like the kind of cryptic responses Sisko got whenever he asked the Prophets for more details about the Reckoning, but the very notion of Yahweh as "pure being," existing outside of time and space, is not unlike the characterization of the Prophets in general. In addition to being incorporeal forms, the Prophets show providential care for the Bajorans, just as Yahweh cared for the people of Israel in the Old Testament.

"am" is the first person singular of the verb "to be," God must be saying that He is pure Being—"Being" in the highest sense. Thus, since the degree of being corresponds to the degree of goodness, God must also be pure Goodness.

This leads us to the matter of creatures. According to Christian teachings, all things receive their being from God; the being of creatures is derivative from God's being. Since everything that exists has some trace of God's own being, and since His being is the same as His goodness, then everything that exists must also have some trace of God's goodness.

$$\text{PURE BEING} = \text{PURE GOODNESS (GOD)}$$
$$\text{(act of creation) being} = \text{goodness (of creatures)}$$

I know what you're thinking: that sounds way too abstract. All right, then, let's do what a Christian Platonist would do—pull out the Bible and open to the first page of the Book of Genesis. Right there, in black and white, it says God looked at His creation and pronounced it good. Therefore, based on both Christian religious beliefs and Platonic philosophical arguments, Augustine concluded that all things that exist are good.

AUGUSTINE EXPLAINS GORGAN

Now, since God's creatures have less being than God, they must also have correspondingly less goodness—the lesser the being, the lesser the degree of goodness. After all, no created thing can be totally good; since Augustine believed the universe was created, he reasoned there must have been a time when the being and goodness of the universe did not exist. If something is capable of "not existing," it must have an absence of being (and, therefore, of goodness) in its very nature.

Yet there's a limit to how little goodness a thing can have and still exist. No creature can be totally without goodness; if it has any being at all, it will also have some goodness. In other words, a totally evil being could not possibly exist; even the devil (or, in the case of our first *Star Trek* episode, Gorgan of Triacus) has some degree of goodness in it. In fact, Augustine would say, it's because of that goodness that Gorgan and the devil are even alive in the first place.

Conversely, the presence of evil is really an absence of good. This is not meant to minimize evil in any way; rather, Augustine merely emphasized his basic point that evil, like all other things, is somehow rooted in good. Therefore, if evil has no real being in itself, it cannot possibly exist without the presence of something good. That would make evil a parasite that preys on its host (goodness).

Now, let's apply Augustine's theory to "And the Children Shall Lead." According to the legend of Triacus, the evil that possessed the marauders who terrorized the planet centuries ago will "live again" and spread throughout the galaxy. As Professor Starnes observed in one of his last recorded messages, "one of the [last members of this] race apparently took refuge in the cave" on Triacus. So let's assume Gorgan is the remnant of evil from long ago, and that he resides in the cave. Though he can make his presence felt (as we see with Kirk at the top of the show), he still needs an appropriate host—a source of goodness—in order to act. After all, as Spock puts it, "Without followers, evil cannot spread." For Gorgan, young children are the perfect vehicle because they can be more easily controlled; unlike most adults, they don't have the wisdom or experience to withstand his power. Gorgan keeps his hold over the children by "suppressing the truth" (as Spock observes) or "misleading the innocent" (McCoy, finishing the thought). Because the parents on Triacus are capable of opposing him, they are in Gorgan's mind an "enemy" that must be eliminated.

Augustine would also say that when Gorgan orders the children to bring out the hidden fears in the crew members (as well as in their parents on Triacus), he is committing, and the adults are suffering, an evil. The youngsters use their power to extract each crew member's "beast"—that is to say, their innermost fears. When Gorgan says, "The fear in each one of them is the beast that will consume them," he's reiterating the Aristotelian notion that our emotions, if not checked by our reason, can lead to destruction. (Interestingly enough, shortly before his death, Professor Starnes referred to this all-consuming fear as "the enemy within." This is entirely appropriate, considering that *Star Trek,* as we know from our discussion in Chapter 6, explored this very notion in an episode by the same name.) We soon catch a glimpse of the various phobias that plague Kirk and his officers. Sulu has a fear of swords (presumably he never quite got over the time he terrorized everyone with a foil, as he did in "The Naked Time," *TOS: #*7); Uhura is frightened of growing old; Chekov is afraid to disobey orders; and Kirk is paranoid about losing his ability to command (again, shades of "The Enemy Within").

However, Augustine might add, Gorgan can make the crew feel fear only insofar as he is good, because it's that "goodness" (in the persons of the children) that makes his existence possible. Although the means Gorgan uses to effect evil—the mirror in which Uhura sees her reflection, the sensation with which the crew members experience their fears—are good in and of themselves, his actions are evil precisely because of something he lacks: namely, a good will. Likewise, the evil experienced by Kirk and his crew is due entirely to their lack of mental wholeness. As we again know from Chapter 6, their "enemy within" makes them less than they should be. Indeed, Augustine would say, evil is always a failure to do something good or to be something good.

"And the Children Shall Lead" also touches on one of the key themes of "The Savage Curtain": evil forces often bring about their own destruction. Whereas Plato believed that evil beings are defeated because of their inner weakness, Augustine felt that they are so due to the absence of good. Gorgan disintegrates once he loses his hold on the children because, as an evil being, he cannot exist without depending on something good.

Of course, when you think about it, the two concepts aren't that far apart. Like Plato, Augustine thought that ethics is rooted within reality itself; the way we come to know it is through analyzing the nature of the one reality we all share.

SISKO'S LEAP OF FAITH

Clearly, the Original Series isn't the only version of *Star Trek* that tackles Christian themes; *Deep Space Nine,* as we know, is replete with them. In fact, as we mentioned briefly in Chapter 2, the notion of an Emissary is very much akin to such messianic figures as Moses and David in the Old Testament, and Christ in the New Testament. Just as the Bajorans believe the Emissary is the legendary "deliverer" promised to them long ago, so Christians believe Christ is the Messiah sent by God to save His people.

Besides borrowing from the story of the Ten Commandments (Sisko smashes the B'hala tablet, just as Moses smashed one of the holy tablets on Mount Sinai), "The Reckoning" provides us with an excellent introduction to a form of Christian ethics quite different from Augustine's. Whereas Augustine believed we can know ethics only by studying reality, the Danish philosopher Søren Kierkegaard (1813–1855) held that ethics is but a prologue to religion. Christianity, he maintained, brings the truth to our reason—a truth at which we cannot arrive by our own powers.

That's an interesting concept, considering that Christianity (or the idea of faith in general, for that matter) would seem to be completely irrational and absurd; indeed, incapable of standing up to reason. As Kira tells Odo in "Accession," the thing about faith is that "if you don't have it, you can't understand—and if you do, no explanation is necessary." Yet that's precisely the point. For the Christian (or Bajoran, or whichever religion you might practice) to realize the truth, he or she must be willing to take actions that might defy explanation.

In other words, as the Bruce Springsteen song goes, it takes a leap of faith to get things going.

For Kierkegaard, a "leap of faith" requires a person to forgo the standards of society, including reliance on reason and the demands of morality, and to trust completely in God— or, in the case of Sisko and Kira in "The Reckoning," the Bajoran Prophets. Such a leap means disregarding traditional church teachings and the pronouncements of theologians (the Kai Winns of the world), so that we experience the presence of God through Him only. Not everyone is capable of making this leap; in fact, Kierkegaard might add, only a person of exceptional, unconditional faith in the divine will can be expected to do this. Once we make the leap, God's voice becomes so authoritative, it transcends all our societal obligations (including, in the case of Sisko, familial) whenever we hear it.

Of course, Kierkegaard didn't have the luxury of watching *Star Trek* episodes at the time he wrote *Fear and Trembling;* if he had, one suspects he might have referred to "The Reckoning" in his book because it embodies his "leap of faith" concept so well. What he did use as a model, however, is the Bible— particularly, the epic story of Abraham and Isaac in the Book of Genesis.

Abraham, as the saga goes, is ordered by God to sacrifice his son Isaac on Mount Moriah. Even though he doesn't quite understand why, he is nonetheless prepared to do it. Now it's important to note, Kierkegaard would say, that Abraham never questions whether God's command is rational, or even if it's a figment of his imagination. Rather than limit God by logic and say that He cannot command an irrational act (or restrict God in terms of morality, as Augustine in effect did, by assuming that He cannot order anything immoral, or create anything that's entirely evil), Abraham unreservedly accepts God's command and is ready to carry it out.

For Kierkegaard, the story of Abraham is the perfect example of the paradoxical nature of faith (a concept we visited briefly in Chapter 2, as part of our discussion of "Accession"). To illustrate just how paradoxical faith is, consider that Abraham goes to Mount Moriah convinced of two propositions:

God will give him his posterity through Isaac.
He will kill Isaac.

Of course, since Isaac is still a boy who has yet to father any children, logically speaking the two propositions are incompatible. In other words, it's irrational for Abraham to believe both propositions simultaneously. Moreover, how is it possible for a good God to order an evil act? This brings us back to another question we raised in Chapter 2: Euthyphro's notion that ethics and God are one in the same. If that's the case, what do we do if He asks us to abandon ethics?

Unlike Socrates, though, Kierkegaard believed that Euthyphro was right all along. The way he saw it, religious choices always supersede ethical choices. From a purely ethical point of view, we cannot possibly justify Abraham's act; morality, after all, requires that a father love his son, not kill him. For Kierkegaard, however, the ethical level is insufficient because it doesn't allow us to make exceptions—and Abraham, known as the "father of faith," was certainly an exception. In his case, ethical requirements were suspended in deference to absolute obedience to God.

SISKO'S THREE STAGES OF EXISTENCE

Now, to make sense of this discussion (not to mention Sisko's behavior in "The Reckoning") on both an ethical and religious level, we need to understand an important component of Kierkegaard's philosophy: the three stages of existence. The first level is that of the aesthetic; the second, that which is ethical; the third (and highest), the level of the religious. As we take a close look at what it means to live at each of these stages, not only will it shed light on Captain Sisko's behavior in "The Reckoning," we'll also understand how he develops as a character over the course of the entire *Deep Space Nine* series.

Indeed, Kierkegaard likened the process of a person moving from one level to the next with the progressive development of an individual. In each case, he or she graduates from one level to another through an act of choice. The person at the aesthetic level, for example, behaves according to his emotions and impulses—someone like the irrational Kirk in "The Enemy Within," Jean-Luc Picard when he was an ensign,* or a young Saint Augustine. Having no specific religious beliefs, he is motivated simply by a desire to enjoy the pleasures of the senses.

Sisko also seemed to be this type of person when he was young. As we learn in "Take Me Out to the Holosuite" (*DS9:* #154), he's been engaged in an ongoing rivalry with Vulcan Captain Solok ever since their Starfleet Academy days, when Sisko got drunk with some buddies and began a heated argument with Solok at an off-campus bar called The Launching Pad. Certainly, Kierkegaard would say, this is a classic case of a person behaving according to his emotions and impulses. We also know from episodes such as "A Man Alone" (*DS9:* #3) that

---

*In "Tapestry" (*TNG:* #141), Picard characterizes his youthful self as "Arrogant, undisciplined, with far too much ego and far too little wisdom." The only thing that mattered to him at the time was enjoying the pleasures of the senses.

he learned to appreciate the pleasures of taste from his father, a gourmet chef who insisted the family dine together so that his "test-tasters" (as he called them) could sample his new recipes. Lastly, he became friends with Curzon Dax, a joined Trill and Federation official with whom he made frequent jaunts to the planet Risa. Curzon, a tireless Casanova, joined Sisko as a carouser on countless occasions when the captain was in his twenties.

Now the time may come, Kierkegaard would say, when one living purely at the aesthetic level realizes there has to be more to life than indulging his own emotional needs. The internal conflict triggered by this sudden awareness might even lead to despair and anxiety. Again, this is not unlike the turmoil Augustine went through prior to discovering Christianity, or the three-year angst Sisko endured following the death of his wife, Jennifer. When this happens, the person at the aesthetic level is confronted with an either/or decision: either remain at this present level of existence or move up to a higher level. The captain's moment of reevaluation came at the time he was offered command of Deep Space Nine—he could either remain in despair, or move on to a new level of commitment (namely, the ethical level). Like Sisko, the person who chooses to live at the ethical level abandons the attitude of selfishness and detachment, and becomes interested in self-improvement and establishing equality, freedom, and justice for others. Unlike the aesthetic person, who has no universal standards (other than following his own tastes), the ethical person accepts a code of conduct formulated by reason. At this level, the choices the person makes are serious, since he must decide how his personal code applies to the concrete situations in which he finds himself.

Though Kierkegaard may have disagreed with Socrates' conclusion on the matter of the *Euthyphro,* he considered the ancient Greek sage to be the perfect example of an ethical person. Had the Danish philosopher lived to see *DS9*, he undoubtedly would have put Sisko in the same class, for the captain personifies life at this second stage of development during the initial years of the series. We saw in "Accession," for example, how Sisko supported the Socratic position that good actions can be discerned through reason alone, not by unquestioned adherence to the divine will. (Obviously the captain has changed his mind about this by the time we get to "The Reckoning," but we'll address that in just a bit.) In this episode, as well as in others early on, Sisko acts as the ethical person who takes a firm stand on moral questions and accepts the limitations upon his life that moral responsibility entails. This accounts for his position in "Playing God" (*DS9*: #37), when he decides to preserve a proto-universe even at the risk of destroying his own.* While grappling with this dilemma, Sisko's mind keeps "going back to the Borg—how I despised their indifference as they tried to exterminate us. I have to ask myself, would I be any different if I destroyed another universe to preserve my own?" Deciding ultimately not to act as the Borg would, Sisko orders the risky venture of saving the proto-universe by returning it to its home in the Gamma Quadrant. Believing in human perfectibility, he invests his energies in Federation activities that aim at achieving that perfection.

Nonetheless, Kierkegaard would say, a crisis such as the one Sisko faced in "Playing God" only goes to show just how hard life at the ethical stage can be. At some point, an ethical person will realize that no matter how hard he tries, he cannot possibly satisfy all aspects of moral law—that, indeed, some instances might require him to deliberately violate the law. And yet, being ethical, he cannot break the law without encountering concomitant feelings of guilt. At that point, he

---

*This, in effect, is the basic question posed by the ethics of duty, a subject we'll discuss in Chapter 11.

finds himself at another crossroads: either remain at the ethical level (and lunge into ethical programs with even greater dedication), or respond to this newfound awareness of his own limitations and exist at the religious level. This movement from the ethical to the religious level can be achieved only by an act of total commitment—indeed, a leap of faith that surpasses the demands of rationality or morality.

Using Kierkegaard's analysis, we can better understand Sisko's decisions and conduct in episodes such as "Accession," "Rapture" (*DS9:* #108), and, of course, "The Reckoning." We saw in Chapter 2 how the captain began to evolve from a purely ethical being to a man living at the religious level. Whereas at the beginning of "Accession" Sisko was still uncomfortable with being perceived as a religious icon, by the end of the show he embraces his role as Emissary after his profound experience with the Prophets inside the wormhole. Even so, Kierkegaard would say, Sisko hasn't quite made it to the religious stage at this point. Though the captain now accepts his office as the Emissary, because he assumes he can somehow balance his responsibilities as a Starfleet officer and his life as the Emissary, he's still functioning on an ethical level.

Things begin to change, however, in "Rapture," the episode that sets the stage for the captain's actions in "The Reckoning." Upon discovering an ancient Bajoran painting illustrating the long-lost city of B'hala, Sisko has the portrait scanned into the holosuite computer in order to decipher the city's location—a mystery, by the way, that Bajoran archaeologists haven't been able to solve for 20,000 years. While studying an obelisk from the painting, Sisko is knocked unconscious by a severe electric shock. He then has a powerful mystical vision ranging over space and time from the Occupation and the discovery of the wormhole to the coming war with the Dominion—a vision that leads him to discover B'hala itself. As a result of this experience, Sisko is completely dedicated to his role as Emissary to the Bajoran people; as Kierkegaard would put it, he has made the leap from the ethical level to the religious. His entire manner changes, from one of a spit-and-polish military commander to that of a spiritual, serene religious leader.

Of course, obsessed as he is with understanding these incredible visions, the captain still has to deal with his Starfleet career. He soon finds out firsthand what happens when ethical duty and religious duty collide. Admiral Whatley, though concerned that the captain's visions might interfere with his responsibilities, announces that Bajor has been finally accepted into the Federation (which, of course, was the goal Sisko has been trying to accomplish from the moment he took command of Deep Space Nine). Only the captain has another vision in which he learns that disaster will fall upon Bajor if it joins the Federation at that time. Crashing the signing ceremony, he informs the Bajoran ministers that it's too soon for Bajor to join the Federation—and since whatever the Emissary says, goes, the ministers vote accordingly. Clearly the Sisko we see in "Rapture" is so far removed from his agnostic attitude early in the series, he's now willing to sacrifice his own life and career in the interest of his religious visions.

ABRAHAM AND SISKO: THE KNIGHTS OF FAITH

Which brings us to the pivotal moment of "The Reckoning." Sisko, Kierkegaard would say, is clearly the Bajoran equivalent of Abraham. By throwing reason and moral principles to the wind, by not allowing Jadzia and Bashir to release the chroniton particles that could exorcise the Pah-wraith from Jake and save his son's life, the captain finds himself standing at the edge of an abyss. At this point, he takes another leap of faith. Only the surrender of reason can overcome his anxiety for his son—and Sisko certainly does surrender his reason! Just as we saw with Abraham, Sisko must put his stock in two logically incompatible propositions:

The Prophets will exact some sort of penance from him.
The Prophets will protect his son.

Since Sisko cares about Jake more than anything else, it must occur to him that the penance the Prophets are talking about may have something to do with his son. In fact, Jadzia Dax speculates that the best way to exact penance from the captain is precisely through Jake. Nonetheless, Sisko steadfastly believes that the Prophets will also protect Jake. This, of course, flies in the face of reason, duty, and basic paternal instincts.

Perhaps we can better appreciate Sisko and Abraham by contrasting them with a "tragic hero" like Kirk in "The City on the Edge of Forever" (*TOS: #28*). When a drugged-out McCoy flees through a time portal into a small American town in 1930, he saves the life of a social worker named Edith Keeler—and unwittingly sets off a chain of events that radically alters the face of history. Though Keeler actually died in 1930, because of McCoy's intervention she went on to lead a pacifist movement that would delay U.S. entry into World War II and ultimately allow Hitler to vanquish the world. Among the many ramifications of Keeler's movement: space flight as we know it was never developed, which in turn means that the *Enterprise* (not to mention its entire crew) never came to be. Spock's calculations enable Kirk and him to arrive in 1930 a few days before McCoy. Kirk eventually discovers Keeler must in fact die in order to set things right—but not until after he realizes he's fallen in love with her. Thus, Kirk must choose between preventing McCoy from saving Keeler (despite the tremendous personal pain her death would cause Kirk) or letting him (in which case, as

Spock puts it, "millions will die that did not die in what would have been our history").

At the moment of truth, though every fiber in Kirk's being yearns to protect Keeler, his commitment to preserve the future of humanity compels the captain to stop McCoy, thus allowing the car accident that would claim her life to take place unimpeded. Kierkegaard would say that Kirk was acting in accordance with a universal moral requirement—the duty of a leader to preserve his people. In other words, to use Kierkegaard's term, he was a "tragic hero" in this situation. We all know the plight of the tragic hero: the nature of his dilemma is one of divided loyalty, but he decides on behalf of the public good at the cost of his private relationship. We may not agree with his decision, but at least we can understand it.

As for understanding Abraham and Sisko's actions, that's a whole other story. Kierkegaard would call them "knights of faith"—meaning, persons who grasp their own freedom and create their own destiny. They disregard the rational counsel of society because they now answer to a higher call. The knight of faith sees deeply into humanity and realizes that at the deepest level he is alone with his god. At that point, he knows absolutely nothing can faze him. Abraham demonstrates this remarkable steadfastness in the Old Testament story, as does Sisko in "The Reckoning." Indeed, unlike the "tragic hero" Kirk in "City on the Edge of Forever" (whose plight is understood and sympathized with, and whose decision is ultimately supported by Spock, McCoy, and the entire television audience), Sisko's decision to let the battle take place on Deep Space Nine is challenged by his entire staff—with the notable exception of Odo, who supports the captain out of deference to Kira's religious beliefs. Though the security chief doesn't understand the concept of faith any better than he did in "Accession," Odo "has no doubt that Kira would allow the Prophets to use her as their instrument" because he knows her trust in them, like that of a knight of faith, is unshakable. (Just the same, though, Odo tells Kira at the end of the show that he "would have preferred the Prophets chose someone else.")

Like Kira and Abraham, Sisko chooses trust in the divine (in this case, the Bajoran Prophets) over reason, as personified by Jadzia, Bashir, and Worf. By taking the leap of faith, he suspends his ethical reasoning and acts on a purely religious level, choosing to pursue a higher calling that transcends his concern for his familial obligation. Though Sisko takes responsibility for his actions, at the same time he gives up his fate and places it in the hands of the Prophets. For a Christian ethicist like Kierkegaard, this is the most admirable thing we can do.

CHRISTIAN ETHICS IN A NUTSHELL

You might be wondering what Augustine and Kierkegaard's respective ethical theories could possibly have in common. After all, while Augustine upheld Platonic reasoning throughout his philosophy, Kierkegaard said we should ultimately abandon reason and follow our faith. Whereas Augustine arrived at his conclusion through logical analysis, Kierkegaard used a biblical story to make his point. Finally, Augustine maintained that evil consists of a lack of goodness. Kierkegaard, on the other hand, clearly believed that evil lies essentially in disobedience to divine commands. These two guys are about as different as Spock and McCoy, Quark and Odo, or Worf and Lwaxana Troi, right?

Yet both Kierkegaard and Augustine are considered Christian ethicists because they based their arguments on biblical passages, particularly references to the Old Testament. Additionally, though Kierkegaard recommended letting our faith prevail, he did not say we should do so blindly (as Akorem exhorted the Bajorans to do in "Accession"). Rather, like Augustine, he relied on reason to state his case; indeed, he clearly suggested that one cannot make the leap from the ethical level to the religious without a great deal of thought.

Star Trek has certainly borrowed images from the Old Testament on more than one occasion, including both of this chapter's model episodes. We've also seen references to New Testament ideas in stories such as "Bread and Circuses" (*TOS:* #43), wherein the Children of the Sun practice the neo-Christian philosophy of total love and brotherhood. Indeed, as Lieutenant Uhura explicitly tells us at the end of the show, the "Sun" these people worship is not the sun in the sky, but rather Christ—the Son of God, according to the Christian faith.

We'll examine the Children of the Sun's ethics more closely in Chapter 15. For now, though, we can contrast this basic aspect of Christianity with another theme central to Kierkegaard's philosophy. The concept of a special people chosen by God—be it the Israelites and Yahweh, or the Bajorans and the Prophets—is very important to Kierkegaard, Sisko (at least, as he's characterized in "The Reckoning"), and, for that matter, the Old Testament in general. Compare that to the universal, egalitarian code of ethics promoted in the New Testament, where the notion of loving our neighbors as ourselves means we should treat all individuals we meet with the same concern that we have for ourselves. (In other words, we're all God's people.) That's quite different from Kierkegaard, who believed we shouldn't attach so much attention to people since they are finite—whereas God, on the other hand, is infinite. It is essential, he argued, that each of us recognize this relationship and act on it, thereby surrendering ourselves completely to God.

Though sprinkles of Christian ideology certainly pop up in *Star Trek* from time to time, it would be a reach to consider it vital to the ethics of the series as a whole. In fact, given Gene Roddenberry's personal beliefs about religion in general, we could certainly argue that it's not central at all. As we discussed in Chapter 2, in Roddenberry's universe, reason is dominant and religion has little place. In fact, for every episode that espouses Christian themes, there are just as many (perhaps even more) that discredit them. "The Reckoning," for example, portrays spiritual leader Kai Winn as arrogant, ambitious, and ultimately self-serving. She resents Sisko not just for his unique relationship with the Prophets (something to which she feels entitled after a lifetime of service and devotion), but for ultimately showing that his faith is stronger than hers. Just as the defeat of the Pah-wraith is imminent, she activates the chroniton generator and releases the spirits from Kira and Jake. Though the Kai claims she did it "to save the Emissary and his son," Kira isn't fooled one bit. She knows Winn was motivated entirely out of spite for Sisko.

Religion also takes it on the chin in episodes such as "Rightful Heir" (*TNG:* #149), in which Picard grants Worf leave to visit the planet Boreth, where the Klingon clerics have fabricated a false messiah. Also, in "Who Watches the Watchers" (*TNG:* #52), a cultural observation team is accidentally discovered by a planet's native humanoids, who decide that Captain Picard is their God. Picard comments, "We haven't had that kind of belief in hundreds of years." Finally, in *Star Trek V: The Final Frontier,* Spock's half brother, Sybok, hijacks the *Enterprise* to pursue his visions of God near the center of the galaxy; needless to say, "God" turns out to be a hoax.

Given *Star Trek'*s overt hostility toward organized religion overall, we can probably attribute the numerous references to Christian ethics throughout each series to the simple fact that because so many facets of Christianity have permeated our culture, the writers were probably influenced by the world in which they live. It may also be *Star Trek'*s way of acknowledging that Christian ethics does touch on some universal truth, even if the series doesn't embrace Christianity per se. Or perhaps both possibilities are true. In any event, having some under-standing of Christian ethics can, at the very least, help us bet-ter appreciate the episodes that address it.

Interestingly enough, as much as *Deep Space Nine* explores spiritual values more than the other *Star Trek* series, the show also extols the principles of good old-fashioned capitalism by virtue of its other primary resident humanoid life-form. Could it be that, deep down, everyone's really a Ferengi at heart? Are we more inclined to look out for number one than espouse a life of total brotherhood? Let's see what Quark and his culture tell us about the ethics of *Trek* in our next chapter.

CHAPTER 10

THE FERENGI AND THE SOCIAL CONTRACT

"The Nagus"
DS9: Episode 11
Stardate: Unknown
Original Air Date: Week of March 22, 1993

At a major trade conference held on Deep Space Nine, Grand Nagus Zek announces that the future of the Ferengi financial empire lies in using the wormhole to find new customers in the Gamma Quadrant. The revered czar then shocks everyone by resigning his position—and naming Quark his successor! Quark's glee over his newfound power is short-lived once he realizes being leader of the Ferengi means always having to look over his shoulder. Worse yet, Zek dies before he can fully advise his replacement what to do! Needing someone he can trust, Quark names his brother, Rom, as his bodyguard—only to anger Rom by refusing to let him run their bar. Though Quark avoids an assassination attempt at Zek's funeral, he is nearly jettisoned into space by his own brother, who has conspired

*with Zek's son Krax to overthrow the new head Ferengi.
The coup d'état is soon thwarted, however, by none other
than Zek himself. The erstwhile Nagus used a sleeping
trance to fake his death in order to test Krax's suitability to
replace him—a test Krax failed miserably because he's not
sufficiently mercenary. After Zek resumes command, Quark
deals with Rom as only a Ferengi would: he rewards his
brother's "wonderful treachery" by promoting him to "assis-
tant manager of policy and clientele."*

Well, here we are, roughly halfway through our search for the
ethical foundation of *Star Trek*. We're beginning to have a good
sense of where each series stands, morally speaking. Along the
way we've gleaned insight from all manner of life-forms—Vulcans, Klingons, Risans, Betazoids, Bajorans, Borgs, Trills, Gorns,
Qs, even rocks.

You know whom we haven't really heard from, though? I'll
give you a couple of hints: their ears are more pronounced than
Spock's, and their values are about as far removed from New
Testament philosophy as you could possibly get.

Indeed, no examination of *Star Trek* ethics would be complete without a visit from those lovable princes of commerce,
the Ferengi. They may be sexist and utterly devoid of charm,
but they're very good at what they do—and what they do is
make money (or what passes for money in the *Star Trek* universe). Like Bret Maverick, the legendary gentle grafter of the
Old West, the Ferengi never miss an opportunity to turn a
profit. Unlike Maverick, though, the Ferengi have no limits. In
fact, their "need for greed" is so extreme, it's almost tempting
to write them off as caricatures. But we won't, naturally, and
with good reason—for the Ferengi characterize a basic part of
ourselves that we don't always like to acknowledge.

FERENGI PRINCIPLES IN THE STATE OF NATURE

The Ferengi, of course, are card-carrying capitalists; most people, they believe, are inherently egotistical self-serving beings who perpetually seek personal gain in everything they do. The Ferengi are ruthless businessmen who aren't above stealing from each other (or, as we see in "The Nagus," doing each other in) if they can get away with it. The 285 Rules of Acquisition are as intrinsic to the Ferengi lifestyle as the Articles of Faith are to Christianity. Perhaps no Rule is more quintessential to their values and principles than Rule 52, "Never ask when you can take" ("Babel," *DS9:* #5).

Doubtlessly Thomas Hobbes (1588–1679) would have found a kindred spirit in the Ferengi, for he saw humanoid behavior in as dubious a light as they do. (Though the 17th-century philosopher specifically had *Homo sapiens* in mind when he wrote *The Leviathan,* one suspects had he lived to see the many humanoid species in *Star Trek,* he would have amended his classic analysis of human nature to include them as well.) Like the Ferengi, Hobbes believed true altruism is impossible, given basic human nature: "Of the voluntary acts of every man, the object is some good to himself." No selfless act, in other words, is really what it seems because there's always a hidden agenda—to wit, our own. We feel bad that Uncle Buddy took a bath in the stock market not out of any decency toward him, but rather a concern for ourselves (after all, but for the grace of God, that could have easily happened to us!). The way Hobbes saw it, even the great acts of generosity we read about all the time are basically publicity stunts. Meaning, the corporate millionaires and financial institutions who dole out artist grants and massive donations to charity do so partially to remind the world just how rich, powerful, and superior they are—so superior, in fact, they can take care of the needs of others, as well as their own.

Hobbes felt the only goodness in humanoid behavior is the goodness each of us feels with regard to her own desires. When it comes to the meanings of "good" and "evil," it's all about "me." Whatever I desire is "good." Whatever threatens me is "evil." Happiness is simply a matter of fulfilling our desires and acquiring the power to do so. However, since your desires will always be different from mine, and since we can never be certain we'll have enough power to fulfill our respective desires, the possibility of serious conflict will always exist.

From this premise, Hobbes imagined how we would act if there were no laws, no courts, no political organization—indeed, no restraints of any kind. Under these circumstances, he reasoned, each of us would do whatever we think we could get away with, taking from each other as we pleased.

Hobbes called this hypothetical condition the "state of nature."

All people in the state of nature are equal. Now, the term "equal" as Hobbes uses it has nothing to do with equal worth, basic human dignity, or any other ideas associated with the word in, say, the Declaration of Independence, or Lincoln's Emancipation Proclamation. Rather, it's closer to "equal" as the Providers might have used it in "The Gamesters of Triskelion" (*TOS:* #46); like the drill thralls on that planet, Hobbes believed that in the state of nature we're all equally physically capable of killing one another.* "Even the weakest," he observed, "has strength enough to kill the strongest, either by secret machination, or by confederacy with others." We see this very point illustrated in "The Nagus," when Rom (who's usually portrayed as being slower-witted, or "weaker," than his brother, Quark) joins forces with Krax and nearly succeeds in doing Quark in. Hobbes also claimed that people are mentally

---

*Given this theory, had Hobbes lived in the 20th century, one imagines him viewing the Cold War conflict with particular interest.

equal in the state of nature, since prudence, which makes one person more intelligent than another in practical matters, is "but experience, which equal time, equally bestows on all men, in those things they equally apply themselves unto." Granted, some people might actually acknowledge their equality with others in these respects. But since most of us, according to Hobbes, are so utterly conceited, we're more likely to exaggerate our own worth and uphold our hyperbole through comparison and competition.

In Hobbes' view, people are by nature both vain and competitive: when two people desire the same thing, and only one of them can have it, they compete with one another and "become enemies." This is the same principle Zek expresses at the trade conference just prior to naming Quark the new Grand Nagus. "It is becoming more and more difficult to find truly lucrative business opportunities here in the Alpha Quadrant," he observes. "Why? Because no matter where we go, our reputation proceeds us, a reputation tainted by the lies of our competitors who maliciously spread the erroneous impression that we are not to be trusted." Like all Ferengi, Zek sees "competitors" (or "enemies," as Hobbes would put it) as those who would take away whatever they can from their rivals. The competitors do not trust the Ferengi, and of course, the Ferengi do not trust their competitors.

Zek further illustrates Hobbes' point by telling Quark that when it comes to being in power, threats to one's life come with the territory. Since only one Ferengi can be Grand Nagus, Quark naturally finds himself the "enemy" of any other Ferengi who covets the position. A particularly belligerent entrepreneur named Gral offers to become Quark's "new best friend" (that is, he'll protect the new Grand Nagus from harm) for a price — his pick of "the most lucrative Gamma opportunities." Gral, as Hobbes would quickly point out, is motivated not by friendship, but purely out of greed. Realizing that he must now live in a constant state of warfare with those around him, Quark seeks Zek's advice. "To survive," the Nagus emeritus replies, "you must surround yourself with loyal men—but not *too* loyal."

What does Zek mean by "not too loyal"? Well, to be truly loyal means being somewhat unselfish, such that you'd put the welfare of another person on the same level as your own. In some instances, such as the case with Secret Service agents, that could also mean putting this person's life *above* your own. As far as a true Ferengi is concerned (or a disciple of Hobbes, for that matter), that's completely absurd. He would see unselfishness as no more than a cunning hoax masterminded by someone scheming to rip off, overthrow, or otherwise dupe the unsuspecting person in power. As Zek explains to Krax at the end of the episode, "You don't *grab* power. You accumulate it quietly, without anyone noticing." A truly clever Ferengi would have let Quark hold the scepter, thus letting him think he was in charge, without letting on that someone else was running things from behind the shadows. Hobbes would add that although we, like the Ferengi, no longer live in the "state of nature," our competitive drive is always close at hand, ever awaiting the appropriate opportunity to strike.

Hobbes called the natural psychological outcome of our competitive condition "diffidence," meaning distrust or suspicion. Diffidence is natural in the state of nature, because you never know when someone might konk you from behind and pick you clean. Quark is the picture of diffidence when Zek arrives on the station at the top of the show. Though the good-natured Rom expresses pride that the Grand Nagus would visit their bar, Quark is ever vigilant. "I hope you can live on pride," he tells his brother, "because that's all we'll have left once he's through with us." At this point Quark isn't aware of the trade conference Zek wants to convene; he simply thinks the shrewd old Ferengi wants to buy him out "at a fraction of what [the bar is] worth." Quark's diffidence typifies how the Ferengi view humanoid nature. Not surprisingly, many of the Ferengi Rules of Acquisition* exhort suspicion, as we see from the sampling below:

Rule 7   "Keep your ears open."
          ("In the Hands of the Prophets," *DS9:* #20; also "The
          Siege of AR-558," *DS9:* #158)
Rule 8   "Small print leads to large risk."
          The Ferengi Rules of Acquisition
Rule 47   "Never trust anyone whose suit is nicer than your
          own."
          ("Rivals," *DS9:* #31)
Rule 48   "The bigger the smile, the sharper the knife."
          ("Rules of Acquisition," *DS9:* #27)
Rule 59   "Free advice is seldom cheap."
          ("Rules of Acquisition")
Rule 86   "Never let the competition know what you're
          thinking."
          The Ferengi Rules of Acquisition
Rule 99   "Trust is the biggest liability of all."
          The Ferengi Rules of Acquisition
Rule 190 "Hear all. Trust nothing."
          ("Call to Arms," *DS9:* #124)

---

*The Rules of Acquisition were written over ten millennia ago by the first Grand Nagus, Gint. All Ferengi boys are expected to memorize the Rules and repeat them on command. According to the episode "Rules of Acquisition," there are 285 Rules, though not every Rule was made known by the time *DS9* ceased production. Though additional Rules have been named in *Star Trek* novels, comic books, and other sources, only those Rules originating from either *DS9* episodes or the companion book by Ira Steven Behr, *The Ferengi Rules of Acquisition* (New York: Pocket Books, 1995), are considered "canon" among Trekkers.

Rule 194   "It's always good business to know about new cus-
           tomers before they walk in your door."
           ("Whispers," *DS9:* #34)

Rule 203   "New customers are life razor-toothed Greeworms —
           they can be succulent, but sometimes they bite
           back!"
           ("Little Green Men," *DS9:* #80)

Zek also demonstrates Ferengi distrust by having his servant Maihar'du taste his food before he eats it. And of course, Quark becomes even more diffident after an airlock bomb nearly kills him. While investigating the matter, Security Chief Odo asks Quark whom he suspects — a rather pointless question to Quark, since like a true Ferengi he suspects everyone.

Hobbes also insisted that we love self-glorification. Because we're basically vain, we expect others to value us and assume they'll think of us as highly we do ourselves. Quark's vanity becomes apparent when, shortly after the first assassination attempt, he considers taking along a Dabo girl on his business trip to the Gamma Quadrant because he thinks that "might enhance his prestige." Krax feeds Quark's ego when he replies, "One look at your imposing features, and the negotiators will give us everything we ask for." Knowing that Quark can't resist basking in someone else's flattery, he manages to rise above suspicion at a critical time by appealing to Quark's conceit. (Hmmh. That *is* pretty sneaky. Maybe Zek was wrong about Krax after all.) On the other hand, when people undervalue us, Hobbes believed, we seek to compensate ourselves by retaliating against them. We see this point illustrated in "The Nagus" when the maestro behind the coup attempt turns out to be the last person Quark suspects: his brother, Rom.

Given this analysis of humanoid nature as a perpetual state of distrust, Hobbes listed three principal causes of quarrel:

competition, diffidence, and glory. The respective objects or goals of these drives are gain ("profit"), safety, and reputation— all of which are certainly worthy of a Ferengi! Indeed, the Ferengi also project their distinctly Hobbesian view of humanoid nature onto nearly every other species. The traders of the galaxy, they frequently remind each other of the 284th Rule of Acquisition: "Deep down, everyone's a Ferengi." By their words and deeds, the Ferengi see all humanoids as essentially competitive, distrustful, and vain.

Hobbes called the condition of violence produced by the scarcity of resources "war." War is seen as a time during which each person is known to be a threat to every other person—a disposition that can flare into battle at any moment. Consequently, the state of nature is a time of extreme insecurity predisposed to violence and mayhem. If you doubt this in any way, Hobbes would say, then ask yourself why else do we deadbolt our doors at night, avoid traveling alone whenever possible (or carry mace when we do), advocate the right to possess a firearm in one's home, buy encryption devices and antivirus software for our personal computers, or keep our valuables safely locked away. If we do these things despite the many laws, peace officers, and boundless other means of appeal in place in the event of injury, just imagine how distrustful we would be if there were no remedies at all!

Given his outlook on human nature, it might occur to you that perhaps Hobbes was a bit of a pessimist. (You wouldn't be alone in your assessment.) You might also wonder why we're even bothering with a notion so negative it couldn't possibly have anything to do with the ethics of *Star Trek*. After all, *Star Trek* basically says that we're okay, warts and all. So we're a little paranoid about our own possessions, or capable of fighting with each other from time to time. Big deal! The Metrons told Kirk that, despite these tendencies, we're "a promising species." Why can't we just go from there?

Well, because there's more to it than that. First of all, Hobbes would say, there's a distinction between being a pessimist and constantly perceiving others as a threat. Just because we're serious about protecting our belongings and upholding our own personal safety, that doesn't necessarily mean we expect the worst in others; that's just common sense. Without rules or safety mechanisms in place, the possibility of lapsing into the state of nature still exists. Likewise, all of us are occasionally guilty of being vain, overly competitive, or unduly suspicious. Though most of us would rather not admit having these less-than-flattering personality traits, they are part of the makeup of being human. Therefore, Hobbes might say, characterizing humankind (or humanoids) in this way is not pessimistic, but rather realistic.

Of course, like any other argument, Hobbes' theory (and his own assessment of it, for that matter) comes down to one thing: either you buy it, or you don't. One privilege of creative license is the ability to comment on issues you might personally oppose without necessarily being subversive. One way to do this is through exaggeration. Though Quark, Zek, and the other Ferengi characters are clearly capitalism personified, they're also basically *Deep Space Nine*'s comic relief. In other words, though *Star Trek* knows how much capitalism pervades our culture—not to mention how deeply Hobbes has influenced our economic system as we know it today—the show is ultimately poking fun at it.

LIVING TOGETHER FERENGI STYLE

Now that we understand *Star Trek*'s take on the whole thing, let's return to our analysis of Hobbesian and Ferengi thought. If competition, diffidence, and glory are the basic drives of humanoid nature, then it would appear that humans and Ferengi are temperamentally unfit to live together in society. Of course, we know that's not the case: in fact, they coexisted quite well for seven seasons, and will continue to do so eternally in syndication.

Ever wonder how they managed to pull that off? That's the kind of question Hobbes would ask, if he had the chance to watch the show. Naturally, he'd have some thoughts on the matter—in fact, he would posit that many of the characteristics that create competition and warfare among divergent peoples can also pave the way for a peaceful coexistence.

Take death, for example—a fear common to humanoids and Ferengi alike. The fear of death can certainly lead to competition and warfare, as we try to "do onto others" before they do it to us. Indeed, Quark seeks Zek's counsel because he hopes to learn how to detect his enemies before they can hurt him. But this same fear of death can also lead to a mutual desire for peace and a willingness to accept rules. After all, logic tells us we'd have a much better chance to survive (and therefore garner profits) under peaceful conditions than otherwise. As the 125th Rule of Acquisition puts it, "You can't make a deal when you're dead" ("The Siege of AR-558"). That's why we're willing to abide by rules or laws laid down by Grand Naguses, Starfleet, or the various branches of our federal, state, and local government.

In fact, think of business as a competitive endeavor, and you can see Hobbes' point expressed in another Rule of Acquisition: Rule 35, "War is good for business" ("Destiny," *DS9:* #61; also "The Siege of AR-558"). The ruthlessly competitive nature of the Ferengi drives them to outdo each other at any cost, even if it means instigating a war. At the same time, however, their competitive nature makes them want to seek peace; thus, Rule 34, "Peace is good for business" ("Destiny").* Of course, if all

---

*Apparently Rules 34 and 35 are frequently confused. Though Dax in "Destiny" identifies "Peace is good for business" as Rule 34, Quark corrects her, saying that it is No. 35. However, *The Ferengi Rules of Acquisition* clearly lists "Peace" as No. 34, and "War" as No. 35; since that book is presumably the "bible" as far as this matter is concerned, we will defer to it accordingly.

Ferengi were competing with one another to the point of killing each other off, eventually there'd be no business to transact. So in order to pursue their business dealings more efficiently, the Ferengi desire peace, and sign contracts with one another to preserve that peace. Rather than being a self-contradiction, Hobbes would say, Rules 34 and 35 show that the same motivator (business or competition) can thrive under two opposite conditions.

The human and Ferengi desire for luxuries can likewise lead to competition, since luxuries and latinum are not available in sufficient quantities for everyone to acquire them. But the love of luxury can also lead us to accept rules in order to retain the possessions we already have. We know that if we steal from someone else, he or she can turn around and do the same to us. Conversely, if we limit our acquisitive inclinations, then others might also refrain from harming us. Therefore, Hobbes would conclude, we prefer living together in peace in order to protect what's ours.

Now, we need two things for a peaceful coexistence to occur. First, we must guarantee that we won't harm one another; we must be able to live together without fear of theft, treachery, or assault. Second, we must rely on one another to keep our promises; as Worf explained to young Alexander in "Cost of Living," "You're supposed to agree. That's what an agreement is." These two conditions form the basis of what Hobbes called the "social contract." Only after these guarantees are in place can a society develop wherein everyone lives a better life than they would in the "state of nature."

Of course, Hobbes wasn't the first to view the creation of society as a harsh necessity forced upon egotistical people by their own aggressive competitiveness. As we discussed in Chapter 3, Plato said the same thing (in the person of his brother Glaucon) when he wrote *The Republic* nearly 2,000 years before:

They say that to do injustice is, by nature, good, to suffer injustice, evil; but that the evil is greater than the good. And so when men have both done and suffered injustice and have had experience of both, not being able to avoid the one and obtain the other, they think that they had better agree among themselves to have neither; hence there arise laws and mutual covenants; and that which is ordained by law is termed by them lawful and just.

Like Hobbes, Glaucon argued that we agree to abide by the rules of society—that is, to live under a "social contract"—only because we don't want to suffer injustice. Of course, Plato also went on to pull the rug out from under that theory, but we already covered that. The point is, Hobbes took Glaucon's basic premise and went from there, as we're about to see.

"A CONTRACT IS A CONTRACT IS A CONTRACT..."

Hobbes believed everyone has a natural right to preserve his own life. This right of self-preservation provides that we can use any and all means necessary for self-defense, and allows us to be our own judge as to what's necessary and good for us. This also means we have the right to do anything we want to others, and to take anything we want from them to ensure our survival. This is the basic idea behind the 52nd Rule of Acquisition, "Never ask when you can take" ("Babel"). If we found a sack full of cash in a bank parking lot, or a Ferengi came across a horde of gold-pressed latinum, the principle behind Hobbes' natural right and Rule 52 means we could keep the money without turning it in or asking if anyone lost it.

Based on this natural right, Hobbes sets down certain laws of nature, which are general rules "found out by reason" that tell us what to do and what not to do. The first law of nature is that everyone ought to "seek peace and follow it." Of course, this law is pretty much common sense, especially for a capitalist society: we have a better chance to survive and accumulate profit if we live under peaceful conditions.

The second law of nature is that we have the right to give up our natural right to do anything we want to others and take anything we want from them. We can lay aside our right to interfere with others by transferring it to someone who becomes the beneficiary of our action. Whenever there's a mutual transfer of rights, we have a contract—a mutual promise of performing what is to be done. The Ferengi, as we know, are just as fond of contracts as Hobbes was; not surprisingly, they consider the inviolability of a contract to be the foundation of their society. As the 17th Rule of Acquisition states, "A contract is a contract is a contract—but only between Ferengi" ("Body Parts," *DS9: #97*). Of course, as definitions go, this isn't very clear. Hobbes' definition of "social contract" is much better: a set of laws designed to ensure maximum freedom combined with personal security. Both the U. S. Constitution and the Constitution of the United Federation of Planets are examples of what Hobbes meant by a social contract.

There are two stages in any contract: the covenant, which is an exchange of promises, and the actual performance. If one or more parties fail to abide by the terms of the contract, we are no longer obliged to live up to it. Though no contract is forever binding (Hobbes believed we never forfeit our right to defend our property and ourselves), the enforceability of a social contract is nonetheless crucial. "Without the fear of some coercive power," Hobbes observed, the parties "are no better off" than they were in the state of nature. Unlike ants and bees, who can live together by their natural instinct of sociability, Hobbes insisted that humanoids are basically antisocial; our lives (and those of the Ferengi, for that matter) are constantly marked by competition, envy, hatred, and other things that otherwise have no effect on naturally social beings. Whereas ants and bees don't distinguish between private goods and the common goods, humanoids and Ferengi do; according to Hobbes, we live in constant tension because sometimes we can't attain our private goals except at the expense of public goals.

Given this view of human nature, people can't be trusted to sacrifice their private goals unless they are motivated to do so by fear. It is out of this fear that contracts are formed in the first place, and only because of this fear that they're obeyed. As Lwaxana Troi put it in "Cost of Living," "Contracts are usually between people who don't really trust one another." Similarly, Hobbes did not trust us to act ethically unless we're fairly certain we'll face the music for acting unethically. Thus, to prevent a backslide into the state of nature, we must institute rules to govern our relations with one another, and set up a power necessary to enforce those rules (as the Ferengi did by establishing the Rules of Acquisition, and as our forefathers did with the Constitution). For Hobbes, the form of government is relatively unimportant; our obedience to our chosen ruler is what matters, regardless of whether we call that ruler president, king, or Grand Nagus. The ruler should provide his subjects not only with safety, but also with "other contentments of life" through instructions and the laws. Hobbes (as I'm sure you've figured out by now) was quite a "law and order" man. In essence, he believed that a powerful government with the strength to enforce the law is necessary for both moral action and social peace.

CONTRACTUAL PROBLEMS

The social contract theory not only offers an explanation of the origin of civil society, but tries to explain the nature of morality as well. Society exists to enforce the most important rules necessary for living together, while morality consists of the entire set of rules that promote living together. Rational beings agree to accept these rules for their mutual benefit, provided that everyone agrees to follow the same set of rules. Those who accept the terms of the contract have rights created, recognized, and protected by the contract.

The problem with Hobbes' social contract theory is that it doesn't guarantee that everyone will have a chance to participate equally in framing the rules of morality—only the signatories are covered directly. So what happens to those who are not asked to sign? As we see very clearly among the Ferengi, this approach to ethics could very well sanction the most brazen forms of political, economic, moral, and social injustice. The sexual discrimination practiced by the Ferengi, for example, has its roots in their contractarian moral theory. If we can make the connection between Ferengi morality (as codified in their Rules of Acquisition), and their blatant discrimination, we may also come to recognize the source for various other injustices inherent in other societies that promote the social contract theory—including our very own.

Another flaw with the social contract theory is that it assumes Hobbes' analysis of human nature is actually right. If that's the case, then Sisko was off the mark when he told his son in "The Nagus" that "Human values and Ferengi values are very different." Certainly that's what Hobbes would have us believe; it's the captain's conceit that makes him think we're different. Our values are derived from analyzing our natures. Since Hobbes believed we're basically egoistic, competitive, and distrustful of one another, we're naturally motivated to compare ourselves to other cultures in the most favorable light. If he's right, that means, among other things, that altruism (that is, a purely unselfish act meant to help another for that individual's own sake) is not only a bad idea—it's not even possible.

LET'S COMPARE SISKO TO ANOTHER ABRAHAM

Glaucon, Hobbes, and the Ferengi weren't the only ones who believed we always act to benefit ourselves, and ourselves alone. According to one famous newspaper account, so apparently did Abraham Lincoln. As the story goes, Lincoln was riding in a coach with a friend one day when he passed a mud hole where several piglets were drowning. The mother sow was screaming in distress, but she apparently couldn't help her babies. Upon asking the driver to stop the coach, Lincoln waded into the mud hole and rescued the piglets. What a guy! Only the way Lincoln saw it, what he did "was the very essence of selfishness. I should have had no peace of mind had I gone on and left that suffering old sow worrying over those pigs. I did it to get peace of mind, don't you see?" Of course, Lincoln was known for his self-deprecating sense of humor, so it's possible he could have made these remarks with tongue in cheek. But let's assume for argument's sake that he was talking straight.

With that in mind, let's imagine an encounter between Sisko and Lincoln—either the same Honest Abe generated by the Excalbians in "The Savage Curtain," or more probably, a replica created by one of DS9's holodeck programs. Let's say their conversation went something like this:

SISKO: With all due respect, Mr. President, just because someone derives pleasure from helping others, that doesn't make him or her selfish. After all, it's usually the unselfish person who derives pleasure from assisting others, not the selfish.

LINCOLN: But, Commander, I only helped those poor animals to ensure my peace of mind.

SISKO: Would it have mattered to you whether you

saved the piglet or not? Either way, you would have done the right thing and therefore been able to feel good about yourself.

Now, would Lincoln really have felt as good had he been unsuccessful, and had to drive off hearing the mother's frantic crying? Probably not. Perhaps then it was really the anguish of the mother pig that he cared about far beyond his own "peace of mind." After all, if a person were truly selfish, why would it matter to him whether others suffered? Because most of us care about the welfare of other people (particularly our family and friends), we're usually compelled to help them. When we do, we hope that our efforts are successful. Otherwise, if all we cared about was whether we felt good (or got "peace of mind") about doing the right thing, then nothing else would matter. We wouldn't worry over the outcome of our actions, nor be concerned over what ultimately happens to the individuals we're trying to help. "Bottom line," Sisko might say to Lincoln, "because these things do matter to us, maybe we're not as purely self-centered as Hobbes and the Ferengi would have us believe."

If the president needed more convincing, perhaps the captain might tell him the story about his own son, Jake, and Rom's son, Nog—which, as luck would have it, also happens to be the "B" story of "The Nagus." Rom pulls Nog out of school in order to please Zek (the Grand Nagus thinks humanoid-taught classes will not teach the boy proper Ferengi values). Despite the fact he cannot read, Nog was trying to do well; more importantly, he enjoyed being in school with his closest friend, Jake. When Zek's ridicule distresses Nog, he takes his anger out on Jake, and at one point blurts out "Humans and Ferengi don't get along!" This remark bothers Jake enough to ask his father about it. "Usually they don't," Sisko replies. "Human values and Ferengi values are very different." Now, we should add that Sisko has mixed feelings about this newfound crack in the boys' relationship—he thinks Nog has been a bad influence on Jake, especially after learning that Jake lied to help cover for Nog when the young Ferengi was nailed for not completing his homework.* A little later on, when Jake doesn't come home for dinner, the captain goes looking for him. Though he expects that Jake and Nog are out causing trouble, Sisko's agitation turns to pride when he overhears Jake patiently teaching Nog how to read.

Jake's example of pure altruism stands in stark contrast to the pure egoism exhibited by the Ferengi (or inherent in human nature, as Hobbes saw it). Jake cares about Nog's education; it matters to him, far beyond any personal satisfaction he gets from knowing that he has helped Nog. If Lincoln asked Sisko why Jake tutors Nog, the captain would probably say, "Because my son is the kind of person who cares about his friends so much, he's willing to take action to help them. He wants Nog to know how to read because he knows that would make Nog a better person."

Now, it's true that if we have a positive attitude toward attaining some goal, we may derive satisfaction from achieving it. However, we must desire to reach the goal before we can find any satisfaction in it. Humans/humanoids want all sorts of things—new clothes, a fulfilling marriage or relationship, double chocolate ice cream sundaes (without the fat), a state-of-the-art computer or car, to be published, to travel in space, to be like Michael Jordan—you name it, we want it. Since we desire these things, we're pleased once we get them. It's also true that when we think about the welfare of others, we're pleased when we help them—but that's not the reason why we help

---

*The homework assignment, interestingly enough, was to write an essay on "what ethics mean." Nog's reason for not having his assignment done: "Vulcans took it," which is, presumably, the 24th-century equivalent of the classic excuse "My dog ate it" (although that claim is even more outrageous, considering that Vulcans are known for their integrity).

them. We do not seek the pleasure; it is not our goal. When that happens, when we strive to help others for their own sakes and not ours, we are acting altruistically. Altruism is certainly much more in step with *Star Trek*'s overall philosophy — especially among members of Starfleet.

Nonetheless, there's no escaping that the Hobbesian aspects of our nature are still very much prevalent in our culture today. Describe Hobbes' social contract theory to just about any introductory college class, for example, and most students will agree that he captured modern morality in a nutshell. That's why Hobbes is worth considering, even though, other than the Ferengi, his philosophy is embraced by just a few rogues in the Alpha Quadrant of the *Star Trek* universe.

TOXIC WASTE IN THE DELTA QUADRANT

We do see Hobbesian values upheld in the Delta Quadrant, too, in a species known as the Malon. In "Night" (*VGR:* #95), a Malon named Emck expects to be compensated when he helps drive off an alien vessel that was attacking the ship. Like the Ferengi, the Malon believe that the only reason to help anyone is to gain something in return; they also value competitive advantage, even going to war in order to protect their self-interests. Janeway learns that the Malon are poisoning the space of another species by using it as a toxic dumping ground; when she confronts Emck about this, he answers simply that it's a "perfect" disposal site. When Chakotay reasons that the site can't be all that "perfect" (after all, another species inhabits it), Emck justifies his actions by saying, in effect, "It's only one species." Janeway, of course, argues that "only one species" is enough of a reason to stop.

Attempting to resolve this problem amicably, Janeway offers to teach the Malon how to eliminate their toxic waste problem by using clean energy instead. Though Emck agrees that the Federation technology would solve a lot of problems on his world, he objects on the grounds "it would also put me out of business." Having accumulated substantial profit under the current system, he would become "obsolete" were the Malon to revolutionize their technology. Diplomacy having failed, Janeway, ever the philosopher-queen, decides to take the side of the species native to this particular region of space and close the vortex Emck regularly used in his forays to dump theta radiation. Thus the episode takes a stand in favor of environmental concerns over worry about financial profit.* When the two conflict, the welfare of the environment should take priority (whereas anyone championing Hobbes' perspective would see it Emck's way, the environment be damned).

STAR TREK CONTAMINATES SELFISHNESS

As we said, Hobbes' analysis of human nature goes against the optimism that is at the heart of *Star Trek*. While his theory on the state of nature does help us understand the ethics of the Ferengi, it doesn't shed any light on the ethics of the series as a whole. The Malon, of course, are presented as *Voyager*'s unprincipled opponents, while the Ferengi are almost always portrayed humorously. Overall, though, capitalism clearly has no place in the ethics of *Star Trek*—perhaps because, as Captain Picard once put it, "The acquisition of wealth is no longer the driving force in our lives" (*Star Trek: First Contact*).

Even Quark, of all people, realizes that not all actions are motivated by selfishness. In "The Ascent" (*DS9: #107*), he and his archrival Odo crash-land their shuttle on a frozen, desolate planet. They have minimal rations, no supplies, and a damaged communications system that cannot permeate the atmosphere.

---

*Of course, in the episode "Thirty Days" (*VGR: #103*), *Voyager* draws the line at using sabotage, or ecoterrorism, in support of environmentalism.

Their only option is to ascend a nearby mountain where the atmosphere may be thin enough to send out a signal before they either freeze or starve to death. It's a long shot, made even more daunting after Odo breaks his leg on the way up. Now, you'd think, like a true Ferengi, Quark would have left Odo behind to fend for himself. But what does he do? He builds a stretcher and carries Odo up the rest of the mountain—an act of true goodness that flies in the face of such Rules as "Never place friendship before profit" ("Rules of Acquisition"), not to mention Hobbes' theory about human nature in general.

Of course, "The Ascent" takes place several years after "The Nagus," during which time Quark has evolved as a character, due in part to his ongoing interaction with human beings. Spock talks about the kind of impact frequent "exposure" to humans can have on other species in "The Gamesters of Triskelion." When Kirk, Uhura, and Chekov mysteriously vanish from the ship, Spock tells McCoy, "We shall continue sensor scans, Doctor. At the moment that is all we can do—except hope for a rational explanation."

Naturally, Bones can't resist tweaking the Vulcan over his peculiar choice of words: *"Hope?* I always thought that was a human failing."

"True, Doctor," replies Spock. "Constant exposure does result in a certain degree of contamination."

Given Spock's theory on the human capacity to "contaminate" alien species (not to mention the overall altruism that pervades in all four series), Quark's act of kindness should come as no surprise. In fact, in our next section, we'll take a close look at an ethical theory that not only extols altruism, but even insists on it. Perhaps here we'll shed even more light on the ethics of *Star Trek*.

PART FOUR

WHEN
DUTY CALLS

"My duty requires that I complete the mission regardless of my personal feelings."

Worf to Jadzia,
"Change of Heart"

DUTY CAN BE A CRUSHER

"I, Borg"
TNG: Episode 123
Stardate: 45854.2
Original Air Date: Week of May 11, 1992

Riker, Worf, and Dr. Crusher investigate the wreckage of a small craft and find that the only survivor is a critically injured adolescent Borg.* Crusher prevails upon Picard to set aside his personal hatred for the species and let her save the young Borg—even though its presence aboard the Enterprise could also alert other Borg. Upon learning

---

*The Borg are a powerful and dangerous humanoid species who implant themselves with cybernetic devices in order to enhance their combat and technological capabilities. Each Borg is tied into a sophisticated subspace network that ensures each member is given constant supervision and guidance. In a word, they're drones. As we mentioned briefly in Chapter 4, Borg society very much embodies the Platonic idea of suppressing individualism for the good of the Collective. In the two-parter "The Best of Both Worlds" (*TNG:* #74 and #75), the Borg captured Picard as part of an ambitious plan to assimilate the entire Federation. While imprisoned, the captain was surgically mutated and transformed into an entity known as Locutus of Borg. During this time he was also forced to participate in a battle that eventually destroyed 39 Federation starships and their crews. Cf. Michael Okuda and Denise Okuda, *The "Star Trek" Encyclopedia,* 2nd ed. (New York: Pocket Books, 1997), pp. 51, 380.

*some of the patient's brain implants must be replaced,
Picard orders Geordi LaForge to install a virus program
that could obliterate the entire Borg species when the
young Borg returns to its Collective. Though Crusher
objects to using one of her patients as a means of killing
others, the remaining officers (as well as Guinan) support
Picard's plan, citing the Borg race's many acts of aggression against the Federation. However, LaForge and Guinan
reconsider their decision once the young Borg (whom they
name "Hugh") begins to display unmistakable signs of personhood. When Picard himself becomes convinced of
Hugh's "singularity," the captain must choose between fulfilling his moral duty and letting Hugh remain an individual (thus, allowing the Borg race to survive)—or carrying
out his own desire for vengeance.*

"Ethics"
TNG: Episode 116
Stardate: 45587.3
Original Air Date: Week of March 2, 1992

---

*Worf becomes paralyzed from the waist down after a heavy
container falls on him and shatters his spinal column. With
no hope for a full recovery, and his warrior pride completely
devastated, the Klingon officer won't permit anyone to see
him—not even his young son, Alexander. Believing his life is
over, Worf asks Riker to assist him in a traditional Klingon
suicide ritual known as the* Hegh'bat. *While Riker grapples
with this decision, Dr. Crusher urges Worf to consider wearing electromechanical implants that will restore up to 70 percent of his mobility. Worf rejects the idea, insisting he'd
rather die than be anything less than the man he was. An*

ambitious neurogeneticist, Dr. Toby Russell, recommends an experimental surgery that theoretically could make Worf walk again. Although Crusher refuses to endanger Worf's life over an unproven medical procedure, Picard, knowing full well that a Klingon warrior lives for risk, believes she should allow Worf to decide for himself. Meanwhile, Riker tells Worf he will participate in the Hegh'bat, *but only in accordance with Klingon tradition. Strictly speaking, that means the death blow must be administered by Worf's own son!*

Well, we certainly have no dearth of issues to discuss in these two episodes—genocide, assisted suicide, and the ethics of medicine in general. We also have plenty of "What would you do if you were...?" questions to ponder, as each *TNG* character faces a situation in which personal feelings or principles come into conflict with professional, cultural, or familial duty.

The idea of honoring one's duty is a theme that's near and dear to *Star Trek*. In fact, we've seen it expressed in different ways throughout the many stories we've talked about so far. Sisko's duty in "The Reckoning" requires him to sacrifice his own needs, even at the risk of losing his son, so that the will of the Prophets can be done. Spock reminds Kirk in "The Enemy Within" that a captain owes it to his crew to look strong on the outside—even when he's divided on the inside. Janeway shows the holographic da Vinci in "Concerning Flight" that we must help our friends see the light, no matter how painful that might be. Kira in "Accession" follows her D'jarra, even though she has neither the interest nor aptitude in being an artist, because she believes Akorem is right. Finally, Lwaxana learns in "Cost of Living" that respecting the practices of another culture doesn't necessarily mean abandoning her duty to her self.

Because the notion of duty recurs so frequently throughout all four series, perhaps we ought to take a close look at this important concept in order to understand its place in the overall picture of *Trek*. After all, to paraphrase our friend Socrates in the *Euthyphro*, it's not enough to know examples of what duty *is*. We need to know what duty *means* before we can really understand it.

ALWAYS ACT FROM DUTY, NOT ACCORDING TO IT

Both "I, Borg" and the aptly titled "Ethics" manifest principles of duty originally expressed by the German philosopher Immanuel Kant (1724–1804). One of the seminal figures in ethical theory, Kant espoused a method of morality that, as it happens, is particularly suitable for the purposes of determining the ethics of *Star Trek*. Because Kant was concerned with right conduct for all rational beings, not just humans, he left the door open for an ethical system that conveniently encompasses extraterrestrials as well.

Kant's rationale was that ethical principles apply to anyone who acts through deliberation and reason. Since every humanoid species in the world of *Star Trek* is capable of making decisions based on reasoning, Kant would argue that any ethical principle applied to us must also be applied to them—a notion, by the way, bolstered by the Original Series in "Return to Tomorrow" (*TOS:* #51). According to that episode, the inhabitants of Sargon's planet, an advanced race of humanoids, colonized various planets throughout the galaxy over 600,000 years ago; as a result, many subsequent humanoid races with similar natures and capacities for reason (including, presumably, Vulcans) came to be. If so, the ethical logic of these diverse species can be distinguished from such factors as culture, language, and physical appearance, insofar as it's rooted in the one reasoning process common to all rational beings in the universe. Therefore, Kant might add, any rational descendant of Sargon can discover its moral duties by way of reason.

Kant believed there are three kinds of actions when it comes to moral duty: those actions that are inconsistent with duty, those in accordance with duty, and those that are from duty. Kant didn't focus much on the first type of actions (encompassing behavior such as stealing, murdering, and torturing people) since they so clearly oppose what moral duty requires of us, it's practically self-evident. He did, however, urge us to pay attention to the difference between acting "in accordance with duty" and acting "from duty," because it's so easy to confuse the two. For Kant, an action done "from duty" is one done with a pure intention—that is, an act done primarily because "it's the right thing to do." The objections Crusher raises in both our model episodes are actions done "from duty." She considers Picard's plan to implant Hugh with a virus that could wipe out the Borg as pure genocide; her duty as a doctor is to preserve life, not participate in the destruction of it. She opposes Worf's planned suicide and the use of Dr. Russell's experimental surgery for the same reason. "The first tenet of good medicine," she explains to Picard, "is never make the patient worse. Right now, Worf is alive and functioning. If he goes into that operation, he could come out a corpse!" (Russell's holographic simulations yielded only a 37 percent success rate. More to the point, she had yet to try it on a living humanoid patient.)

All right, you might ask, how is acting "from duty" any different from acting "according to duty"? Aren't they the same thing? Not for Kant; to him, acting "in accordance" with duty means doing something out of self-interest. While it might look like we're doing the right thing, we really have an ulterior motive. In other words, our intention isn't pure. Russell acts in accordance with duty throughout "Ethics," as do LaForge and Picard in the early stages of "I, Borg." Russell is more concerned with making a name for herself with her genetronic replication procedure than with whether Worf is actually healed; LaForge rigs a nourishment device in Hugh so that it works only if the young Borg cooperates; Picard cites the Borg's many crimes against the Federation to obfuscate his own desire for revenge. (Of course, once Geordi and the captain recognize Hugh as an individual, their motivations change; from that point on, their actions in the episode are done "from duty.")

Kant would particularly disapprove of Picard's decision to wipe out the Borg because it was clearly made out of spite. Not that he couldn't sympathize with Picard, or any other victim of Borg assimilation—indeed, the notion of "personhood" was very important to our 18th-century friend (as we'll see in due time). It's just that Kant also believed acting out of sympathy, hate, or any other feeling just isn't a good idea. Like Plato, he distrusted the emotions, regarding them as unstable and unreliable. Though our emotions often motivate us to acts of compassion and generosity, they can just as easily lead us to destruction and cruelty. Therefore, Kant would advise Picard to overcome his rage and rely on reason in order to act morally— which, of course, is what the captain does in the second half of the show.

THE ROAD FOR KANT IS PAVED WITH GOOD INTENTIONS

Still, it's impossible to act purely from duty without giving at least some thought to our own self-interest—that's human nature. Even Kant knew that. However, he would caution, if we act primarily out of self-interest or a desire for pleasure, then our motive is not what it should be. It's one thing if we act from duty because it brings us pleasure; it's entirely different if we act from duty, knowing it may very well interfere with our pleasure.

For Kant, it's not just what we do that matters, but also why we do it. Not surprisingly, our intentions play the marquee role in his entire concept of morality. This means we cannot possibly act "from duty" unless we intend to do what is right regardless of our feelings or any rewards. Put another way, when considering a course of action, we should always ask whether we would still do it even if we knew we'd get nothing out of it personally. Picard, Crusher, and LaForge all pass this test, while Russell clearly fails it.

How do we figure out what makes an action good? By forgetting about what it accomplishes. Indeed, Kant believed that the consequences of our behavior should never even enter the picture. So long as our intention is pure, then our actions will always have true moral worth—even if they happen to yield unfortunate results.

This, of course, runs counter to the old adage "The road to hell is paved with good intentions," which teaches that merely intending to do good isn't enough: we must also bring about good. Given the destructive nature of the Borg, the risk in showing compassion to Hugh is that he might trigger an action that could endanger everyone aboard the ship—a point Guinan dramatically makes to Picard during their fencing match when she disarms the captain after he lets down his guard. Kant, nevertheless, would insist it doesn't matter what Hugh does upon his recovery, what counts is that Crusher did the right thing by saving the life of another rational being.

Kant's emphasis on intention rather than inclination as the determinant of our moral actions is further explicated in "Rules of Engagement" (*DS9:* #90), wherein Worf faces possible extradition to Qo'noS for destroying a Klingon civilian vessel. Indeed, Ch'Pok, the Klingon advocate who prosecutes Worf, sounds very Kantian in his assessment of the matter. "We Klingons are not concerned with matters of fact and circumstance," he says in his opening statement. "What matters to us is what was in Worf's heart when he gave the order to fire: was he just a Starfleet officer doing his duty, or was he a Klingon warrior reveling in the battle? Because if he was a Klingon lost in the bloodlust of combat, only we can judge him, not you."

Ch'Pok argues that because Worf is Klingon, his violent inclinations got the best of him, causing him to open fire without thinking things through. Since Worf's heart is Klingon, he should therefore be extradited. Though Sisko, representing Worf, objects on the grounds that "you can't put a man's heart on trial," T'Lara, the Vulcan admiral who is presiding over the matter, rules that the question of Worf's motive is relevant—a judgment with which Kant would also agree.

Now, at this point in the *Star Trek* chronology, Worf is considered a traitor among Klingons because he sided with the Federation during the invasion of Cardassia. (This wasn't the case back when he was an officer on *TNG*.) Because of this, Ch'Pok argues, Worf is angry and bent on revenge against the Klingon Empire, even to the point of firing on an unarmed ship. Though Worf insists he would never attack a defenseless opponent, Ch'Pok cleverly provokes Worf into assaulting him, thus demonstrating that Worf could indeed attack unarmed people when angered. Things look bleak for the big guy, till Odo finds evidence at the 11th hour that Klingon government officials falsified the list of victims by using the names of Klingon citizens who had died in an earlier crash on Galorda Prime. Seems the entire affair was staged to gain sympathy for the Empire's plan to annex Cardassian territory—and cause Worf further embarrassment to boot!

Though clearly exonerated, Worf is not as happy as you might think. Upon discussing the matter with Sisko after the hearing, he admits he really *was* looking forward to a chance for vengeance when the Klingon ships first attacked. Sisko proceeds to chew Worf out. Since the purpose of the mission was humanitarian in the first place (delivering aid to a besieged Cardassian colony), Worf never should have accepted the assignment knowing he had ulterior motives. (Our friend Kant, of course, would say the same thing. That Worf lucked out and no one was killed is inconsequential. What matters is that his intentions at the time he took on command were not pure.)

Sisko softens the blow a little by telling Worf he'll "make a fine captain someday," then urges him to attend a victory celebration at Quark's bar. Only Worf, depressed and remorseful over letting his personal desires interfere with his ability to carry out his moral obligations, doesn't want to go.* That's not good enough, says Sisko: "Part of [the duty of] being a captain is knowing when to smile, to make the troops happy, even when it's the last thing in the world you want to do—because they're your troops and you have to take care of them." (Which, when you think about it, is not far removed from what Spock said to Kirk in "The Enemy Within.") Though he'd much rather remain by himself, Worf stoically overcomes his feelings in order to execute his duty.

AUTONOMY RULES IN THE KINGDOM OF ENDS

Kant also taught that when a rational being acts as the source of moral action, he or she has an *autonomous* will—that is, a will that is free and independent—whereas, a person with a *heteronomous* will is easily influenced by desire, emotion, or some other outside interference. Jadzia shows signs of a heteronomous will by yielding to her craving for icoberry torte in "Let He Who Is Without Sin..." The same can be said for irrational Kirk in "The Enemy Within," as well as anyone who overdoses on food, drink, sex, or other pleasures. But you can also have a heteronomous will if your moral judgments are simply those instilled in you by your parents, which they received from their parents, and so on. Your will is het-

---

*An understandable reaction, especially given Worf's Stoic inclinations. Stoicism is quite compatible with a concern for duty and letting reason guide our desires.

eronomous because you allow your principles to be based on an outside source without ever questioning it.

We see another example of the difference between an autonomous will and a heteronomous will in "I, Borg." While running tests on the young Borg's physiology early in the episode, LaForge and Crusher ask the patient if he has a name. The Borg responds, "Third of Five"—meaning, of course, that he was the third of five Borg members on his ship. Eventually they give him a more personal moniker: Hugh. When LaForge asks the Borg what he thinks of his new appellation, he says agreeably, "We are Hugh." Now, the reason, of course, that Hugh refers to himself in the first-person plural is that at this point he still thinks of himself as a Borg. His actions are determined by an outside source (to wit, the Borg Collective); therefore, Kant would say, he has a heteronomous will. LaForge, on the other hand, has an autonomous will. "We are also separate individuals," he explains to Hugh. "I make decisions for myself." A person who decides for himself knows that only his own reason can tell him what to do or not to do. An autonomous being, Kant might add, is capable of discerning what is right and wrong without needing to rely on outside authorities, such as government officials or religious leaders. He or she is therefore free to oppose external pressures, such as those imposed by the totalitarian Borg.

Kant's concept of morality strives for an ideal state in which each individual's goals harmonize with those of everyone else. Kant called his utopia the Kingdom of Ends; "Kingdom" refers to a community of people, "ends" the way in which the people treat each other (as "ends," or individuals who have their own goals in life). Every time we show respect and consideration for one another, we make the Kingdom of Ends a little more possible, a little more real. This philosophy, of course, is alive and well in the world of *Star Trek*. We see it practiced not only among the crews of the *Enterprise, Voyager,* and Deep Space Nine, but in their dealings with new life and new civilizations as well.

Not that it's always easy. Bright as we are (to borrow a line from Chapter 4), we're still capable of making the same mistakes, even after we've learned from them. When that happens, we stray from the Kingdom, just a little bit. Picard strays momentarily from the Kingdom with his highly emotionally charged plan to use Hugh as a means of wiping out the entire Borg species. Upon noticing signs of individualism in the young Borg, LaForge urges the captain to reconsider the matter—but Picard won't even hear of it. When LaForge persists, to the point of referring to Hugh as a person, the captain coldly replies: "Centuries ago, when laboratory animals were used for experiments, scientists would sometimes become attached to the creatures. This would be a problem if the experiment involved killing them. I would suggest that you unattach yourself from the Borg." Like a scientist who disregards the sentiency, individuality, and intrinsic value of lab animals, mitigating their deaths by considering them things to be used for the advancement of science, Picard in this scene objectifies Hugh (he insists that the young Borg is an "it," while LaForge speaks of him as a "he") in order to justify his plan to destroy the Collective.

To be fair, though, scientists aren't the only ones who talk in this manner. As we all know, sometimes when we're angry— or "have issues," as Deanna Troi might put it—we'll refer to other people as "its" just to show how little we think of them. (Of course, Deanna knows Picard has major issues with the Borg, but the captain wasn't willing to talk about them when she sought him out at the beginning of the show.)

HUGH JOINS THE KINGDOM, WHILE GUINAN BRINGS PICARD BACK

Prior to meeting with Picard, LaForge voices his concerns to Guinan, resident bartender aboard the *Enterprise*. Now, Guinan is an ideal bartender because she belongs to an advanced race of humanoids known as "listeners." Guinan also has major issues with the Borg, since she's one of the few survivors of a Borg attack that devastated her planet nearly a century before. When Geordi asks her to visit Hugh, Guinan seizes the opportunity to vent her anger at his people for destroying her own. To her surprise, however, the young Borg is genuinely sympathetic: "What you are saying is that you are lonely. So is Hugh."

This remark is significant because it's exactly what Crusher said to Hugh in the scene in which she and LaForge gave him a new name. Hugh appeared scared and confused when he first regained consciousness because he no longer heard "other voices" in his head. Like all Borg, he was accustomed to having the thoughts of the other members of his Collective play endlessly inside his mind. When Hugh plaintively asked what happened to the voices, Crusher deduced that the young Borg was lonely now that he was separated from his people. The fact that Hugh makes the same remark after hearing Guinan's own story of separation (as opposed to simply repeating it indiscriminately, much like a parrot would) shows that he has associated the words with the feeling—a clear sign that he is beginning to develop an independent thought process. (Hugh's words also render Guinan speechless for perhaps the only time in the series, but that's another story.)

Like LaForge, Guinan questions the morality of Picard's plan upon seeing Hugh emerge as an individual. Appearing before the captain in the ready room of his quarters (a privilege she alone has, given their special relationship which goes "beyond friendship and beyond family"), Guinan implores Picard to talk to Hugh before carrying out the plan: "If you are going to use this person to destroy his race, you should at least look him in the eye once before you do it...because I am not sure 'it' is still a Borg."

As much as it pains him (the psychological scars from his own assimilation still run deep), Picard knows Guinan is right.

He tests Hugh's autonomy by assuming the identity of "Locutus" (the name the captain was given by the Borg during his captivity) and demands that he help assimilate the *Enterprise* crew. Picard then attempts to bring out Hugh's full Borg-like nature by repeating the Borg's signature mantra, "Resistance is futile." Only Hugh stands his ground: "Resistance is *not* futile. Some have escaped." Picard continues to verbally pound away at the young Borg until he finally blurts out, "I will not assist you!" Hugh not only demonstrates loyalty to his newfound friends, but in doing so he adamantly refers to himself in the first-person singular. This proves to the captain beyond a shadow of a doubt that Hugh is no longer Borg, but rather a "fully realized individual." After all, the word "I" is not in the Borg vocabulary!

Having recognized Hugh as an autonomous being, Picard knows he must now accord him the same dignity he would grant to any other person. Not only does he abandon his plan to annihilate the Borg, he lets Hugh decide for himself whether he wants to return to the Collective. Though Hugh strongly wishes to remain aboard the *Enterprise* with his new friends, he chooses to go back in order to ensure their safety— if he stays, he knows too well that "[other Borg] will follow." Of course, this sparks another debate: Riker suggests removing Hugh's memory of his experience, while LaForge firmly opposes it ("We can't make him an individual, then take that away from him!").* Knowing that would make them no better than the Borg (who will almost certainly reprogram Hugh

---

*Apparently one of *Star Trek*'s favorite ethical dilemmas, the issue of granting individualism to a humanoid or other life-form, only to remove it from their memory later on, is the focus of "Latent Image" (*VGR:* #105), as we know from Chapter 6, as well as "Pen Pals" (*TNG:* #41). Just as LaForge fights for Hugh's interest, so Seven argues on the Doctor's behalf in the *Voyager* episode, and Data likewise young Sarjenka's in "Pen Pals." Interesting enough, prior to ordering the deletion of Sarjenka's memory in "Pen Pals," Picard also objectifies Sarjenka (he refers to her as "the alien"), presumably to detach himself, much as a scientist would, from the morality of his decision.

themselves upon his return), Picard ultimately decides to leave Hugh intact. Besides, this way, it's possible Hugh might yet "infect" Borg consciousness with his newfound singularity. "Perhaps," concludes the captain, "that's the most pernicious program of all."

By divesting himself of his personal enmity for the Borg, thereby putting Hugh's interests ahead of his own, Picard, Kant would say, fulfills his moral duty. Whether Hugh succeeds in contaminating the Borg with the individualism "virus" is inconsequential. What matters is that the captain treats him with the respect due a fellow rational being in the Kingdom of Ends.

RIKER AND PINOCCHIO

Worf may make the wrong decision in "Rules of Engagement," but at least, like Picard in "I, Borg," he seems to have some element of choice in the matter. (Kant, of course, would say we have no option but to do our duty. The point is, each character's situation is such that he can just as easily go one way as the other.) We don't always have that luxury; sometimes the nature of the situation thrusts us into performing our duty with no ifs, ands, or buts.

This is another favorite ethical dilemma of *Star Trek*'s, one that seems to happen particularly to Riker more often than others. No matter how agonizing the circumstances, though, Number One always manages to live up to his duties (except when his libido gets in the way). He has a serious commitment to duty that would make Kant proud.

Take, for example, "The Measure of a Man" (*TNG:* #35), in which cybernetics expert Bruce Maddox attempts to dismantle and study Data so that more androids can be manufactured for Starfleet's use. Though Data initially agrees to the procedure, he balks upon realizing Maddox may not be able to reassemble him. Maddox, anticipating this, produces an order transferring

Data to his command. When Picard is unable to fight the transfer, Data resigns from Starfleet. Maddox challenges his resignation on the grounds that Data is the property of Starfleet—not an individual with rights. Picard and Riker take the matter before Starbase Judge Advocate General Phillipa Louvois, who allows the captain to represent Data at the formal hearing. However, because Louvois is short-staffed, she orders Riker, as the second-highest officer aboard, to prosecute the case for Starfleet. Worse yet, the JAG officer warns Riker that unless he gives a 100 percent effort, she will automatically decide in favor of Maddox and order Data dismantled.

Now, does that suck, or what?

Left with no choice, Riker must argue that his friend is nothing more than a man-made creation. Gut-wrenching though it is, he fulfills his duty to the best of his ability— exactly as Kant prescribes. In fact, as far as Picard is concerned, Riker performs his office a little too well, dramatically emphasizing his point by approaching Data from behind and switching him off, leaving the android lifeless in his seat. "Pinocchio is broken," concludes Riker. "Its strings have been cut." The captain believes the case is lost, until Guinan helps him see that the term "property" is merely a euphemism for slavery. Duly inspired, Picard argues that while all of us are created, that doesn't necessarily make us the property of our creator. Data may be a machine, but he's also displayed time and again the truest measure of a rational being: the ability to think and choose for himself (which, again, is an essential Kantian idea). Taking this into consideration, Judge Louvois rules in favor of Data.

Like "Rules of Engagement," the episode ends with a victory celebration that one crew member doesn't wish to attend. In this case, Riker is despondent over coming so close to sealing Data's doom; indeed, one suspects this may have been his "most painful moment in Starfleet" (the words Kirk used to describe the torment of prosecuting Spock in "The Menagerie"). The android, however, comforts his friend: "This action injured you and saved me. I will not forget it." Data knows that Riker was only performing his duty—a duty that clearly went against his personal inclinations.

KANT'S TWO-PRONGED MEASURE FOR KNOWING YOUR DUTY

Given the examples we've discussed so far, let's assume Kant was right—that duty, rather than emotions or inclinations, is indeed the basis of morality. That still leaves us with the problem of determining which actions are our moral duties. Meaning, if the measure of a rational being is the ability to choose individually, what's the measure of duty? How do we know where our duty lies?

Kant would say that if we honestly believe that an action we're considering reflects some general rule of behavior, then we can feel confident about its morality and proceed on with it. However, if what we intend to do contradicts a general rule of thumb, we should consider it immoral and not do it.

Now, what exactly did Kant mean by this? Was he suggesting we should be like a lot of elected officials, and base our decisions entirely on opinion polls or some other barometer of public consensus? Far from it—indeed, no ethicist would prescribe that. What Kant was saying is that, in deciding what to do, we should always ask these two questions: (1) What's the principle behind our actions? and (2) Can this principle be applied to all other rational beings (or, as Kant would put it, could we *rationally will* that everyone act like this)?

Suppose you're a college freshman who's trying to choose a major. You want to be a TV news anchor, so you're thinking about a degree in communications. Mom and Dad want you to get a business degree "so you'll have a better chance of succeeding in the real world," and besides, they're paying your tuition. You'd still have to ask yourself what your underlying principle is for choosing a major. Perhaps you decide on a degree in electronics because you want a high-paying job, and that's where the money is. Now you have to ask what would happen if everyone else based their choice on the same principle. If everybody chose a career in electronics (or any other field, for that matter) because that's where the big bucks are, eventually the market would be flooded. All the high-paying jobs would then become low-paying jobs. That would cancel out your original intention, which was for *you* to make the big money. Therefore, you can't pass this principle on to everybody (or, Kant would say, you can't "rationally will" the principle), if it proves to be irrational or inconsistent with your original intention.

Or let's say you want to borrow money from the bank. The terms of the promissory note require you to repay the loan within five years. Though you're not really sure you can pay it back in that amount of time, you also know nothing will be lent to you unless you sign that note. Your reasoning might be, "Banks loan money all the time. When I need money, I will ask the bank for a loan and promise to repay it, although I know I may not be able to do so." If you applied that same principle universally (that is, if for love of money we all signed off on promissory notes we couldn't honor), then eventually every bank would either fold or stop lending money altogether. That, again, would be inconsistent with your original intent.

Wait a minute, you may be saying. If Kant wanted us to consider what would happen if we applied the principles behind our actions to everyone else, wouldn't that in itself be inconsistent with the rest of his concept of morality? In other words, wouldn't he really be asking us to consider the consequences—not just the pure intention—of what we do? Yes and no. On the one hand, because the essence of reason is consistency, and the test of consistency is universal applicability, Kant implied that we should consider the consequences of our actions *before* we do them (that is, we must ask ourselves if they pass the measure of consistency). However, once we've committed our actions, Kant, as we mentioned before, would say we should judge them solely by what we intended to do, not by how they turned out.

ASSISTED SUICIDE IN *STAR TREK*

Now, let's apply Kant's two-step method to "Ethics" and the matter of assisted suicide. Once again, our man Riker finds himself in a duty-related pickle when Worf asks him to assist in the *Hegh'bat* ceremony: "You and I have served together for many years, fought side by side. I know you to be a brave and honorable man. If you truly consider me a friend, help me now. Help me end my life as I have lived it, with dignity and honor!" Like Crusher, Riker believes suicide is wrong; the loss of one's mobility does not necessarily mean the end of one's life. Though Picard agrees with his officers on this point, he also understands the Klingon notion of honor and believes Worf's wishes should be respected.*

After several days of pondering where his duty lies, Number One decides that if he has to help Worf, he's not going to make it easy for him. "I've been studying this ritual of yours,"

---

*Though the impassioned nature of most Klingons goes against Stoicism in general (a point we raised in Chapter 8), the notion of the *Hegh'bat* is very much consistent with the Stoic position on suicide. The Stoics believed that the harshness of reality might disturb one's inner balance, leading to anxiety and pain. Therefore, they advocated suicide under certain circumstances. As the Roman Stoic Seneca once observed, "To die well is to escape the danger of living badly." Worf (or any other Klingon warrior, for that matter, whose pride had been destroyed) would certainly qualify as one of those exceptions.

he says. "I think it's despicable... the casual disregard for life, the way it tries to cloak suicide in some glorious notion of honor. I may have to respect your beliefs, but I don't have to like them."

Riker proceeds to rattle off the names of several friends and officers who died in the line of duty: "Every single one of them fought for life until the very end." (The implication, of course, is that we all have a moral duty to fight for our lives.) Though Worf denies that he "welcomes death," Riker says he isn't so sure. "I get the sense you're feeling pretty noble about this whole thing.... Let me remind you of something: the Klingon does not put his desires above those of his family or his friends. How many people on this ship consider you a friend? How many owe you their lives? Have you even thought about how we might feel about your dying?"

Then Riker goes for the jugular, so to speak, by reminding Worf of what Klingon law mandates: in a traditional *Hegh'bat*, the eldest son must assist in the suicide. That means if Worf is really serious about this stuff, he must ask young Alexander to drive a knife into his father's heart. Knowing he can't bring himself to do that, Worf changes his mind.

Now, Riker makes the principle on which he based his decision not to assist in the *Hegh'bat* very clear when he flat out tells Worf, "I will not help a friend commit suicide." For argument's sake, though, let's pretend Riker made the opposite decision. If that were the case, his reasoning would be, in effect, "For love of my friend, I make it my principle to shorten his life when a longer life seems more unhappy to him than satisfying." Now, if Riker were truly Kantian in his approach to duty, he would have to also ask himself whether he'd want all other people to follow this same principle. Once he raised this question, however, he'd see this principle would result in a contradiction, because it asks us to destroy the life of our friends out of love for them. After all, Kant might add, the love of friendship is supposed to improve our lives, not end them.*

Kant's measure also comes into play in "I, Borg." When Picard considers implanting Hugh with a virus that could destroy the Borg, he must ask himself whether he could advocate genocide as a principle for all of us to follow. He must rationally recommend using someone for an evil purpose without their consent as a universal practice. Because neither action is one he can "rationally will," Picard's intended action cannot be morally good.

KANT AND THE IMPORTANCE OF PERSONHOOD

When considering what we must do, Kant said, we should consider what all rational beings must do. If a moral law is valid for you and me as rational beings, it must therefore be valid for all rational beings. Suppose Picard decided to implant Hugh with the virus after all, provided the Borg could not retaliate. In other words, the principle is that it's okay for the Federation to use an individual Borg as a means for destruction, but not the other way around. The captain's decision would still be morally wrong because it contradicts a principle he would "rationally will" to everyone (namely, that it's wrong to use anyone strictly as a means). In other words, it calls for an exception—and for Kant, there could be no exceptions in ethics.

Put another way, Kant held that there's something about a rational being that deserves the respect due a person, as opposed to being treated as a thing. To be a person in his "kingdom" is to be an end in itself. A phaser is not an end in

---

*Indeed, this example is a paraphrase of one of Kant's own arguments against suicide.

itself; it's a thing, a tool made to be used as a means of pro-tection. Whenever we treat fellow rational beings as things or means, we are disrespecting them. Commander Maddox, of course, treated Data as a thing in "Measure of a Man." Picard considered Hugh to be the same for much of "I, Borg," as did Dr. Russell her patients in "Ethics" (particularly, the man who died after failing to respond to one of her experimental techniques).

The notion of personhood was very important to Kant. Because all rational beings have intrinsic worth as persons, no one has the right to treat another rational being as a tool to achieve knowledge, power, or any other end that fails to give that person the respect he deserves. From a moral standpoint, that means we can never manipulate other rational beings to achieve our goals, regardless of how good these goals may be. This inviolable moral rule is clearly evident in Dr. Crusher's approach to medicine. Consider her objections to Russell's prac-tices throughout "Ethics," especially her scathing denouncement of the neurogeneticist at the end of the show.

Worf, as we know, elects to undergo the high-risk gene-tronic replication surgery after Riker dissuades him from com-mitting suicide. Although his vital signs function normally during the early stage of the operation, the Klingon unexpect-edly goes into cardiac arrest . . . and soon dies on the table. However, just as Crusher breaks the news to Alexander, Worf suddenly comes back to life! Though Worf's recovery had more to do with his peculiar anatomy than anything else, that doesn't stop Russell from taking all the credit.* Crusher, naturally, knows it was a fluke, and doesn't shrink from giving her col-

---

*Klingon physiology includes redundancies for nearly all essential bodily func-tions. The idea apparently is that if one organ fails, one of the reserves eventu-ally kicks in. For the record, Worf has 23 ribs, 2 livers, an 8-chambered heart, a double-livered neural pia matter, and a backup synaptic system.

league a final scolding: "I am delighted that Worf is going to recover. You gambled. He won. Not all of your patients are so lucky.

"You scare me, Doctor," she continues. "You risk your patients' lives in the name of research. You take shortcuts right through living tissue. You put your research ahead of your patients' lives—and as far as I'm concerned, that's a violation of our most sacred trust!"

The notion of the intrinsic worth of each individual forms the basis for Kant's supreme principle of morality: "Act so that you treat humanity, whether in your own person or in that of another, always as an end and never as a means only." This principle, which weds individualism and altruism, doesn't mean we can never use the services or skills of rational beings who happen to be merchants, engineers, or physicians. What it does say is that we should never use them simply as a means. We must always recognize them as ends, as individuals with intrinsic value over and above our own needs.

In other words, our most essential duty is recognizing the dignity each of us has. It's a principle that should be familiar to us—perhaps so familiar, we sometimes pay it lip service and no more. How else can we account for the concept of "downsizing" a company via the wholesale elimination of jobs on which an entire community may have depended for its survival and well-being? We may now have a more efficient means of doing business and increasing our profits, but at what cost?

I don't mean to single out employers. All of us are accountable. Whenever we poke fun at someone, for example, without any consideration of how he or she might feel, we violate this supreme principle. When the Federation in *Star Trek: Insurrection* deceives the Ba'ku in order to acquire their "fountain of youth," it also breaches this sacred law of morality. This aspect of Kant's ethics has far-reaching practical implications on such issues as death with dignity, sexual relationships, forced relocations of people, and discrimination. We should regard each other as rational beings worthy of respect, treating each other as individuals, not as means for achieving our own ends.

But let's go back to Picard's example of lab animals. They clearly do not have the same rational capacities that we have. Does the same standard apply to them? Are animals and other nonrational creatures entitled to less respect, or even any at all? Let's see what Kant had to say about that in our next chapter.

OUR DUTY TO OTHER SPECIES

"Hunters" and "Prey"
VGR: Episodes 83 and 84
Stardates: 51501.4 and 51652.3
Original Air Dates: February 11 and 18, 1998

These two self-contained but interrelated episodes originally aired in consecutive weeks. In the first story, Tuvok and Seven of Nine are captured by the Hirogen, a savage breed whose entire culture is based on the thrill of the hunt. Lacking any moral center, the Hirogen view all other species as "game" to be hunted, killed, gutted, and mounted. Janeway rescues her officers from being slaughtered, and swears that her crew will "show our teeth, like any cornered animal" if the Hirogen prey on them again. In the second hour, Voyager encounters a vessel carrying a critically wounded Hirogen hunter. Though Seven strongly advises against bringing a Hirogen aboard, Janeway nonetheless has the injured alien beamed into sickbay. The captain's act of compassion backfires, however, when the Hirogen's quarry—a member of the highly dangerous Species 8472—makes its way onto Voyager. With the lives of her crew in the balance, Janeway must decide which side to choose in the deadliest game of all.

"Scientific Method"
VGR: Episode 75
Stardate: 51244.3
Original Air Date: October 29, 1997

One by one, the crew members begin to suffer extreme medical problems. Janeway is plagued by piercing headaches; Chakotay and Neelix find their metabolisms hyperstimulated; Torres has severe trouble breathing. A genetic analysis enables the Doctor to detect a microscopic tag on one of Chakotay's DNA cells that appears to be responding to a nearby signal. With the help of Seven of Nine, the Doctor determines that Voyager has been invaded by a mysterious species barely visible to the naked eye. The intruders have implanted invisible metal devices on many of the ship's personnel, recording their findings on them as though they were subjects in a series of experiments. Janeway vows to fight back upon realizing her team has been involuntarily recruited as "lab rats" in the name of science. But the perpetrators insist they're in control of the situation—and threaten to exterminate her crew if she resists.

Kant made it clear that we have a moral duty to recognize the intrinsic worth of all rational beings. A "rational being" in his view is anyone capable of applying impartial moral principles in determining what morally ought to be done. Does the same hold true for individuals of other kinds? Are we obliged to recognize the intrinsic worth of creatures or animals who are not necessarily capable of thinking rationally and morally for themselves? Given our purposes, this is a valid question, especially considering the vast diversity of alien species our heroes encounter throughout the *Star Trek* universe.

Suppose you took a short hiatus on a pastoral planet very much like the so-called amusement park planet Kirk and his crew visited in "Shore Leave" (*TOS:* #17), complete with the sophisticated technology that can read your mind and material-ize your thoughts. The only apparent life-forms on this place are creatures similar to the Horta in "The Devil in the Dark" (*TOS:* #26), the spaceborne being known as Junior in "Galaxy's Child" (*TNG:* #90), or the sea creature in "Thirty Days" (*VGR:* #103). Meaning, these are benign living things that possess thoughts and desires; a definite capability for perception, mem-ory, and a sense of the future (particularly their own future); a discernible emotional life, including feelings of pleasure and pain; a capacity for preferences; and the ability to initiate action to pursue their goals. About the only characteristic dis-tinguishing this species from you, me, and other humanoids is that they're not "rational beings" in the Kantian sense.

Now, let's say this place reminds you of those hunting trips in the great outdoors that you went on with your father long ago. Next thing, you know...poof! You've got a rifle in your hands. You see one of the native creatures sprinting in the dis-tance. Suddenly, you have this urge to shoot it—not out of fear, mind you, but purely for recreational purposes. Your ethical principles are based entirely on Kant's teachings. Would his system of morality prevent you from pulling the trigger?

The answer, it might surprise you, is no. Though Kant would-n't necessarily encourage shooting the creature, he'd see nothing morally wrong with doing so. You see, Kant's notion of "per-sonhood" doesn't include nonrational beings; in fact, he believed creatures of this kind have value only insofar as they serve human needs. In other words, he saw them as means to our ends. Not only would he allow you to hunt them down for pleasure, he'd also sanction Harry Mudd, Cyrano Jones, and any other entrepre-neurial mind who might see fit to export these creatures through-out the galaxy in the name of science and/or mass consumption.

THE GREAT BIRD SPEAKS OUT
ON HOW WE TREAT ANIMALS

Does *Star Trek* agree with Kant on this point? Again, the answer is no—but this should come as no surprise, considering how disreputably the Original Series characterizes Mudd, Jones, and those like them. The stories we'll discuss in this chapter are among the many episodes that comment (some more subtly than others) on our treatment of nonhuman animals. The views expressed by each series on this matter, of course, reflect the evolving personal beliefs of franchise creator Gene Roddenberry (who was nicknamed the Great Bird of the Galaxy by producer Robert Justman): "My philosophy about the use of animals has changed [over the years]," he told David Alexander in 1991. "I am not yet a vegetarian, but I don't feel comfortable as a meat eater knowing a lot of the things that go on to put meat on the table. . . . I look forward to [the day when] we would have our juicy T-bone steak without having to kill the animal.* I feel way different about domestic animals now. I am a bit queasy about the way we raise our chickens and beef [in factory farms]. It's really ugly."

Of course, Roddenberry is really talking about two different things here. Not only does he have reservations about how animals are processed or raised in factories, he also has reservations about eating animal meat per se. We'll get back to this distinction a little further on. For now, let's just say he has a lot to be queasy about. Factory farms, like automobile factories, are ruthlessly efficient in their operation. Accordingly, the

---

*Alexander punctuated these remarks by recalling a *TNG* episode that commented on how "it was no longer necessary for animals to be raised for food," and that "24th-century technology could create an analog of meat so that all the things associated with bringing meat to the table were no longer necessary." So it would seem that Roddenberry's dream is very much alive in the world of *Star Trek*. See David Alexander, "Interview of Gene Roddenberry: Writer, Producer, Philosopher, Humanist," *www.philosophysphere.com/humanist.html,* pp. 12–13.

234 | THE ETHICS OF STAR TREK

animals in these places are treated more like machines to be processed than live creatures with needs. The animals are rarely allowed to engage in their normal habits. Shade and shelter are practically nonexistent for pigs, cattle, and sheep in feedlots, while those animals who are raised indoors never get to feel the soil underfoot. Cattle are forced to stand in their own wastes. Egg-laying chickens have their beaks clipped to keep them from pecking each other; pigs likewise have their tails cut off to prevent their chewing on one another. Finally, most animals are confined in crowded, unnatural, stress-producing environments; chickens, for example, are often jammed four at a time inside a cage barely large enough to hold one.

"Hunters" gives us two graphic examples of the kind of indignities these animals suffer. Upon examining the deceased passenger whose ship was detected by *Voyager* early in the show, the Doctor determines the body had been "gutted" perhaps as much as a month before. Indeed, as we learn a bit later on, the Hirogen remove the intestines and other body parts of their victims, and often wear them as a symbol of status. Finally, when Tuvok and Seven regain consciousness upon their capture, they find themselves trussed like animals about to be slaughtered.

Roddenberry also feared that our treatment of nonhuman animals as means rather than ends could extend to all other nonhuman species we might encounter in the future, including extraterrestrial beings.* "If we are not careful, we may

---

*While the Great Bird of the Galaxy worried about our attitude toward extraterrestrial beings who "don't act and interact as we do," others have speculated as to what might happen if extraterrestrials treated us the way we currently treat other animals. One author, for example, described a race of "Troogs" who take over our planet and divide humans into four castes: pets, capons (farm products), hound-men, and wild humans. See Desmond Steward, "The Limits of Trooghaft," in *Animal Rights and Human Obligations,* ed. Tom Regan and Peter Singer (Englewood Cliffs, N.J.: Prentice-Hall, 1976), pp. 238–45.

see sentient life that is so different we won't realize it is sentient," he told Alexander in 1991. "Because the creatures we meet don't act and interact as we do, we might consider them valuable—much as many people disdain dolphins and whales today."

You may be puzzled over this last remark if you used to watch *Flipper* and assumed the concept expressed by the show's theme song ("Everyone loves the king of the sea") held true. But if that were the case, then why does the military endanger the lives of dolphins in some cases by attaching detonation devices to them while conducting radar experiments? Roddenberry's point is that we use and exploit all animals. Sometimes we're even threatened by them simply because we don't understand them. We've seen this idea expressed often on *Star Trek*, usually by an "alien" character such as Spock or Seven of Nine. For example, *Star Trek IV: The Voyage Home* imagines that humpback whales will become extinct by the 21st century due to humankind's shortsightedness. Spock summarizes the film's attitude in one sentence: "To hunt a species to extinction is not logical."

Roddenberry's concerns are also reflected in episodes such as "Captive Pursuit" (*DS9: #6*), wherein O'Brien violates the Prime Directive in order to save the reptilian-skilled humanoid Tosk from being hunted down purely for sport. Tosk, whom O'Brien befriended after his ship was docked at DS9 for repairs, belonged to a species that was bred and raised for the sole purpose of being hunted by a race known as . . . well, Hunters. If that's not humiliating enough, a code of silence prevents Tosk from telling anyone about his role as the hunted. Sisko and O'Brien learn the truth about their friend when three Hunters beam aboard the space station and angrily demand that Sisko release him. Though the captain has "no tolerance for the abuse of any life-form," compliance with the Prime Directive demands that he turn Tosk over to the Hunters.

O'Brien, however, disobeys Sisko by allowing Tosk to escape, thus fulfilling his friend's deepest wish: the chance to die with honor. Though Sisko reprimands O'Brien for taking matters into his own hands, the show makes it clear that the captain approves of his actions. Like the Great Bird of the Galaxy, Sisko believes killing simply for the sake of sport should not be allowed in any star system.

Of course, game hunting is denounced even more emphatically in the allegorical episodes "Hunters" and "Prey," which pull no punches in depicting the Hirogen as unconscionable, bloodthirsty, brutal savages. The Hirogen taunt their captives ("You were pathetic prey, easily taken," they say to Seven and Tuvok) and get a clear adrenaline rush just before "making their first kill." The episode plainly suggests that game hunters, like the Hirogen, experience a similar kind of pleasure from the "thrill of the kill." Furthermore, the Hirogen's lack of moral center makes them "extremely dangerous" (as Tuvok tells Janeway), since our moral center is what restrains us from committing violent acts. Without it, the episode implies, we're no better than the Hirogen—liable to inflict violence on those we construe as weaker, inferior, or simply different from us.

THE "HARM PRINCIPLE" AT WORK IN THE *STAR TREK* UNIVERSE

Obviously, this is a touchy subject, one that could very well make a lot of people uncomfortable—especially those who have pets. Roddenberry said as much himself when he admitted his reservations about eating animal flesh, despite feeling "queasy" about the way we treat animals. "Hunters," "Prey," and "Scientific Method" come down strongly on this issue by asking us to imagine what it would be like if we were in the animals' place. As noble as that sentiment is, though, it doesn't do us much good as an ethical theory. We need an argument based on more than just emotion to stake our claim. We need something that can stand to reason.

Clearly we can't turn to Kant, for reasons we already covered. Aristotelian virtue ethics doesn't really discuss this problem. Since Hobbes' social contract theory only includes those who have signed the social contract, that would certainly exclude animals, among others, from moral consideration. Though Christian ethics has some guidelines on how to treat animals, they're not spelled out in any systematic or consistent way.

So where does this leave us? In the hands of Tom Regan, a contemporary philosopher whose duty-based ethics includes direct duties to nonhuman animals and other life-forms. Let's take a look at his theory and see how it applies to our *Star Trek* episodes. Who knows... perhaps some of these principles might even hold true for us as well.

Though emotionally charged, the "what if we were in their place" argument does raise a valid point: the harms we do to other animals can just as easily be done to us. This is another one of those truths that we all know, yet all too often pay no more than lip service to. Sometimes it takes a rude awakening (though perhaps not as extreme as what the *Voyager* crew goes through in these episodes) for the truth to kick in. As Janeway puts it in "Scientific Method," "I'm sure you'd see things differently if your people were the ones subjected to these experiments." Though we, like the alien scientists in that story, may justify the "discomfort" we inflict upon animals in the name of progress, our perspective would undoubtedly change if we were the ones being pursued, processed, pricked, or probed.

With that in mind, the episodes suggest, we have a direct duty not to harm individuals of all kinds—a point on which Regan would agree. To affirm this duty in the case of humans, but not other species, violates the formal principle of justice, which requires that all similar cases be treated similarly. Based on these considerations, we can formulate a principle stating, again, that we have a direct duty not to harm individuals. This principle, which Regan calls the "harm principle," has a broad scope, covering human and nonhuman beings alike (even extraterrestrials). To inflict gratuitous suffering on a life-form, be it human or otherwise—or to bring about his or her untimely death—means to harm the one just as surely as it means to harm the other.

THE SUBJECT-OF-A-LIFE CRITERION...
OR, WHY BETAZOIDS MAKE
LOUSY ANIMAL TRAINERS

Widely inclusive though it is, the harm principle does not cover *all* living things. Regan, for instance, would say we have no such moral obligation to potatoes, individual blades of grass, or cancer cells. So where do we draw the line? How do we distinguish those life-forms to whom we have a moral duty from those to whom we do not? What characteristics must a living thing have in order for us to extend it moral consideration?

According to Regan, the key thing common to humans and all other animals is what he calls the "subject-of-a-life" criterion. Individuals are subjects-of-a-life if they have (1) beliefs and desires; (2) perception, memory, and a sense of the future, including their own future; (3) an emotional life, complete with feelings of pleasure and pain; and (4) preferences and the ability to initiate action in pursuit of their desires and goals. Regan argues that since all normal mammalian animals who are at least one year of age have these capabilities, they therefore fit the criteria for being subjects-of-a-life—a conclusion he bases on our commonsense view of the world, ordinary language, similar physiology, animal behavior, and an evolutionary understanding. Other life-forms may also be subjects-of-a-life, provided they have all the relevant mental and emotional traits that Regan mentions. Since the Horta, Junior, the "Thirty Days" sea creature, and the inhabitants we encountered in the hypothetical situation with which we began this chapter all meet this criterion, it would therefore be wrong in Regan's view for us to do them harm.

Star Trek also seems to believe that mammalian animals are subjects-of-a-life. Consider the exchange between Picard and Deanna that begins "Pen Pals" (*TNG: #41*). Deanna accompanies Picard as he runs the holodeck equestrian adventure program, but declines his invitation to actually ride the horse. This surprises the captain, who assumed that Deanna would make an "outstanding animal trainer" because of her innate telepathic ability. But that's not the case, Deanna explains: "[Betazoids] become too involved in the thoughts and shifting passions of the beasts. We lose our way and get swept up in emotion." Because of this, she adds, she prefers a mode of transportation that does not "have a mind of its own." Deanna's response certainly supports the notion that horses and other mammalian animals have thoughts, preferences, emotions, and the ability to initiate actions to pursue their desires and goals. That, of course, makes them subjects-of-a-life and therefore entitled to the right not to be harmed.

How can we tell whether an animal has beliefs, desires, preferences, and perception? By testing their behavior or reactions after exposure to certain stimuli. For example, my dog Robin believes there's a big bag of chewbones stashed away in a kitchen cabinet because he saw me put them there. If I wanted to test that—or, Regan would say, if I wanted to see if Robin believes the bones are in the kitchen—I'd simply walk to where I put them. If Robin follows me expectantly, or starts wagging his tail in front of the cabinet, that proves he believes the bones are in the cabinet. His behavior shows me his belief. Similarly, the Horta in "Devil in the Dark" shows Kirk she is a conscious being by backing away from him as soon as he whips out his phaser. The Horta believes the phaser will hurt her because she was wounded by a phaser beam moments before. Kirk tests the creature's beliefs by observing her reactions to the weapon. Every time he lowers his phaser, the Horta advances, whereas every time he points it at her, she retreats.

This particular scene also illustrates the harm principle in action. Kirk's attitude toward the Horta changes once he recognizes her as a conscious animal. From that point on, Regan would say, the captain knows he has a moral duty to protect her from harm — the same as he would Spock, his crew, or any other individual subject-of-a-life. Indeed, Kirk no longer sees her as a savage monster that killed countless Federation personnel (as well as one of his own "red shirts"); instead, he insists on keeping the animal alive so that he might learn the motives for her destructive behavior. With the help of Spock and the Vulcan mind-meld, Kirk learns the Horta is simply a mother trying to protect her eggs. Though benign in nature, she fired on the Federation miners who had inadvertently broken into the chamber where the eggs were stored — much as any other mother would fight to protect her children. Just as Regan obliges us to recognize and respect the behaviors and beliefs of all conscious beings, so Kirk and Spock negotiate a level of understanding between the Horta and the mining expedition that enables them to coexist peacefully.

The subject-of-a-life principle is also evident in "Scientific Method," albeit again in a metaphorical way ("These lab rats are fighting back!" says Janeway once she realizes what's been happening to her crew). When the Doctor discovers microscopic tags on the DNA cells of Chakotay, Neelix, and several other patients, he suspects the ship has been invaded and asks Seven to help him investigate. With her Borg sensory nodes adjusted to a phase variance of .15, Seven now is able to see what the rest of the crew can't. As she surveys each deck of the ship, she notices that strange metallic devices have been clamped on the bodies of most of the crew—some on their heads, some on their chests, some on their backs, some on their legs. Brown-robed aliens hover all over the place, taking readings from their scanners or performing adjustments on the equipment by hand.

This particular sequence is intended to leave us with the impression that we, like Seven, have just entered an animal research laboratory. Indeed, what we see on *Voyager* is not far removed from what goes on in actual research facilities. In a widely broadcast videotape from the University of Pennsylvania, for example, we see a monkey with electrodes fastened to her chest, as well as tubes inserted into the base of her skull and down her throat. Injured with severe brain damage, she has four electrodes bolted into her head, from which tubing descends to what the experimenters describe as "a stab wound" in her neck. In other footage, from the University of Connecticut, researchers fused the bones of conscious, unanesthetized rabbits with steel screws and acrylic cement, then cemented a steel bar with steel screws to their skulls so that the rabbits were completely immobilized during subsequent surgery and testing sessions. Simulating electrodes were then thrust through the covering of the rabbits' brains and cemented into position with acrylic cement. These devices, of course, are quite similar to the stereotaxic metal spikes implanted in Janeway's skull in "Scientific Method."* (No wonder her head was killing her.)

Seven manages to render visible an alien named Alzen and brings her to Janeway. While Seven and Tuvok try to capture the other aliens and free the rest of the crew, Alzen tells the

---

*However, what happens to Janeway is a little less gruesome than what actually goes on in contemporary laboratories. For instance, in order to learn how humans perceive color, one Berkeley researcher removed portions of the skulls of monkeys and cats in these stereotaxic devices, and then inserted electrodes into their brains for up to 48 hours at a time. At least the captain didn't lose any of her skull!

captain that the *Voyager* crew has been selected to undergo tests and observations for the purposes of medical research. None of this flies with the captain. "Tests?!?" she responds angrily. "I'd call them mutilations." Though Alzen claims she doesn't like to make other people suffer, "sometimes it's a necessary part of [her] work." Regan, of course, would say that any work that knowingly causes harm to a conscious subject-of-a-life—even if it's for a noble cause—is nonetheless morally wrong.

R-E-S-P-E-C-T AND OTHER PRINCIPLES *STAR TREK* COULD AGREE WITH

Regan also believes that those who satisfy the subject-of-a-life criterion have inherent value—that is, value in their own right. That means they're capable of experiencing life for better or worse, depending on what happens to them. This idea leads to what Regan calls the "respect principle," which calls for us to treat those individuals who have inherent value in ways that respect their inherent value. This idea, of course, is intrinsic to "Hunters," "Prey," "Scientific Method," and the other stories we've discussed so far. Borrowing a phrase from Kant, Regan says we must never treat individuals who have inherent value merely as a means for our purposes.

The respect principle not only rules out treating such individuals as a means, it also imposes the duty to assist those who are victims of injustice at the hands of others. This principle accounts for why, in "Prey," Janeway chooses to help Species 8472, even at the risk of inciting the more dangerous Hirogen. After the injured Hirogen is beamed aboard, Tuvok receives a telepathic message from Species 8472. The creature's ship was damaged during the conflict with the Borg, and has been stranded in space ever since. "It has no desire for conflict," Tuvok reports to Janeway. "It only wants to return to its domain." But it can't, of course, because it's been chased by Hirogen hunting parties for the past six months.

Ever the Aristotelian, Janeway looks at the context of the situation. She knows Species 8472 is ruthless and dangerous. In this particular case, however, she sees the alien is more akin to a deer we might encounter on a country road—it doesn't want any trouble, it just wants to get home. For this reason, she decides to help the 8472 alien escape. The captain's decision displays courage and compassion, as well as an acute understanding of the respect principle. After all, while the 8472 alien means no harm, it is clearly being persecuted by one who does intend harm (namely, the Hirogen). Therefore, Regan would say, *Voyager* has a moral obligation to help it.

Of course, given the Borg's history with Species 8472, it's not surprising that Seven disagrees with the captain and refuses to cooperate. Though Janeway tries to sway her protégée toward thinking otherwise ("A single act of compassion can put you in touch with your own humanity"), Seven refuses to comply. "Objection noted," replies the captain. "We'll do this without you." Before that can happen, though, the 8472 alien and the Hirogen become engaged in hand-to-hand battle. During their struggle, Seven activates a wall console and transports both the 8472 alien and the Hirogen to one of the attacking Hirogen ships. Although the Hirogen break off the attack, Janeway is furious at Seven for leaving an innocent member of a species, who only wanted to return home, to die at the hands of another. (Of course, one wonders why Seven would choose to help the Hirogen when she was nearly skewered by them in the previous week's episode, but that's another matter.)

Needless to say, Regan would share the captain's indignation. We fail to treat individuals who have inherent value in ways that respect their value if we treat them in ways that harm them (or, in Seven's case, put them in a position where they can be harmed). Anyone who would harm another individual, or allow others to do so, must somehow justify her actions not only by appealing to other moral principles but also by showing that these principles morally outweigh the right not to be harmed in a particular case. Seven might justify her actions by reminding everybody that all Borgs past and present hate Species 8472, but again that's more an emotional argument than a moral principle. (Besides, Janeway and Regan would say, two wrongs don't make a right.)

But why should anyone harm anyone else at all? Well, you could argue some instances justify harming one individual to help many others. That would make sense, provided both the "one individual" and the "many others" were all harmed equally. (Harms are equal only when they detract equally from the welfare of two or more individuals.) Let's say you had the choice of treating one individual for a cold or a thousand individuals for a cold, and there are no complicating factors. In that case, it's far better to treat the thousand even though the one individual is harmed by not being treated.

The problem with this argument, of course, is that not all harms are equal. Becoming a quadriplegic, for example, is a much greater harm than breaking a finger. Now, would it be morally permissible to make one individual a quadriplegic to save a thousand others from getting a broken finger? Regan says no. In fact, the respect principle would justify overriding the rights of the many in that very instance. If we're really serious about respecting the inherent value and rights of individuals, we can never consider a lesser harm to an individual to be equal to or greater than a substantial harm. Would it be fair to regard the plight of the quadriplegic as equal to or greater than that of an individual with a broken finger? Of course not. We can't possibly respect each individual's rights unless we count only equal harms equally—not unequal harms equally. If we could prevent only one injury, equal respect for both individuals requires that we override the one who will suffer a broken finger and choose to help the one who would otherwise become a quadriplegic.

Regan calls this principle the "worse-off" principle. More generally expressed, it means that when we "must decide to override the rights of the many or the rights of the few who are innocent, and when the harm faced by the few would make them worse-off than any of the many would be if any other option were chosen, then we ought to override the rights of the many." In this case, the magnitude of the harm done to the individual who would thereby become quadriplegic, versus that sustained by the individual with the broken finger, is what determines whose right should be overridden. Since a quadriplegic would clearly be "worse-off" than the other would be, equal respect for both individuals' rights requires overriding the other's rights in favor of the one who would otherwise suffer paraplegia.

WHAT REGAN WOULD SAY TO THE GREAT BIRD

Now, let's see how these two principles apply to our *Voyager* episodes, as well as the issues Roddenberry raised in his comments to David Alexander. First, turning to Roddenberry's concern about how animals are raised on factory farms, Regan would say factory farming is unjust because it treats farm animals not with the respect they are due, but as renewable resources whose value is only relative to human interests. As for the Great Bird's discomfort over eating animal meat (he would like the taste of the steak without killing the animal), Regan supports his moral intuition, arguing that even if the animals were raised "humanely," animal agriculture would still be wrong. It is not ethically justifiable to bring an individual's life to an untimely end in order to serve someone else's interests. In other words, the harm done to an animal by ending his or her life is far worse than the harm you and I experienced by switching to spaghetti with tomato sauce, or not eating meat altogether. Animal agriculture, therefore, violates the respect principle, the harm principle, and the worse-off principle.

Game hunting in general assumes that the value of wild animals can be reduced to how useful they are to human interests—a notion that clearly breaches both the harm and respect principles. The hunter harms the individual being hunted, which in turn violates the respect required by his or her inherent value. Of course, some hunters justify their practice by claiming that they are saving the animal from an even worse death—namely, starvation. But there's a lot of other ways you could save animals from a slow death that have nothing to do with killing them. As it happens (especially in the case of bowhunting), the animal rarely dies quickly. Even rarer is the hunter who goes into the woods actually wanting to help the animals; after all, that would defeat the purpose of the hunt. Like the Hirogen, most hunters receive some pleasure from killing that has nothing to do with helping their victim.

As for how game hunting fares against the worse-off principle . . . who suffers the greater harm, the hunter deprived of his sport, or the animal deprived of his life? The answer should be obvious.

Regan's principles would also refute the morality of using animals in medical research. To justify the harming of animals on the chance it might ultimately benefit others is to say, in effect, "These animals are only valuable insofar as they are useful to us." But that's not the case. Animals have an inherent value of their own that clearly transcends their usefulness to others—and that, in turn, entitles them to our respect. Because the use of animals in research clearly fails to treat them with the respect they deserve, that practice would be considered wrong and unjust on all three counts—harm, respect, and worse-off principles.

Naturally, there will be those who, like Alzen in "Scientific Method," will always insist there's a "greater purpose" to their tests. "Your perspective would change," she dispassionately tells Janeway, "if your people were [among the millions who might] live longer and healthier lives as a result." While this may seem like a reasonable argument, it's clearly not one *Star Trek* upholds. "My people decided a long time ago," retorts the captain, "that [exploiting one species for another's benefit] was unacceptable, even in the name of science."* Consider that many 24th-century medical experiments (as we know from "Ethics") are performed on holosimulations. Presumably, once Starfleet recognized the immorality of using sentient life-forms in medical research and banned such procedures, it found alternatives that did not involve killing or harming anyone.

Regan, of course, would tell Alzen that even the most noble of scientific achievements can never be justified if the means used to secure these ends are ultimately unjust. This is not to say that scientific research should be abandoned. By all means, it should continue—just not at the expense of those animals who qualify as subjects-of-a-life. We should find some other way to get the job done.

Regan's ethical theory provides us with a rational series of principles for not eating, hunting, and performing scientific experimentation on subjects-of-a-life—be they human, nonhuman, or extraterrestrial. While it's clearly not necessary for us to eat animals to live in good health, nor hunt them down to be entertained, the question of whether individual human beings could survive and be healthy without animal research is not as certain. Regan's point, again, is that even a good goal is not worth pursuing if it means violating the respect due an individ-

---

*In *Star Trek: Insurrection,* Picard and his crew reject the chance to use another species for the health and greater longevity of almost everyone else in the galaxy on similar moral grounds.

ual with inherent value. On this point, *Star Trek* would seem to agree.

There's one thing you can say about Regan. All this talk about equal or unequal harms and determining exactly what constitutes a subject-of-a-life sure makes one wonder about the many situations we face in life that aren't so clear from a moral perspective. What if, for example, we were in a moral dilemma such that we had to violate one duty in order to carry out another? Since this situation seems to happen a lot on *Star Trek* (particularly to Commander Riker), perhaps it's worth exploring. We'll do just that in our next chapter.

HONOR AMONG THIEVES AND KLINGONS

"Honor Among Thieves"
DS9: Episode 139
Stardate: Unknown
Original Air Date: February 25, 1998

Starfleet Intelligence recruits Miles O'Brien to infiltrate the Orion Syndicate—the top crime ring in the Alpha Quadrant—and flush out the informant believed to be responsible for the recent deaths of five Starfleet operatives. Posing as a down-on-his-luck handyman, O'Brien quickly ingratiates himself to Liam Bilby, a petty criminal with close ties to a Syndicate leader named Raimus. Bilby not only reveals the identity of the informant, he presents O'Brien to Raimus and "witnesses" (i.e., vouches for) his character. When O'Brien discovers Raimus is linked to a representative of the Dominion, Starfleet Intelligence extends his assignment so that he can ascertain more about the alliance between the Syndicate and the Dominion. By this time, however, O'Brien has developed genuine concern for Bilby's welfare, making him torn between his duty to

Starfleet and his loyalty to his new friend. The moral conflict reaches a boiling point when Raimus orders Bilby to assassinate a Klingon ambassador with a Klingon rifle—an act intended to wreak havoc among Klingons, as well as sever the Klingon alliance with the Federation. O'Brien tips off Starfleet Intelligence, only to learn Starfleet plans to warn the Klingons—a move that will all but seal his friend's fate. Does O'Brien dare violate his duty to Starfleet by warning Bilby about the trap?

Remember the scene in "I, Borg" where Picard reminds LaForge of how scientists detach themselves from lab animals to avoid the emotional conflicts that would otherwise occur when the time comes to kill them? Because the captain at this point in the episode still intends to use Hugh as a weapon of destruction, he advises Geordi not to become too attached to the young Borg for the same reason. When you think about it, that's basically what Starfleet Intelligence agent Chadwick says to O'Brien in "Honor Among Thieves." After all, if you're going to be a spy, it's not a good idea to sympathize with the man you're about to turn in. (Which goes to show why not everyone is not cut out to be a scientist or a secret agent.)

The point is, from time to time we all find ourselves in a spot where, like O'Brien, our professional duties might collide with our relationship with our friends or family. According to Kant's ethical system, all moral duties are absolute because they're derived from reason. Since the essence of reason is consistency, and the test of consistency is applicability without exception, Kant concluded there can be no exceptions to any moral duty. Therefore, he would say, O'Brien must honor his duty to Starfleet no matter what—just as Riker fulfills his duty to Starfleet by arguing that Data is a machine, even though he believes otherwise, in "Measure of a Man."

But does *Star Trek* really believe that? True, as we saw in Chapter 11, many of Kant's ethical principles appear to be alive and well, particularly among the officers aboard the *Enterprise-D*. But if Picard, Riker, and company are truly neo-Kantian, how do we account for their breaching the Prime Directive in "Justice" (among many other occasions)? Certainly the agony the captain feels over Wesley's safety (not to mention his empathy for Dr. Crusher over the welfare of her son) is no less than the anguish that wracks O'Brien in "Honor Among Thieves." Yet as we know, Picard, having examined the circumstances and all possible consequences in that particular situation, decides that his duty to uphold justice—which, in this case, means sparing the life of an innocent young boy—far outweighs his sworn duty not to interfere with the laws of Edo society.

Should O'Brien act no less equitably? If he does choose his friendship to Bilby over his oath to Starfleet, what guidelines should he use to base his decision?

Scottish philosopher W. D. Ross (1877–1971) recognized that breaking an oath might be the result of a conflict in moral duties. We have other duties to consider besides keeping oaths and promises, such as protecting the lives of others, relieving them of distress, and not doing them harm. The "others" to whom we owe these duties could be the members of our family, our friends, or, in the case of a Starship captain, those under his or her command. Ross argued that absolute rules of morality such as "never break a promise under any circumstances" are self-destructive because they assume the various situations we encounter in our daily lives are such that exact rules of moral action are always possible. We know, and *Star Trek* knows, that isn't always the case. Indeed, sometimes—as Kirk, Picard, Sisko, and Janeway have shown us on numerous occasions—breaking a promise may be the only right course of action. Therefore, Ross would tell O'Brien, when making an ethical decision he must weigh his alternatives (that is, he must consider his other moral duties) and then decide which obligation is most important for the particular situation at hand. In other words, to borrow from Aristotle, our moral duty is always based on context.

SIX DEGREES OF PRIMA FACIE DUTIES

To get a better picture of how Ross would handle cases that involve conflicts of duties, we need to understand the difference between "prima facie" duties and our actual duty. For Ross, prima facie duties are self-evident moral rules that may on occasion be overridden by stronger moral claims. O'Brien's prima facie duty in "Honor Among Thieves" is his promise to Starfleet to find out how the Orion Syndicate compromised Starfleet Intelligence. Ross would say that O'Brien should keep that promise simply because he made it, unless some other prima facie duty appears to be more binding.

Our actual duty, on the other hand, is what we should actually do in a given set of circumstances. If the situation at hand involves only one prima facie duty (such as honoring his promise to Starfleet), then that is what O'Brien should actually do. If, however, there are conflicting prima facie duties (which is certainly the case in "Honor Among Thieves"), he must carefully weigh and consider all prima facie duties relevant to the situation in order to determine what he should actually do.

Now, it's important to note that by "duty" Ross was not referring to our motivations, but rather our duty to perform certain actions. We have no obligation to feel grateful or to regret past harms that we have caused. It is, however, our duty to perform certain actions regardless of our motives.

How do we know which prima facie duty we should actually do in a given moral dilemma? Well, there's no set formula, said Ross. Though the general duties themselves may be self-evident, our judgments about our duties in a particular set of circumstances often are not. When faced with conflicting duties, Ross held that we should take all factors into account and then use our best judgment as to which prima facie duty is more binding. This idea, again, is very similar to Aristotle's notion of basing actions of virtue "at the right time, on the right occasion, toward the right people, for the right purpose, and in the right manner."

But note how vague the factors Aristotle lists are! This is a problem because in a concrete situation, how do we know what is the "right" time, occasion, and so forth? Although Aristotle and Ross agree that many different factors must be taken into account when considering what to do in a given situation, Ross is less vague about what these factors are. His list of prima facie duties spells out what is right in more detail than Aristotle did, while retaining the flexibility of theory.

Ross named six categories of prima facie duties. This is by no means an exhaustive list, but rather one that all reflective people would recognize as moral duties. Ross believed that if each of us sat down and really thought about what our moral duties truly are, we'd all arrive at the following list: (1) duties based on prior acts; (2) duties of gratitude; (3) duties of justice; (4) duties of beneficence; (5) duties of self-improvement; and (6) duties of non-maleficence. Let's look at each of these separately and see how they apply to "Honor Among Thieves."

1. *Duties that rest on previous acts of our own.* Ross broke this particular duty into two categories:
   a. *Duties of reparation* stem from past harms we have caused others. These harms may have been direct or indirect, individual or collective, intentional or unintentional. Reparation requires that we respect the intrinsic worth of the individual we have harmed, acknowledge

our wrongdoing, and take action to compensate the individual we have harmed. How much reparation we owe depends on the magnitude of the harm done, as well as the extent of our active participation in bringing about the harm.

Part of O'Brien's assignment was to get "as close to Bilby as possible." Though Agent Chadwick may have meant that strictly in terms of proximity, obviously Miles became close friends with Liam, especially after the thief "witnessed" for him. "I will take care of you," Bilby told O'Brien. "I don't forget my friends, because friends are like family. Nothing is more important. *Nothing.*"* O'Brien gradually becomes concerned with Bilby's welfare, to the point where he seeks assurance from Chadwick that Bilby will be no worse than imprisoned by the time the mission is over. Once he realizes that he has effectively set up Bilby for assassination, O'Brien knows that he has harmed his friend and seeks reparation. Having acknowledged his wrongdoing, O'Brien tries to compensate Bilby for the harm he caused him by confessing — a confession that could very well cost him his life. After all, the chief saw Bilby kill a man who sold him flawed disruptors, so he knows he could conceivably kill again. However, because O'Brien hopes he might somehow save Bilby's life by coming clean, his confession, Ross would say, is the appropriate reparation. Of course, given the extent of Miles' participation in bringing about the harm, one might argue whether his reparation even fit the crime — he wasn't directly responsible for Bilby's predicament,

---

*Bilby's belief that "family is the most important thing" is a significant part of his character, so much so that he reiterates it four times over the course of the episode.

but only indirectly so. Yet O'Brien recognizes, as most ethicists do, that we should be held accountable not only for those acts we are directly responsible for but also those acts we are indirectly responsible for. In fact, one imagines him asking whether his reparation was indeed enough.

b. *Duties of fidelity* are based on past commitments we have made, such as duties to be honest with our friends and family, to remain faithful to our spouses or significant others, to deliver the manuscript on time, to keep promises such as taking our kids to the zoo, and so forth. We keep our promises because of our past action in making the promise and because we know it's our duty to keep it. When we fail to keep our commitments, our loved ones feel betrayed, editors become angry, the kids get upset, and so on down the line. We can count on those people who take their duties of fidelity seriously to keep their word, and to remain loyal, even in the face of temptation.

We see the concept of fidelity illustrated twice in "Honor Among Thieves." O'Brien's allegiance to Starfleet Intelligence was implicit the moment he went undercover, and he remains faithful even in the face of an agonizing moral conflict. Chadwick, on the other hand, breaches his duty of fidelity when he assures Miles that Bilby will be safe in a Federation prison—a promise he apparently makes just to keep O'Brien at bay. Once O'Brien realizes he's been deceived (and more importantly, that his friend is now in danger), he decides all bets are off. His fidelity to Bilby is now the more pressing prima facie duty to uphold.

2. *Duties of gratitude* rest on previous acts of other people toward us, such as past favors and unearned services. Note that "gratitude," as Ross used the term, is not merely a

matter of emotion, but one that also requires the use of our reason so that we know when duties of this kind are morally appropriate. Ross knew that we are often bound by obligations arising from our personal relationships, such as those between friends and relatives.

Ross would say that once he becomes Bilby's friend, O'Brien owes him respect, loyalty, and reciprocation of his many acts of kindness. Bilby took O'Brien into his confidence and staked his own life on his trustworthiness. Moreover, Bilby bought him gifts (including a stylish green suit), took him to the races, and invited him to meet his family. Bilby's genuine esteem and affection do not go unnoticed. O'Brien knows these acts of friendship create obligations he would not have to someone to whom he was not so close. That's why he agrees to look after Bilby's cat Chester at the end of the episode.

3. *Duties of justice* involve the duty to give each person equal consideration. These duties, according to Ross, rest on the "fact or possibility of a distribution of pleasure or happiness which is not in accordance with the merit of the persons concerned; in such cases there arises a duty to...prevent such a distribution."

This, again, is very similar to the Aristotelian principle of equity. Certainly Picard believes the distribution of pleasure the Edo would receive by punishing Wesley Crusher in "Justice" is "not in accordance with the merit of the persons concerned." Given Wesley's unfamiliarity with Edo law, the captain recognizes his prima facie duty to prevent "such a distribution" in that situation. Likewise, though the death of an Orion Syndicate member would likely please Starfleet Intelligence, O'Brien recognizes "such a distribution" is not justified in Bilby's case. Bilby was being "set up" by the Federation. Even if the Federation will be pleased by the outcome of its act, the "setup" itself is unjust. O'Brien, therefore, has a duty to prevent it.

4. *Duties of beneficence* come from the notion that there are always other beings in the world whose virtue, knowledge, or pleasure we can improve. This is certainly intrinsic to the optimism of *Star Trek,* which imagines a world in which all people (at least those who belong to the United Federation of Planets) have a much deeper appreciation of the importance of sharing and learning from each other than perhaps we do today. In fact, the idea is so pronounced in the 24th century, Starfleet basically established the Prime Directive, as Picard suggests in "Pen Pals," to "protect" starship captains from interfering with societies whose normal development they believe they can "improve." Of course, most starship captains would say that this is always a judgment call. As we know from Chapter 8, Kirk decides the Prime Directive doesn't really apply in the case of "The Apple" because, under Vaal's leadership, the humanoids of Gamma Trianguli VI have never been allowed to grow in the way most "normal" humanoid cultures need to grow. Ross would say the prima facie duty of beneficence prevailed upon Kirk to "interfere" by teaching the Gamma Triangulans about the importance of love, freedom, and individualism in their daily lives—all of which certainly improved their virtue, knowledge, and pleasure.

Bilby also displays beneficence in "Honor Among Thieves" by constantly showering O'Brien with things that would please him, to the point where he even recruits a prostitute so that his new pal won't be "lonely." (Of course, happily married Miles, ever mindful of his fidelity to Keiko and their young daughter, Molly, tactfully declines.)

5. *Duties of self-improvement* rest on the fact that we can improve our own condition of knowledge or virtue. O'Brien may not realize it at the time, but his acts of adopting

Chester and risking his career and own life to save Bilby help to improve his own virtue. Of course, this isn't the first time we've seen O'Brien act unselfishly, or even put his life on the line. The point is, every time we do a virtuous action, we solidify the virtuous nature of our characters all the more. Each unselfish act we do makes it easier to act unselfishly again when the opportunity next arises. Who knows... if we practice it often enough, unselfishness could become so natural it's practically imbedded in our characters. If Ross were reading along with us, he'd say that Kirk's courageous sacrifice in "City on the Edge of Forever," which clearly improves his virtue, is among the many other dramatic examples of self-improvement we've discussed so far in this book.

6. Last, but certainly not least, are *duties of non-maleficence* (that is, duties of "non-injury"). These include the duty to do no harm, as well as the duty to prevent harm. For Ross, non-maleficence is the most important duty of all, and therefore should be "prima facie more binding." O'Brien fulfills this duty when he warns Bilby that he's about to walk into a trap, a decision that reflects Ross' teaching that "We should not, in general, consider it justifiable to kill one person in order to keep another alive." By notifying the Klingon Empire of the impending assassination attempt, Starfleet Intelligence basically uses Bilby as a sacrificial lamb in order to keep the Klingon ambassador alive. Though O'Brien certainly wants to protect the ambassador, he nonetheless believes given the circumstances that doing so at the expense of another man's life is not justifiable.

PAINTING FROM THE SAME PALETTE

We know what O'Brien did. How can we tell whether it was the right thing to do? Using Ross' list of prima facie duties, we can see that he had only one duty to Starfleet Intelligence: fidelity. If he hadn't become friends with Bilby, or if the situation he faced in "Honor Among Thieves" was such that fidelity to Starfleet was the only prima facie duty at play, then breaking his oath and revealing his identity to Bilby would have been morally wrong.

Obviously, that wasn't the case. Because O'Brien did befriend Bilby, his duties of reparation, gratitude, justice, and non-maleficence prevailed upon him to try to save Bilby's life. Looking at it purely by numbers, the four prima facie duties owed to Bilby clearly outweigh the one obligation to Starfleet. Taken all together, the four duties to Bilby would seem to outweigh fidelity to Starfleet qualitatively speaking as well. Therefore, it would appear that our friend Miles O'Brien did the ethical thing.

But let's go back to the issue we raised at the beginning of the chapter. Being a secret agent, by definition, requires a certain degree of deception. If that was going to be a problem, then why did O'Brien accept the assignment in the first place? If he really felt guilty about betraying Bilby, why he did put off telling him about the operation until the last possible minute?

Good questions. Unfortunately, there's no pre-set formula we can apply to O'Brien's situation—nor any other moral dilemma, for that matter. Part of the problem has to do with the complex nature of moral decision making itself. Ross believed we should approach moral issues as though we were creating a work of art, not solving a mathematical problem. Though the finished paintings might look very different, we're all painting from the same palette. Moral principles, like the artist's palette, may provide the form of our final decision, but never the specific content.

Carrying the metaphor a step further, each moral dilemma we face is a blank canvas with its own peculiar texture.

("Texture," in this case, stands for the set of circumstances peculiar to each dilemma.) To demand that an ethicist provide us with a paint-by-numbers scheme for every moral decision is about as reasonable as an artist demanding his mentor to tell him exactly how the finished picture should look. What was ethically right before may not be appropriate this time. We need to develop the moral sensitivity to judge each case separately and act accordingly. And that, like any other skill, is something we can only learn by doing.

THE BRIDE OF SPOCK

Conflicting prima facie duties are also at issue in "Amok Time" (*TOS:* #34), an episode we've mentioned briefly in two previous chapters. When the normally placid Spock begins exhibiting violent outbursts of emotion (slamming a tray of food against the wall, biting Nurse Chapel's head off, and acting pretty much like an ornery SOB), it doesn't take a rocket scientist to know something's terribly wrong. Though Spock won't tell Kirk what the problem is, the captain knows his friend is stressed and, acting from a duty of beneficence, grants him a leave of absence on his home planet. Changing course from Altair VI, where the crew is scheduled to attend an inauguration ceremony, the *Enterprise* heads for Vulcan—only to receive a priority message from Starfleet indicating that the ceremony has been moved up seven solar days! Like O'Brien in "Honor Among Thieves," Kirk must weigh concern over a friend's well-being against his duty of fidelity to Starfleet. What does he do?

At first Kirk believes his duty to obey Starfleet is more pressing, so he reverts course back to Altair VI. Only this decision troubles the captain, so he asks Chekov how long it would take if the ship increased to maximum speed and diverted to Vulcan just long enough to drop off Spock. This baffles Chekov, who tells Kirk they're *already* on their way to Vulcan, per Spock's command. Whatever's bothering Spock must really be serious, since it's uncharacteristic of him to disregard the captain so blatantly. Upon ordering Spock to undergo a complete medical examination, Kirk learns from McCoy that unless Spock is returned to Vulcan within eight days, the first officer will die due to the extreme stress produced by a chemical imbalance in his body. Spock eventually reveals that the problem stems from the *Pon farr,* the blood fever of mating, which strips logic away from Vulcans and causes their basic instincts to surface. The *Pon farr* occurs every seven years in a Vulcan's adult life, during which time he must return to the mother planet and take a bride. As much as Nurse Chapel would *love* to help Spock with his problem, this overpowering drive compels Vulcans to mate with other Vulcans.

Again acting out of beneficence, Kirk asks Starfleet Command for permission to divert to Vulcan. However, Admiral Komack says no, citing the importance of the Altair VI mission on the heels of the region's recovery from an interplanetary war. That would appear to be that. After all, Bones reminds Kirk, "You can't go off to Vulcan against Starfleet orders. You'll be busted." Though the captain realizes this, he also knows there are other prima facie obligations at stake besides his fidelity to Starfleet. For one, Spock's life is on the line, so the duty of non-maleficence certainly comes into play. Equally important, Kirk knows that Spock has saved his life time and again. In the captain's mind, that debt of gratitude far outweighs his duty to Starfleet in this particular situation. "I can't let Spock die," he says to McCoy. "I owe him my life a dozen times over. Isn't that worth a career? He's my friend."

Kirk has the courage to act on his convictions, based on an ethical sense of what is essential to honor, friendship, and personal integrity. Rigid regulations and orders will never come first with him. He directs the *Enterprise* to continue its journey to Vulcan. Ross would say the captain did the right thing by recognizing that the duties of non-maleficence and gratitude were clearly "prima facie more binding" under the circumstances.

Upon landing on Vulcan, Kirk, Spock, and McCoy find themselves in a place called *Koon-ut-kal-if-fee,* the place of marriage or challenge. As we know from Chapters 7 and 8, Spock's intended wife, T'Pring, arrives on the scene and immediately calls for a challenge—which, according to Vulcan ritual, means she must choose a champion to fight Spock for possession of her. Though T'Pring chooses Kirk, the captain learns that because he is a foreigner, he has the right to turn down the challenge. If he does, Spock's intended bride will choose another—most likely Stonn, the tall, muscular man we see by her side. (As we learn later on, T'Pring prefers Stonn over Spock because Stonn is "simple and easily controlled." In other words, your basic boy toy.)

So here are the fight card options: either Spock vs. Kirk, or Spock vs. Stonn. McCoy thinks that Spock, in his present condition, is no match for Stonn, but he doesn't want him to fight Kirk, either. Kirk, however, thinks he can knock out Spock without really harming him, so he agrees to the fight—a decision again based on the duty of non-maleficence (to do no harm, and to prevent harm). Worse comes to worst, he figures he can always surrender, which would satisfy Vulcan honor and enable Spock to have T'Pring. Only T'Pau, the Vulcan elder, tells the boys this is a fight to the death! Now what do they do? Thinking quickly, Bones injects Kirk with a neural paralyzer, causing the captain's heartbeat and breathing to stop long enough to create the appearance of death. That way, Spock can win the fight without actually having to kill his commanding officer. (Of course, Spock lets T'Pring have Stonn after all, for reasons we already covered in Chapter 8.)

TO DIE LIKE A KLINGON

Like O'Brien, Kirk chooses the prima facie duties of non-maleficence and gratitude over the duty of fidelity because in his judgment the needs of his friend at this particular time are more urgent than the need to uphold his oath to Starfleet. This isn't to suggest that either man completely abandons his oath, or ceases to perceive it as a duty. It's just that, in each case, they temporarily suspend their duty of fidelity in favor of a more morally compelling obligation.

But don't get the impression that fidelity is not important in the *Star Trek* universe. Far from it. Consider, for example, "A Matter of Honor" (*TNG: #34*), wherein Riker volunteers to serve aboard the Klingon bird-of-prey *Pagh* as part of the Officer Exchange Program. According to the episode, this cultural exchange program enables members of the Klingon Defense Force and Starfleet officers to serve aboard each other's ships in an effort to promote intercultural understanding. Riker becomes the first Federation officer to serve on a Klingon vessel. As he prepares for the exchange, Riker learns from Worf that he'll be expected to assassinate Kargan, his temporary captain, just as his second-in-command Klag will try to assassinate him. (That's just the way Klingons are.) Worf also gives his friend an emergency transponder to ensure his safe return to the *Enterprise* in case of trouble.

Upon Riker's arrival, Kargan asks, "Exactly where are your loyalties, Commander?" Klingons, as we know, like to get straight to the point.

"I've been assigned to serve this ship and to obey your orders," assures Riker, "and I will do exactly that."

"Will you take an oath to that effect?" asks Kargan. (Klingons, of course, are also a suspicious lot.)

"I just did," says Riker. Thus, Riker has taken on a duty of fidelity to the Klingon captain and his ship. Aware that "Number

One" has made a similar pledge to Starfleet, Second Officer Klag questions Riker's authority and challenges him to a fight—just as Worf predicted. Riker, however, promptly flattens Klag, putting to rest any doubts that he could command a Klingon crew effectively.

Meanwhile, back on the *Enterprise,* Picard discovers a strange organism eating away at the hull of his ship, as well as the *Pagh.* The captain changes course to warn the Klingon vessel, while his officers try to find a way to remove the parasite. Naturally, when Kargan detects the parasite, his reaction is quite different—he assumes it's some kind of *Enterprise* attack! Riker tries to convince him otherwise, but the Klingon captain will have none of it. Kargan changes course and cloaks the *Pagh,* preventing the *Enterprise* from communicating with it. Picard becomes concerned and orders the ship to raise its shields—an act of precaution that Kargan interprets as an act of aggression. The enraged captain is now determined to attack and destroy the *Enterprise.*

This sets the stage for another dramatic confrontation between Riker and Kargan. Since their exchange is particularly interesting from an ethical point of view, perhaps we should look at it in detail. As Kargan orders his ship to prepare for battle, Riker implores him to reconsider. "They may be here to help you—don't be a fool!"

That, Kargan sharply reminds Riker, is not the way to address an Klingon captain. "Do not forget my rank!"

Now Riker knows he's got a big problem on his hands. Kargan's on the verge of making him choose between his oath to Starfleet and his oath to Kargan. "I haven't [forgotten your rank]," he says. "I'm simply trying to help you understand."

"I understand fully," says Kargan. "Now *you* understand. I am still captain of this vessel. And you are still crew and sworn to obey me. You gave me your oath."

"Yes, I did."

"Then fulfill your oath and serve this ship as you swore to! Tell me the surest method of attack against the *Enterprise!*"

Not surprisingly, Riker refuses. Though Kargan insists he capitulate as "a matter of honor and loyalty to your oath," our hero holds his ground: "I will not surrender the secrets of the *Enterprise* to you. I will not break any vow that I have taken in the past. I have also taken an oath of loyalty to your ship. I will not break that oath."

The Klingon captain may be blinded by anger in this instance, but even he can see Riker has dug himself into a deep ethical hole. "They are in conflict!" he screams.

(Ross, by the way, would say that Kargan is right. Considering that the philosopher specialized in matters of conflicting duties, he would know one when he saw one.)

Nonetheless, Riker insists there is no conflict. So how does he wriggle out of this precarious scrape? Very carefully. "I will obey your orders," he tells Kargan. "I will serve this ship as first officer and in an attack against the *Enterprise* I will die with this crew. But I will not break my oath of loyalty to Starfleet."

Given how obsessed Klingons are with the notion of honor, Riker's reply pleases Kargan: "If you had told me the secrets of the *Enterprise*, I would have labeled you a traitor and killed you where you stood. But instead you will die with us. You will die like a Klingon." Riker nods his assent.

Meanwhile, aboard the *Enterprise*, a Benzite exchange officer named Mendon determines that the organisms can be removed from the hull by using a tunneling neutrino beam. Though Picard informs the *Pagh* of this discovery, Kargan persists in his delusion and orders his crew to prepare for attack. Hoping to buy time, Riker recommends not firing "until [we're] within 40,000 kilometers. It will cut down their response time."

"You are honoring your promise to serve us?" asks a Klingon officer.

"Would you do less?" replies Riker.

"[Then] you will give the order to fire, Commander Riker," says Kargan. "Any questions?"

"I question your judgment," says Riker, a response clearly motivated by his duty of fidelity. "In my opinion your reason for forcing this confrontation is not valid."

Kargan, of course, is unmoved. "Commence the attack as ordered."

At this point, Ross would say, the most important prima facie duty (non-maleficence) becomes crucial. Riker must find a way to prevent harm to the crews of both ships he has sworn to defend—which he does, with the help of the handy-dandy emergency transponder Worf gave him at the top of the show. Riker pulls the transponder out of his boot and activates it in plain sight, knowing full well Kargan will likely confiscate it. Sure enough, Kargan grabs the device...just as Worf triggers the switch that beams the captain aboard the *Enterprise*! Now in command of the *Pagh*, Riker decloaks and demands that Picard "surrender"—a move that enables the Klingons to maintain their honor as warriors.

While Kant and Ross were both concerned with the ethics of duty—a philosophy that clearly permeates *Star Trek*—it would seem that Ross' concept of prima facie duties is more compatible with the overall ethics of *Trek* than Kant's ethical system. Though the *Next Generation* characters certainly embody many of Kant's ideas, his failure to recognize the intrinsic worth of nonrational animals is inconsistent with the respect *Star Trek* promotes for creatures of all kinds. Moreover, his insistence that moral duties are absolute goes against the equitable approach to justice that each series holds dear.

Thus, as much as Ross would approve of how O'Brien, Kirk, and Riker comported themselves in the episodes we've analyzed in this chapter, Kant would disapprove—except in the case of Riker, because he alone did not violate his oaths. Kant would insist O'Brien had a duty not to deceive Bilby in the first place, despite his commitment to Starfleet. (Imagine what the world would be like if we all deceived one another whenever we wanted information nobody's willing to give. Pretty soon, communication as we know it would grind to a halt.) Kant would also have Kirk consider what would happen if all Starfleet captains disobeyed Starfleet orders. Eventually, wouldn't Starfleet become ineffectual and perhaps even cease to exist?

Of course, Kant also said we should never consider the consequences of our acts—in his system of morality, only our intentions are important. In Chapter 14, we'll look at an ethical way of thinking that asks us to act in ways considerably different from the way Kant prescribes. According to our next theory, consequences are the *only* thing we should consider.

PART FIVE

RECEPTACLES, RESPONSIBILITY, AND RECONCILIATION

"We always feel better if we think we're in control of our own circumstances."

Kathryn Janeway,
"One"

DOES THE GOOD OF THE MANY OUTWEIGH THE GOOD OF THE FEW?

"The Mark of Gideon"
TOS: Episode 72
Stardate: 5423.4
Original Air Date: January 17, 1969

The prime minister of Gideon abducts Kirk as part of a desperate plan to win his planet membership in the Federation. Gideon's germ-free atmosphere once made it a veritable paradise. But an epic population explosion, brought on by the inhabitants' spiritual inability to practice birth control, severely deteriorated the environment, rendering the planet a crowded hell where no one dies. Prime Minister Hodin schemes to alleviate this crisis by transporting the unsuspecting Kirk onto an exact replica of the Enterprise *built on the planet's surface. The captain soon finds himself alone with Odona, Hodin's beautiful young daughter, who has volunteered to sacrifice her life as part of Hodin's drastic scheme to save the planet. Hodin wants to infect Odona with* Vegan choriomeningitis, *a disease in*

Kirk's bloodstream that, if spread, could cause an epidemic that could drastically reduce Gideon's population and free the planet from its suffering. Kirk discovers the plan and tries to save Odona, arguing that she doesn't need to die in order to transmit the disease. But Hodin hopes his daughter's martyrdom will inspire other Gideons to surrender their lives so that the planet might "once again be the Paradise it once was." For that to happen, Odona's death cannot be stopped.

"Man of the People"
TNG: Episode 129
Stardate: 46071.6
Original Air Date: Week of October 5, 1992

An unwitting Deanna Troi becomes the latest pawn of an ambitious ambassador. Picard comes to the aid of Ramid Ves Alkar, a Lumerian envoy whose ship was attacked en route to Rekag-Seronia, where he is slated to mediate a bloody dispute. Alkar and Sev Maylor, an elderly woman who he claims is his mother, are transported aboard the Enterprise. Alkar asks Deanna to assist him in the negotiations, even though Maylor shows nothing but hostility toward her. Even stranger, when Maylor suddenly dies, Alkar refuses to permit an autopsy, insisting that Troi join him in a traditional death ceremony instead. Unbeknownst to Deanna, the "ceremony" is really a means that enables Alkar to suck the positive, tranquil feelings out of her system, while transferring his negative, hostile emotions onto hers. The diplomat has used many women, including Maylor, as similar instruments to maintain an unflappable demeanor in his peace talks. The transfer causes Deanna to

behave erratically and age rapidly, resulting in a danger-
ously high neurotransmitter level. Crusher prevails upon
Picard to let her perform an autopsy on Maylor, and deter-
mines that Maylor was in fact a young woman whose death
was caused by symptoms identical to those exhibited by
Deanna. Though Picard angrily confronts Alkar, the ambas-
sador refuses to reverse the process, claiming that Deanna
is a "receptacle" through whom he can save thousands of
lives. Crusher determines an alternate way to break Alkar's
spell, but it's not without risk. For the doctor's plan to
work, Deanna Troi will temporarily have to die.

Hodin's willingness to sacrifice Odona for the good of the
planet certainly seems noble, especially given his role as the
leader of Gideon. The way he sees it, by giving up his own
daughter, he's showing his people that he's not asking them to
do anything he wouldn't do himself.

Still, that begs the question of whether Hodin and Odona's
actions are morally commendable in the first place—not to
mention whether it's reasonable for them to expect others to
make the same sacrifice.

Since Hodin implies that he has a duty to lead other
Gideons by his example, what would Kant have to say about
the matter? From an ethical point of view, a leader has a duty
to serve his people, even if this service conflicts with his personal desires and relationships.

If that's the case, then why does Kirk try to stop them—especially since Odona apparently *wants* to sacrifice herself? Having
consciously risked his life on many occasions for the benefit of
his crew, you'd think the captain would appreciate the concept of
self-sacrifice for the sake of achieving a greater goal. Isn't that an
integral part of what *Star Trek* is all about?

Before we chew on these and other important questions, let's
ask the Guardian of Forever to take us back once more to the

18th century, where a British contemporary of Kant laid the groundwork for an influential ethical theory that's about as opposed to Kant's system of morality as you could possibly get.

HODIN'S PLAN AND THE GREATEST GOOD

As it happens, this particular way of thinking also grew out of suffering—not from overpopulation, mind you, but rather the enormous economic, social, and political upheavals that plagued 18th-century England as a result of the American Revolution, the Napoleonic Wars, and the early stages of the Industrial Revolution. Because of the tremendous affliction he saw all around him, Jeremy Bentham (1748–1832) sought a basis for morality that was both practical and social in nature. Very interested in social reform, he held that any act or institution of government must justify itself through its contribution to "the greatest good for the greatest number." Since Bentham claimed all acts and institutions must justify themselves through their utility, his theory eventually became known as utilitarianism.

Bentham, as well as his intellectual disciple John Stuart Mill (1806–1873), held that the happiness of any individual consists in a favorable balance of pleasure over pain. Those actions that tend to increase pleasure are considered "good," while those disposed to increasing pain are considered "bad." For example, the germ-free atmosphere of Gideon certainly increases the pleasure of its inhabitants, enabling the people of Gideon to flourish in such physical and spiritual perfection that life itself is practically eternal (death comes only to the very ancient). From a utilitarian perspective, the germ-free atmosphere is good because it brings pleasure. If Bentham and Mill had the chance to see "Mark of Gideon," they'd undoubtedly agree with Kirk when the captain tells Hodin that "Most people would envy you." On the other hand, "Births," as Hodin tells

Kirk, "have increased our population until Gideon is encased in a living mass of beings, without rest, without peace, without joy." That, from a utilitarian point of view, is a bad thing, because the immense overpopulation has caused the planet great pain.

Pretty simple and straightforward, wouldn't you say?

Now, since the ultimate goal of utilitarianism is pleasure, that would make this theory a form of hedonism. The only difference is that Bentham and Mill strove for a social hedonism, whereas the goals of Aristippus and Epicurus were purely egoistic. Social hedonism insists that we should act to increase the pleasures of others as well as our own pleasure—a pleasure that should be as great and as all-encompassing as possible. In fact, the theory goes, it is every person's duty to do two things: (1) increase to the utmost the total amount of pleasure in the world, while at the same time (2) strive to reduce the total amount of pain in the world as much as possible. The fundamental moral ideal behind utilitarianism is that we should always try, as best we can, to be impartial in choosing between our own pleasure and that of others.

The ultimate value of any kind of hedonism—namely, pleasure—is held to be "intrinsically valuable." Anything that helps us obtain pleasure, or avoid pain, is said to have "instrumental value." Things with instrumental value serve as instruments that enable us to obtain something we desire. Since Odona agrees to sacrifice herself as an instrument for her people to obtain future happiness, her actions have instrumental, but not intrinsic, value.

A utilitarian ethicist would consider Hodin's plan to sacrifice his daughter morally right, since it would ultimately reduce the total amount of pain on a planet where people desperately dream of being alone. "There is no place, no street, no house, no garden, no beach, no mountain that is not filled with people," Odona poignantly explains to Kirk. "If he could, each one would kill to find a place to be alone. If he could, he would die for it."

Sure enough, Kirk feels empathy for Odona as soon as he listens to her story. Mill would say that the captain, like most of us, is naturally sympathetic and concerned about the well-being of others, as well as his own. These feelings of compassion are what spur us on to increase the pleasure of others—or decrease their pain, as the case may be—rather than be solely concerned with our own pleasure and/or pain. Our desire to be one with our fellow creatures, in turn, forms the basis for our capacity to develop moral feelings. (Of course, considering Odona's costume—an outfit best described as something straight out of Frederick's of Hollywood—it's possible Kirk's concern for her welfare might be temporarily distracted by another kind of desire. But let's not digress.)

KANT AND MILL DEBATE "THE MARK OF GIDEON"

We know that Mill would consider Hodin's decision to sacrifice Odona ethically sound. Should we? How we answer that question depends on whether we prefer the utilitarian way of thinking over Kant's system of morality. Remember that with Kant, when it comes to evaluating the moral quality of our actions, the consequences of our behavior should never enter the picture. So long as our intentions are pure (that is, so long as we are acting from a sense of duty), our actions will always have true moral worth, regardless of whatever results they yield.

That's the complete opposite of utilitarianism, which judges the morality of a particular action *entirely* on its consequences. For Mill, we perform our duty only when our actions bring happiness to all who are affected by them—regardless of what our original intentions happened to be. For example, say you're swimming in the ocean. Suddenly you're swept away by a killer wave, and you start to panic. You flail your arms and yell for help. A Good Samaritan sees you in the distance, signals for a lifeguard, then jumps in after you. The lifeguard also eventually comes to your aid, and between the two of them you're rescued. Now, let's say the only difference between the lifeguard and the Good Samaritan is that while the Good Samaritan saves you out of the goodness of her heart, the lifeguard saves you only because that's what he gets paid to do. Does that make the Good Samaritan more noble than the lifeguard? Utilitarianism says that neither of these points are relevant. What matters is that your life was saved. As Mill himself once observed: "He who saves another from drowning does what is right, regardless of his motives, even if he is to be paid for his trouble."

Similarly, Mill would say that so long as Hodin's plan saves his people from misery, it wouldn't matter whether he truly wanted to relieve his world of distress or was actually more concerned with his own legacy. Either way, the same action would bring about the same results; ergo, according to Mill, it has the same moral value.

Mill would add that Hodin's intentions are relevant only insofar as evaluating his character as a person is concerned—not his actions. And that's a whole other ball of wax. Therefore, we should not assume an action to be good just because it's performed by a "good" person, or bad because it's done by a "bad" person. The results are ultimately what matters, not the character or intentions of whoever does them.

Utilitarianism does, however, insist that we strive to further the common good, not simply our own. With that in mind, before committing ourselves to an action, we should always ask the following question: *Will my society be better off because of this action?* Had Hodin asked himself this question as he contemplated sacrificing Odona, he certainly would have answered yes. After all, he believes that the agony of

Gideon can otherwise be alleviated only by introducing disease and death at a young age, given what Hodin calls their "unshakable tradition" of not "interfering with the Creation" they love so deeply. Though the prime minister realizes inflicting his daughter with *Vegan choriomeningitis* will cause an epidemic that will claim many lives, he also knows the reduced population will ultimately enable Gideon to "[become once again] the Paradise it once was." His action, Mill would therefore conclude, is intrinsically valuable and must be considered morally right.

But wait . . . if the moral question we should ask is whether society "would be better off" for what we're about to do, isn't that a measure of intention? Mill says no. Intention, after all, is a window into the inner motivation of an individual. But the inner motivation of the individual is not the focus of utilitarianism. Rather, it's the good of society.

Give me a break, Kant might interject in addressing the prime minister. "*These* are the questions you should be asking: *Would I really want everyone to act the way I intend to act? Can I 'rationally will' that all people somehow contract a fatal disease to serve as an example for others to follow?* Because if you did, a contradiction would result. If the rest of the planet followed Odona's lead and shortened their own lives in order to relieve the suffering of others, then eventually there would be no Gideons left to follow her example. Life would be destroyed by the very process employed to improve it. And besides, to treat your daughter as a means with only instrumental value is to disregard her intrinsic worth as a person. Therefore, you cad, what you intend to do has no moral worth."

IS SELF-SACRIFICE A GOOD THING?

We'll come back to the debate between Kantian ethics and utilitarianism shortly. First, though, because "The Mark of Gideon" is primarily about self-sacrifice, we ought to take a look at what Mill himself had to say about this very subject.

It's worth noting, for example, that some detractors of utilitarianism like to say the theory itself is a contradiction insofar as it promotes self-sacrifice. As a type of hedonism, the argument goes, utilitarianism should be concerned only with pleasure—whereas acts of personal sacrifice clearly bring pain. Mill responded to objections of this kind by pointing out that those actions of self-sacrifice we acknowledge to be good obtain their value from increasing the happiness of society. Thus, self-sacrifice is only good to the extent that it increases the greatest happiness overall. When that happens, those actions simply reinforce the altruistic view "that the happiness which forms the utilitarian standard of what is right in conduct is not the agent's own happiness, but that of all concerned."

On the other hand, acts of self-sacrifice that do not benefit "all concerned" in society accordingly do not deserve moral credit. As Mill wrote in his famous essay *Utilitarianism:*

> All honor to those who can abnegate for themselves the personal enjoyment of life, when by such renunciation they contribute worthily to increase the amount of happiness in the world; but he who does it ... for any other purpose, is no more deserving of admiration than the ascetic mounted on his pillar. He may be an inspiring proof of what men can do, but assuredly not an example of what they should.

Without a doubt, Hodin believes his sacrifice of Odona would "contribute worthily to increase the amount of happiness" on Gideon. In fact, were he more familiar with Mill's writings, the prime minister probably would have used the very same words when he explained his position to Captain Kirk.

Where does *Star Trek* stand on this issue? It's hard to tell—at least based on the way "The Mark of Gideon" ends. Though Kirk manages to save Odona's life (Spock beams them off the ersatz *Enterprise* and onto the real ship, enabling McCoy to cure her), he can't prevent the annihilation from taking place. Because Odona's blood still carries the communicable disease, she is nevertheless able to spread it and cause the plague that will eventually reduce Gideon's overpopulation. This conclusion suggests that *Star Trek's* position on the morality of sacrificing one life for the sake of saving many more is, at best, ambiguous. We're left with the impression that personal sacrifices such as Odona's are acceptable, provided the victim is truly acting on her own consent.

Of course, if that indeed is *Star Trek's* contention, then why does Kirk insist on saving Odona? If she really wants to give up her life, why doesn't he just let her do it? Both of which are good questions, neither of which the episode really answers. As I say, it's confusing. That's not the case, however, with "Man of the People," wherein Picard again takes a Kantian stance against using another person only as a means. *Star Trek's* position is much stronger in our second story, perhaps because the circumstances of the two victims are much different. Whereas Odona volunteered to give up her life, Deanna was clearly recruited against her will.

A DRAIN ON DEANNA'S ENERGY

Like Hodin, Ambassador Alkar in "Man of the People" embodies many inherent utilitarian principles. We see this right off the bat, when he tells Picard that he wants an immediate end to the fighting between the Rekag and the Seronians: "To delay a week, even a few days, could cost thousands of lives." Utilitarians are almost obsessed with the social cost and benefit of any particular action. Maximizing the balance of social benefits over social costs is a utilitarian criterion of right action.

Though Deanna's sudden aging clearly surprises Alkar ("Usually my receptacles survive for many years"), he is otherwise unmoved by the gravity of her situation. The way he sees it, the hapless Troi has long since proven her instrumental value to his ultimate mission. "It seems hopeless," he explains to Picard, "but [now is when] I can be most effective. If I'm focused, free of disquieting thoughts, I can turn these factions toward peace."

Naturally, Picard is aghast to hear the devious diplomat speak of his victims as "receptacles." Kant, for that matter, would react the same way. In fact, utilitarianism is frequently criticized for treating sentient individuals as mere receptacles of what has positive or negative value, so the use of that word in "Man of the People" is certainly appropriate. To a utilitarian, "receptacles" have no value of their own. What has value is that which the receptacles contain—namely, experience. As contemporary ethicist Peter Singer explained in his criticism of classical utilitarianism, "It is as if sentient beings were receptacles of something valuable, and it did not matter if a receptacle got broken, as long as another receptacle were available to which the contents could be transferred without getting spilled in the process."* Utilitarianism urges that we strive for the best balance of good experiences over bad experiences among all who are affected by the things we do. We shouldn't concern ourselves with the experience of a particular individual (Deanna or Odona, in the case of our two episodes), but rather with the best total balance of good over bad experiences (be it peace in the Rekag-Seronia system, or the end of suffering on the planet Gideon).

---

*Peter Singer, "Animals and the Value of Life," in *Matters of Life and Death,* ed. Tom Regan (New York: Random House, 1980), pp. 369–70.

We see the differences between Kant's principles and utilitarianism illustrated even further in the climactic showdown between Picard and Alkar. The ambassador, for example, implores the captain to look at the big picture. "Come on, Captain, surely you can see that there's a broader canvas here. If I came to their peace talks hindered by unwanted emotions, then the Rekags and the Seronians would be condemned to go on fighting."

"You can't explain away a wantonly immoral act," says Picard, his fury boiling, "because you think it is connected to some higher purpose."

"Captain, do you know how many people have died on this planet in the last 48 hours? Thousands. Deanna Troi is just one individual."

"That does not justify brutalizing her, nor any of the others you have used," replies Picard, voicing the Kantian argument that no rational being should ever be used as a means only — which, no matter how Alkar paints it, is exactly what he's trying to do.

Of course, ever the proponent of "the greatest good for the greatest number," Alkar asks Picard to consider the little Rekag and Seronian children who go to bed each night fearing for their lives. For their sake, his argument implies, it's certainly worth sacrificing a few lives. "Captain, I get no payment," he continues, sounding very righteous. "I have no power base, no agenda... I'm willing to risk my life simply to help others."

Now Picard is really pissed. "You think that makes you appear *courageous*? Because you're mistaken. You're a coward, Alkar. You exploit the innocent because you're unwilling to shoulder the burdens of unpleasant emotions. This time you will be held accountable!"

Despite his impassioned appeal for Deanna's life, the captain might as well have spoken to a wall. Alkar refuses to save her, then sics a pair of thugs on Picard (and on Worf, who has accompanied him down to the surface) to make himself clear. Perhaps he reasons that when utilitarian arguments fail, one should resort to the principle of "might makes right."*

Of course, Picard manages to foil the ambassador after all. With the help of Dr. Crusher, he has Deanna suspended in a deathlike state to sever Alkar's bond with her and force him to chose another "receptacle." Sure enough, Alkar beams back aboard the *Enterprise*, this time accompanied by a woman named Liva. Upon viewing Deanna's "dead" body, he immediately engages poor Liva in the "ancient Lumerian funeral ritual"—only to find her zapped off the ship in the nick of time! This time, *he* suffers a neurological overload, causing him to collapse and die just as Deanna comes back to life.

By his actions, Picard shows that his outrage was not merely personal, but based on ethical principles. Like Kant, he believes that no one, regardless of the circumstances, has the right to abolish the autonomy of an individual.

A NIGHT OF INSURRECTION

Utilitarianism and Kantian ethics clash on several other occasions in the world of *Star Trek*, with the utilitarians taking it on the chin almost every time. In *Star Trek: Insurrection*, for example, Admiral Dougherty wants to relocate the 600 Ba'ku without their consent in order to use the regenerative properties collected from their planet's rings to help "billions." The ring particles have the capacity to double one's life span, a discovery that could revolutionize medical science throughout the galaxy. Though Picard believes the forced relocation will destroy the Ba'ku, Dougherty, like Alkar, asks the captain to

---

*"Might makes right," as we know from *The Republic*, is the principle advocated by Plato's adversary Thrasymachus. We'll revisit this age-old belief in Chapter 15.

consider the big picture: "Jean-Luc, we are only moving 600 people."

Not surprisingly, Picard doesn't buy this utilitarian argument, either. "How many people does it take before it becomes wrong—a thousand? Fifty thousand? A million? How many will it take, Admiral?" Unable to answer this, Dougherty, also like Alkar, forsakes utilitarianism in favor of good old-fashioned "might makes right." (Hmm...maybe it's just a coincidence, but perhaps *Star Trek* is questioning how strong utilitarian principles really are, when they can be so easily abandoned at a moment's notice.)

Voyager also spurns utilitarian values in "Night" (*VGR:* #95), an episode we discussed briefly in Chapter 10. The ship finds itself traveling in a void of space so vast, there are no other star systems within 2,500 light-years. It will take two years to escape this veritable black hole. "It's like being becalmed in the middle of the ocean," observes Chakotay. "If it weren't for sensors, we wouldn't even know we were at warp. We've only been crossing this expanse for two months and we're already feeling the strain. How do we last another two years?"

In fact, morale is so bad, Janeway refuses to leave her cabin! Though *Voyager* at one point had the means to leave the Delta Quadrant and return home, the captain believed doing so would have ultimately put innocent people at risk. So she elected to stay—a decision she has long since second-guessed, especially now that the ship is stuck in a seemingly endless void. "I made an error in judgment," she tells Chakotay. "It was short-sighted and selfish, and now all of us are paying for my mistake!" Convinced she has let everyone down, Janeway isolates herself from her crew for several weeks. A utilitarian, of course, would explain the predicament this way: though the captain believed her crew would be "better off" by remaining in the Delta Quadrant, because her decision caused her crew pain and unsettlement, it was ultimately the wrong thing to do.

Just as the crew goes completely stir-crazy, Seven of Nine reports that long-range sensors are picking up dangerously high levels of theta radiation. Soon afterward *Voyager* is rocked and loses its power. Using flashlights, Seven and Paris encounter a humanoid who angrily rushes at them. Seven disables the alien with her phaser and has him taken to sickbay. By the time the emergency power comes on line, Janeway learns that her ship is now surrounded by three alien vessels, and that 17 intruders are on board. The aliens stop their attack, however, when a fourth vessel comes to *Voyager*'s defense. Identifying himself as "Controller Emck of the Malon export vessel," the new ally tells Janeway about a spatial vortex a few light-years from their position leading directly to the other side of the expanse. This could be the break the crew's been looking for! Not only would this shortcut liberate them from the void, it will shorten the length of their trip by two years.

Ah, but there's a catch. Emck will help *Voyager* only if Janeway releases the alien lying injured in sickbay. Once the captain realizes the Malon are poisoning the space of the other alien species, she tells Emck to buzz off. The alien in sickbay then leads *Voyager* to his people, all of whom are dying from theta-radiation exposure. Naturally, they ask Janeway for help.

This leaves the captain in the following predicament: if she turns over the one alien, her crew will be closer to home and relieved of their extreme malaise. Emck, of course, will be ecstatic. In fact, as far as anyone can tell, the only person likely to suffer in this deal would be the alien in sickbay. In other words, your basic "greatest good for the greatest number" scenario. If Janeway were a utilitarian, she'd give up the alien to the Malon in exchange for the ticket out. But she isn't, so of course, she doesn't. As we mentioned in Chapter 10, the captain not only protects the alien, she thwarts Emck even further by stopping his toxic-disposal business (and protecting the environment, to boot). Like Picard, Janeway believes that because

286 | THE ETHICS OF STAR TREK

all rational beings have intrinsic value, they should never be used only as means with instrumental value. Her actions clearly show that she also prefers Kantian ethics over utilitarian principles.

SPOCK, A MAN OF NUMBERS

Let's stop and take inventory. Picard and Janeway clearly reject utilitarian principles. Given Kirk's opposition to Hodin's plan in "Mark of Gideon," it would appear he leans the same way. That's three out of four *Star Trek* captains (we'll get to Sisko in a moment). Based on sheer numbers, can we safely assume that utilitarianism is not a part of the ethical makeup of the series?

Not exactly—especially when you consider the pivotal moment of *Star Trek II: The Wrath of Khan,* when Spock sacrifices his life to save the *Enterprise.* Surely the words he utters are forever etched in the memory of every Trekker: "The needs of the many outweigh the needs of the few... or the one." For good measure, he repeats this almost verbatim near the end of the movie: "The good of the many outweighs the good of the few or the one." Spock's words, of course, basically paraphrase the utilitarian credo, "the greatest good for the greatest number." The Vulcan's sacrifice certainly appears to be warranted in this situation. Not only that, he takes matters in his own hands—more or less "volunteering" to give up his life, just as Odona volunteers to give up her life for the benefit of her people in "Mark of Gideon."

Which brings us back to the question we raised earlier. Perhaps *Star Trek does* embrace utilitarian thought under certain conditions.

That would be a reasonable conclusion... except that Kirk almost immediately negates this in *Star Trek III: The Search for Spock.* The captain jeopardizes his career, as well as those of his other senior officers, in order to save Spock's life. What does Kirk say when Spock asks him why he did this? "The needs of the one outweighed the needs of the many." In other words, though Spock appears to espouse utilitarian values, Kirk seems as strongly against them in *Star Trek III* as he was in "Mark of Gideon."

This philosophical difference is also dramatized in "The *Galileo* Seven" (*TOS*: #14), a show we visited briefly in Chapters 6 and 8. Spock's first command mission turns disastrous when the shuttlecraft *Galileo* crash-lands on Taurus II, a hostile planet inhabited by "huge, furry creatures." (Don't you love these scientific descriptions?) Though Spock and his six-member crew—McCoy, Scott, Lieutenant Boma, Yeoman Mears, and "red shirts" Latimer and Gaetano—are unharmed, their ship is badly damaged and must be repaired if they're to achieve orbit. Complicating matters, the *Enterprise* cannot locate them due to the planet's atmospheric conditions. Because the *Galileo* has lost a lot of fuel, Scotty determines they can achieve orbit only if the weight aboard the shuttlecraft is lightened by at least five hundred pounds—that is, the weight of three grown men.

Though it's suggested that Spock draw lots to determine who stays behind, the Vulcan shuns that idea: "My decision will be a logical one... arrived at through logical processes."

Naturally, McCoy reacts emotionally: "Life and death are not logical, Spock!"

Ever the utilitarian, however, Spock replies, "But attaining a desired goal is." Like any utilitarian ethicist, the first officer is concerned with the consequences of his actions.

Spock orders the two red shirts to scout the area. Of course, they soon buy the farm at the hands of the "huge, furry creatures." That takes some pressure off Spock, at least for the time being. Though McCoy and Mears collect about 50 pounds worth of equipment that could be eliminated, Scott says the

Galileo is still about 150 pounds overweight. Now the pressure's on again. Spock must choose between leaving one crew member behind or risking everyone's life on a hostile planet. "It is more rational to sacrifice one man than six," he says to McCoy. Again, the Vulcan believes in the concept of "the greatest good for the greatest number"—even when his own life is at stake. Injured himself by a fallen rock during another attack by the "huge, furry creatures," Spock insists that Boma and McCoy leave him behind and return to the ship. From a utilitarian (as well as a logical) point of view, it's simply a matter of numbers. The lives of two men count for more than his own life, just as the lives of six people count for more than the lives of one. (McCoy, of course, disagrees with this logic, and rescues Spock anyway.)

Meanwhile, back on the *Enterprise,* Kirk is on the verge of yet another prima facie ethics dilemma. The captain has been ordered to transport critically needed medical supplies to the New Paris colonies that have been devastated by plague. Quite literally, millions of lives are at stake. Yet Kirk is more concerned with the welfare of his crew members on Taurus II. Mill and Bentham would tell him to deliver the supplies because that would potentially save more lives, or result in the best balance of good experiences over bad. 'Tis better to risk losing seven lives if it ultimately means saving millions more. Though Galactic High Commander Ferris doesn't put it as eloquently, he basically tells Kirk the same thing. Only our hero (demonstrating once again that when it comes to his crew, "The needs of the one outweigh the needs of the many") decides to rescue the *Galileo* seven (or at least, what's left of them)—a decision based on his duty of gratitude. The captain dispatches a rescue team aboard the shuttlecraft *Columbus* that eventually rescues Spock and the surviving crew.

SPOCK, A MAN OF. . . EMPATHY?

Spock's utilitarian leanings certainly make sense, given his proclivity for numbers—his brain, after all, functions very much like a calculator. Just consider how precise he is whenever he responds to a quantitative question! Remember how he convinces Kirk to let him assist in the search for the Horta in "Devil in the Dark" (*TOS: #26*). The captain wants Spock to return to the surface and help Scotty fix the nuclear reactor because he is afraid both he and his second-in-command might lose their lives to a creature that has already wasted several men. Without batting an eye, Spock assures Kirk that "The odds against you and I both being killed are 2,228.7 to one." Similarly, in "Errand of Mercy" (*TOS: #27*), Spock determines that the odds of his and Kirk's both dying as a result of the Klingon attack on the planet Organia are "approximately 7,824.7 to one"—even under fire.*

But Spock's concern for the number of individuals in moral decision making goes much deeper than his affinity for impromptu calculations. Consider his reaction upon realizing the Vulcan ship *Intrepid* has been destroyed in "The Immunity Syndrome" (*TOS: #48*). As you may recall, Spock actually tells McCoy about the disaster before the news is officially confirmed. "How can you be so sure the *Intrepid* is destroyed?" asks the doctor.

"I felt it die," says Spock.

"But I thought you had to be in physical contact with a subject to sense—"

"Dr. McCoy," interrupts Spock, "even I, a half-Vulcan, can sense the death screams of 400 Vulcan minds crying out over

---

* "Errand of Mercy," as we know, marks the first appearance of the Klingons in the *Star Trek* universe. Cf. Michael Okuda and Denise Okuda, *The "Star Trek" Encyclopedia*, 2nd ed. (New York: Pocket Books, 1997), p. 141.

the distance between us." Realizing McCoy doesn't understand, Spock elaborates: "I have noticed this insensitivity among wholly human beings. It is easier for you to feel the death of one fellow-creature than to feel the deaths of millions."

Harsh though this may sound, the Vulcan has a point. It's easy for us to empathize when one person dies—even if it's someone we may not even know. How many of us, for example, were saddened at the passing of DeForest Kelley? Though most of us probably never met him, we all felt as though we knew the man who played "Bones" because *Star Trek* has been part of our lives for nearly 35 years. Those of us who are fans of *Peanuts* undoubtedly mourned the loss of Charles Schultz for the same reason. Now compare that to how we tend to react to the news of plane crashes, hurricanes, or other disasters— where the death tolls are often in the hundreds, or even thousands. Maybe it's the sheer numbers, maybe it's the distance, but for some reason we tend to think of these deaths in a more abstract way. We might shake our heads like McCoy, or say "What a tragedy," but that's about it.

Of course, the prospect of empathizing with millions in the same way we empathize with one death would be absolutely depressing. Which accounts for McCoy's next line: "Suffer the deaths of thy neighbors, eh, Spock? Is that what you want to wish on us?"

Naturally, Spock gets the last word: "It might have rendered your history a bit less bloody." In a nutshell, the Vulcan explains that the reason he so wholeheartedly accepts the utilitarian principle "the greatest good for the greatest number" is that he has a greater sensitivity to suffering and death than most of us.

Of course, you could say that it's impossible for Spock to be a "true" disciple of Bentham and Mill (his tremendous capacity for empathy notwithstanding). Utilitarianism, after all, is a form of hedonism, which ultimately promotes pleasure—which, most would agree, is one concept that's completely incompatible with Vulcan thinking.

Or is it? If we scratch Spock's surface a little more deeply, we'll see that pleasure indeed is very important to him. Remember the poignant moment at the end of "This Side of Paradise" (*TOS:* #25), after the pleasure-inducing Omicron Ceti III spores lose their power over our Vulcan friend. "For the first time in my life," he says to Kirk wistfully, "I was happy." Spock is likewise sympathetic to the space hippies in search of a hedonistic paradise in "The Way to Eden" (*TOS:* #75)—a sympathy that Kirk himself does not share. Similarly, Spock disagrees with the captain's decision to destroy Vaal in "The Apple" (*TOS:* #38) because such action would bring the people of Gamma Trianguli VI "pain, worry, insecurity, and tension." In the same episode, the normally phlegmatic Vulcan even responds to a request to carry out an order by saying, "With pleasure, Captain."

Finally, when Spock risks a court-martial by abducting Pike in "The Menagerie," he presumably has weighed the pain of losing his career against the pleasure that Pike would ultimately receive on Talos IV. Since the Vulcan can repress his feelings of pain, and Pike stands to gain a great deal of pleasure, Bentham and Mill would say that he clearly made the right choice. Therefore, it would appear that Spock (at least to some extent) does indeed agree with the fundamental principle of utilitarianism: pleasure is a good thing we should pursue, while pain is a bad thing we should avoid.

SISKO DECIDES TO LIE, CHEAT, AND BRIBE

Nonetheless, given how adamantly Picard, Janeway, Kirk, McCoy, and most of the other principal series characters oppose utilitarian values, Spock's acceptance of this ethical theory in both word and deed would seem to make him an anomaly in the *Star Trek* universe.

Or is he? Consider the course of action Sisko takes in "In the Pale Moonlight" (*DS9:* #143), wherein the captain lies, cheats, and resorts to bribery—all of which he justifies (albeit, uneasily) by appealing to the utilitarian principle of "the greatest good for the greatest number."

As the episode begins, the captain believes the Federation's only hope of winning the war against the Dominion is to convince the Romulans to join their side. The problem is, the Romulans are officially neutral, having signed a nonaggression pact with the Dominion. To get them to change their mind, Sisko and Garak, a former Cardassian spy, decide to manufacture evidence to convince the Romulans that the Dominion intends to go after them. Knowing that the primary pro-Dominion advocate on Romulus, Senator Vreenak, will soon be visiting a nearby Cardassian colony, the artful Garak suggests that Vreenek "could be persuaded to make a secret detour to Deep Space Nine" if Sisko invited him.

Now, Sisko is not exactly comfortable about the prospect of collaborating with Garak—a point he makes clear in his personal log. Nevertheless, he arranges with Klingon Chancellor Gowron to pardon a criminal named Tolar. In exchange for his release, Tolar agrees to fabricate a holographic recording of a meeting held at the highest levels of the Dominion in which the planned invasion of Romulus is discussed. Sisko then trades a very dangerous biological substance (a compound normally regulated directly by the Federation) for the rare Cardassian data rod needed for the forgery. If that isn't enough, the captain also has to bribe Quark, whom Tolar once tried to kill, not to press charges against the felon. Quark agrees, but not without making a few demands of his own: "Thank you, Captain, for restoring my faith in the 98th Rule of Acquisition: 'Every man has his price.' "

At this point, Sisko makes the following entry in his personal log: "Every day entire worlds are struggling for their freedom—and here I am, still worrying about the finer points of morality. I had to keep my eye on the ball: winning the war." Just as utilitarians emphasize the consequences of actions over other moral considerations, we see Sisko using the same reasoning. Nonetheless, as we watch the episode, we can't help wonder how much longer Sisko will allow the end to justify the means.

Tolar completes his task and prepares to leave Deep Space Nine—only to learn from the captain himself that he can't leave until the forgery produces the desired result. When Tolar objects, Sisko violently slams him against a wall and threatens to kill him if the forged data rod has the least imperfection. Later, Sisko shows Vreenak the recorded "meeting" in which Dominion leader Weyoun and Cardassian leader Damar "discuss" plans to invade Romulus. Sisko then lies through his teeth when the senator doubts the authenticity of the transmission. A suspicious Vreenak, however, sees through the deception and threatens to expose the captain to the entire Alpha Quadrant.

Two days later, Sisko appears to catch a break—Vreenak is killed when his shuttle explodes en route to Romulus. Deep Space Nine's senior officers are ecstatic. In fact, the entire Federation was probably happy to hear the news of the accident, for it almost assuredly means that Romulus will enter the war on their side. If Sisko were truly a utilitarian thinker, he ought to feel pretty good about the whole thing. After all, utilitarianism not only promotes the greatest pleasure to the majority of those affected by a particular action, it holds that we should be concerned only with the consequences of our actions. Clearly, the consequences of Sisko's actions are nothing but positives for the Federation.

But Sisko smells a rat, spelled G-A-R-A-K. Indeed, the former operative admits that he wasn't convinced they could fool Vreenak, so he arranged to blow up the senator's shuttle to ensure the plan's success. Garak reasons that when the Romulans examine the wreckage of Vreenak's shuttle, they'll find the burnt remnants of the data rod "which somehow miraculously survived the explosion." Sure enough, that's what happens—and in due time, the Romulan Empire formally declares war against the Dominion.

A utilitarian would say so long as the plan resulted in the "greatest good for the greatest number"—in this case, drawing the Romulans into the war to help the Federation—it doesn't matter how Sisko and Garak got the job done. Still, the captain is clearly troubled at the end of the episode. Though he realizes that he may have saved the entire Alpha Quadrant, he also knows it was at the cost of a few lives—and his own self-respect. "So, this is a huge victory for the good guys," he records in his personal log. "So I lied. I cheated. I bribed men to cover the crimes of other men. I am an accessory to murder. But the most damning thing of all—I think I can live with it."

Sitting alone in the quiet of his own room, Sisko sounds like a man trying very hard to convince himself that he really can live with the consequences of his actions—so much so, he repeats himself twice. Nevertheless, his rationalizations ring hollow. He is visibly uncomfortable, an agonized man, having made choices that have torn his moral fabric. Though he appeals to the utilitarian argument that the end justifies the means, it's not clear whether he really believes this—or if he's simply using it as a means in order to cope with what he did.

What do you make of this? True, given the circumstances, the choices Sisko made are at least understandable. But were they worth turning his back on all of his Starfleet ethics? If the cap-tain really believes he "can live with it," then why he is so anguished over what he chose to do?

Before we can second-guess the captain—or question the choices we make in any other moral dilemma, for that matter—we need to look at one last ethical theory: existentialism, a theory that focuses on choices and angst. Let's explore this in our next chapter and see if it helps us out of this conundrum.

THE EXISTENTIALIST CONUNDRUM OF MASTER AND SLAVE MORALITY

"Bread and Circuses"
TOS: Episode 43
Stardates: 4040.7, 4041.2
Original Air Date: March 15, 1968

While orbiting near the fourth planet of solar system 892 ("IV-892"), the Enterprise *discovers wreckage of the S.S. Beagle, a survey vessel commanded by Captain R. M. Merrick, which disappeared long ago. Kirk, Spock, and McCoy beam down to investigate and immediately encounter the Children of the Sun, a group of "slaves" who are fugitives from the local authorities, a government of the "strong" patterned after ancient Rome. The Children defy Roman values by preaching nonviolence, love, and brotherhood—a philosophy modeled after the doctrines of the Son of God. Aided by Flavius, a former gladiator who became a slave after converting to the Children's teachings, the* Enterprise *three search for Merrick—only to be captured by Roman forces and taken into the city. There, they learn that Merrick sold out his entire 47-member crew by making them participate in the gladiatorial*

games, a crude yet highly profitable form of entertainment televised nightly throughout the planet. In exchange, Merrick was
awarded the cushy position of "First Citizen" to Proconsul
Claudius Marcus. Kirk soon realizes that Marcus is using Merrick to lure other Starship crews to fight in the games—a point
Marcus makes clear by condemning Spock and McCoy to die
in the arena unless Kirk surrenders all remaining Enterprise
personnel.

"Conundrum"
TNG: Episode 114
Stardate: 45494.2
Original Air Date. Week of February 17, 1992

When an alien vessel scans the Enterprise, Picard and
crew are stricken with a peculiar kind of amnesia—while
all retain their respective navigational skills, they don't
know who they are, nor why they're aboard the vessel.
Though access to the ship's mission reports, crew records,
and personal logs has been strangely prohibited, the computer does indicate the Enterprise is presently at war with
the Lysian Alliance—an operation so covert that absolute
radio silence is in order. Unbeknownst to the crew, however, their memories and data files have been manipulated
by the Satarrans, a species with advanced computer-hack-
ing capabilities that hopes to use the Enterprise to destroy
their rivals—the Lysians! During the confusion, a Satarran
operative slipped aboard the ship, knowing the computer
would eventually identify him as "second-in-command
Keiran MacDuff." Though Picard proceeds to wipe out a
Lysian ship, he increasingly questions the morality of his
"orders," especially once he realizes his "enemy" is actually

a small colony whose weapons technology is vastly inferior to his own. But MacDuff is determined to carry out the "mission"—even if he has to override Picard to do it.

For all its apparent anachronisms (Roman gladiators in outer space?), "Bread and Circuses" was actually eerily prescient on one important count—namely, the way in which Empire TV dictates the format of the gladiatorial games. Within a decade of this episode's first broadcast, network television's influence on professional sports began to increase, from instituting *Monday Night Football* to scheduling playoff and/or championship-level games exclusively at night. Without going too far afield (or ranting about World Series games that last until midnight Eastern time), decisions such as these are based on the advertising rates the networks can charge during prime-time hours, when the TV-viewing audience is at its highest. This is not unlike some of the maneuvers we see in "Bread and Circuses," such as slotting Kirk's execution during the early show so as to be "guaranteed a splendid audience." The higher the ratings, the more Claudius Marcus can charge the manufacturers of the Jupiter 8 automobile to sponsor *Name the Winner!*, Empire TV's nightly gladiatorial games broadcast. Perhaps Hodgkins was on to something after all.*

---

*Hodgkins' Law of Parallel Planet Development is a sociological theory which, according to the episode, suggests that "similar planets with similar populations and similar environments will evolve in similar ways." While IV–892 is technologically and environmentally similar to 20th-century Earth (television permeating society, smog permeating the air), from a cultural standpoint, the planet closely resembles the ancient Roman Empire. Among other things, this explains the popularity of *Name the Winner!* Presumably, this same sociological principle also accounts for such phenomena as the Ferengi system of commerce in *DS9*, which incorporates many of Hobbes' principles; Cardassian labor camps, which parallel the internment camps instituted by both the Axis powers and the Allied nations during World War II; the "space hippies" of "The Way to Eden" (*TOS: #75*), whose mores reflect the counterculture movement of the 1960s; and the Ten Tribes in "Friday's Child" (*TOS: #32*), whose nation-state resembles the feudal societies that pervaded Europe between the 9th and 15th centuries.

"Bread and Circuses," of course, is far more than just a nifty satire of how television works. The dichotomous worlds of the Roman Proconsulate and the Children of the Sun provide us with a terrific illustration of existentialism in action.

Existentialism is a philosophy that emphasizes our existence as individual human beings who must make choices. Since individual human beings must make serious choices in each segment of every *Star Trek* series or film, this theory is highly germane for our purposes of discovering the overall ethics of the show. Existentialism can be broken down into three primary schools of thought—Nietzsche's master/slave duality, Kierkegaard's three stages of existence (a concept we're already a little familiar with), and Sartre's notion of existential angst. By the time we finish exploring each theory and applying it to our episodes, we'll find ourselves in a prime position to determine *Star Trek*'s ethical foundation.

CLAUDIUS MARCUS AND THE WILL TO POWER

Remember the position our Sophist friend Thrasymachus argued throughout *The Republic*? He held that no matter how you slice it, justice always serves the interest of the stronger party—a philosophy better known as "might makes right." Though Plato outreasoned Thrasymachus point for point over the course of the dialogue, many people over the years (including some of history's preeminent thinkers) have nonetheless believed that the concept equating justice with strength is true.

Thrasymachus' idea is clearly alive and well on Planet IV-892. Claudius Marcus embodies the notion that strength is praiseworthy, while weakness is something to be scorned. To Marcus, the most devastating thing he can say to Kirk (other than, perhaps, insulting his mother) is that his species "has no strength." Contrasting humankind unfavorably to his own people, the proconsul boasts that the gladiatorial games "have always strengthened us." As he tries to goad Kirk into beaming down the rest of the *Enterprise* crew to take part in the games, he assures the captain that "only the weak will die."

One imagines Marcus would have been a big fan of Friedrich Nietzsche (1844–1900), a German thinker who based his moral philosophy on the concept of "might makes right." Like Thrasymachus, Nietzsche believed the only true morality is that of the strong imposing their will on the weak. He claimed there is "a twofold history of good and evil" that shows the development of two primary types of morality—namely, the master and the slave moralities.

In the master morality, which Nietzsche obviously held as the ideal, "good" means "noble" (in the sense of "with a soul of high caliber"), while "evil" means "vulgar" or "plebian." As we're about to see, Marcus' beliefs and actions in "Bread and Circuses" parallel this philosophy in many ways. First, the master morality is a code of self-glorification that affirms the demands of the ruling class. Since a person of nobility considers himself the creator of values, he doesn't look beyond himself for any approval of his acts. The haughty Marcus certainly doesn't care whether Kirk agrees with his conduct or approves of his values.

Second, Nietzsche would say that when Marcus contrasts the strength of his own species with the weakness of humans, he is showing his bias toward his race and his disdain of newcomers to his planet. As the German philosopher himself observed: "The profound reverence for age and for tradition— all rest on this double reverence, the belief and prejudice in favor of ancestors and unfavorable to newcomers—is typical in the morality of the powerful." The "powerful," in Nietzsche's view, also value courage, self-reliance, mastery, and creative leadership; thus, the gladiatorial games of Planet IV-892 would certainly appeal to them, for the noble man "takes pleasure in subjecting himself to severity and hardness, and has reverence for all that is severe and hard."

Conversely, the nobility look down on cowardice, humility, compassion, and weakness. In their view, Nietzsche continued, those who are "weak" deserve no respect, because they were only put on the earth to be preyed upon by the strong. Had he been familiar with it, one imagines Marcus might well have quoted Nietzsche's moral theory as he explained to Kirk his exploitation of slaves. Nietzsche believed that

> "Exploitation" does not belong to a depraved, or imperfect and primitive society; it belongs to the nature of the living being as a primary organic function. [It is also the] consequences of the intrinsic Will to Power, which is precisely the Will to Life.

In other words, exploitation is a good thing because it's natural. To express the Will to Power is to compel reality to submit to one's own creative might. We see the Will to Power in nature, which favors life and the strong while shaking out the weak — indeed, "survival of the fittest," as one of Nietzsche's contemporaries, Charles Darwin, once put it. We certainly see this philosophy at work in "Bread and Circuses." Merrick tells Kirk that those members of the *Beagle* crew "who were able to adapt to this world are still alive. Those who couldn't adapt are dead. That's the way it is with life everywhere, isn't it?"

Nietzsche also held that a master may help the unfortunate — not out of pity, but rather from an impulse generated by an abundance of power. Again, we see this ethics in action on Planet IV-892. As much as he "exploits" the slaves in his society, Marcus does provide them with guaranteed medical care and old age pensions, simply because he can, given his superabundance of power. We see another instance of the proconsul's "largesse" when, after sentencing Kirk to death, he provides the captain with a sumptuous final meal of wine and roast pheasant. The proconsul then lets the unfortunate Kirk have a final night of passion by loaning him his slave girl Drusilla. Again, these acts of "beneficence" are not done out of pity, but rather because he's come to respect the captain "as a man." "Since you are a man, Kirk," Marcus explains the following morning, "I gave you some last hours as a man." Alas, because Kirk defied him by not surrendering the rest of his crew, Marcus knows he must execute the captain as a show of strength: "We must demonstrate that defiance is intolerable." However, as a final act of "generosity," the proconsul assures Kirk that he, Spock, and McCoy will all die "quickly and easily." What a humanitarian!

Speaking of Drusilla...though we see no other female characters on Planet IV-892, one gets the impression, based on the way Marcus treats his slave girl, that the Roman Proconsulate has decidedly sexist values. This, again, is very much a characteristic of Nietzsche's master morality: "Every aristocratic morality is intolerant...in the control of women." Now, don't think for a moment that Nietzsche disapproved of this intolerance, for he also observed that aristocratic morality "counts intolerance itself among the virtues, under the name of 'justice.'" The fact is, Nietzsche was a noted misogynist—to him, much of the "slave" still remains in women "which seeks to seduce good opinions of itself." This disdain for women permeates his works.

THE CHILDREN OF THE SUN

This brings us to the slave morality, which, Nietzsche believed, originates with the lowest elements of society: the abused, the oppressed, the slaves, and those who are uncertain of themselves. Naturally, the Children of the Sun fall under this category. In the slave morality, "good" symbolizes those qualities that make suffering easier, such as "sympathy, the kind, help-ing hand, the warm heart, patience, diligence, humility, and friendliness"—all of which, of course, are values espoused by the Children of the Sun. The slave associates "evil" with strength, the arousal of fear, and the will and the power to rule—in other words, every value the master morality holds dear. Naturally, the master would put a different spin on things, insisting that he who arouses fear is good because he "seeks to arouse it." Marcus champions the master's value when he tells Kirk that the Romans do not fear death, then tries to get the captain to exhibit the slave morality ("Admit it, Kirk—you find the games frightening, repellent"). Kirk, how-ever, knows Marcus is trying to arouse fear in him and doesn't give him the satisfaction: "In some parts of the galaxy, Procon-sul, I have seen forms of entertainment that would make this look like a folk dance!"

That the Children of the Sun express Christian values is particularly fitting for our purposes. Nietzsche, as it happens, believed the slave morality is a perverted morality for which Christianity is entirely responsible. The first Christians, after all, were outcasts; thus, the way Nietzsche saw it, they created a value system solely designed to meet the needs of outcasts. Their morality became the morality of the herd, where no one is supposed to raise his head higher than the rest of the herd. Christianity, in short, promotes mediocrity precisely because it favors the weak, the sick, and the old. (Given these views, of course, it's also appropriate to note that Septimus, the leader of the Children of the Sun, is an elderly man.)

The other problem with Christianity, in Nietzsche's view, is that it promotes resentment against those in power. Indeed, he claimed, if the abused, the oppressed, the suffering, the une-mancipated, the weary, and those uncertain of themselves were ever to establish moral codes of their own, they would likely reject the virtues of the powerful and stress those qualities that made their own lives easier. In Nietzsche's eyes, Christian values such as sympathy, generosity, patience, humility, and friendliness are not noble, but rather the products of weak, embittered slaves who hated the independence, strength, and pride of their rulers. As we see in "Bread and Circuses," the Children of the Sun do indeed oppose the virtues of Marcus and the rest of the Roman government. The Children's emphasis on nonviolence, love, and brotherhood certainly makes life easier for them—not to mention Kirk, Spock, and McCoy (especially after Septimus tells Flavius to lay off them at the beginning of the show).

As for Nietzsche's claim that Christianity is responsible for the entire slave morality... if that's the case, *Star Trek* suggests, then what's wrong with that? When Uhura discovers that the "Sun" worshiped by the Children is actually the Son of God, Kirk, Spock, and McCoy deduce that, just as the Christian philosophy replaced that of Imperial Rome on Earth 2,000 years before, a similar philosophy of "total love and total brotherhood" will also replace the Imperial Rome of Planet IV-892 in "their 20th-century." The very thought pleases Kirk to no end: "Wouldn't it be something to watch, to be a part of, to see it all happen again?" Unlike Nietzsche, *Star Trek* clearly believes a nonviolent Christian ethics is an effective counterforce against a morality that promotes aggressive strength.

IS KIRK A MASTER OR A SLAVE?

Still, there's the practical question: how can the weak and downtrodden possibly overtake those who value aggressive strength? Nietzsche would say the reason Christian ethics could replace a society like Imperial Rome is, again, that the slaves resented their masters to the point of rebellion. In his view of Earth history, once the slaves gained power over the masters, the master morality was reversed to the status of evil, while the slave morality was elevated and became the common ideal. The power of the master race was broken by undermining its psychological strength.* By resisting the natural impulse to use aggressive strength, the weak races put forward new values such as pity and humility. According to Nietzsche, this reflects a desire on the part of the weak to undermine the power of the strong. However, in doing so, he added, they created a negative attitude toward the most natural drives of man.

Because Nietzsche claimed the division between slave and master moralities can be found in every culture, to see it depicted in the world of "Bread and Circuses" wouldn't surprise him a bit. But Nietzsche also held that sometimes this division can be found within the same individual. Take Captain Kirk, for example. While he clearly approves of the values of the Children of the Sun, he often acts in a way that Nietzsche would associate with the master morality. He certainly delights in "all that is severe and hard"—though he refuses to take part in Marcus' gladiatorial games, we know he's also willing to duke it out with just about anybody at the drop of a hat. In a crisis situation, he'll often take matters into his hands, regardless of whether Spock or Starfleet approve of his actions. As far as being sexist . . . while it's true that Kirk respects the abilities of Uhura and the other women on his crew, when it comes to other females, he's a bit of a rake. In fact, as one writer put it: "There is little critical support for reading Kirk as anything other than an oppressive patriarch bent on conquering the galaxy and sexually dominating all the young and 'beautiful' women he encounters in the process."†

---

*Nietzsche was not thinking of ancient Rome, but rather of early Greek history, before the time of Socrates.
†Elyce Rae Helford, "A Part of Myself No Man Should Ever See," in *Enterprise Zones,* ed. Taylor Harrison et al. (Boulder: Westview Press, 1996), p. 11.

On the other hand, Kirk certainly does feel pity, often extends a helping hand, truly believes in peace and equality, and generally does not seek to arouse fear in others (unless he or his crew is threatened). All of these characteristics, of course, are contrary to traditional master morality. So the captain clearly does exhibit both master and slave moralities.

Nietzsche, of course, would consider "The Enemy Within" a perfect illustration of the division of master and slave moralities in the same person. Rational Kirk would be considered a "slave" because he is empathetic, unsure of himself, and utterly weakened by his inability to decide. Irrational Kirk, naturally, would be categorized as a "master" because he aggressively seeks to arouse fear in others, cares little for anyone else's approval of his actions, and "controls" Yeoman Rand by sexually abusing her.

THEISTIC EXISTENTIALISM IN THE ALPHA AND DELTA QUADRANTS

Though widely considered a 20th-century phenomenon, existentialism clearly originated in the 1800s. In fact, as long as we're being technical, Nietzsche wasn't even the first existentialist thinker. That honor goes to our friend Søren Kierkegaard (a Christian philosopher, ironically enough), whose teachings frequently spoke of guilt, paradox, anxiety, and other ideas that have since become associated with existentialism. Like other existentialists, Kierkegaard believed existence in itself is absurd and meaningless.

Now what exactly does this mean? Kierkegaard would say life is meaningless because it has no "meaning" that can be determined by reason. In other words, when it comes to answering such burning questions as how we should live or what we should live for—in essence, what our life is supposed to "mean"—our reason will ultimately fail us. The "meaning of life" is not something we can find in a book or glean from any-one else; it doesn't "exist" in a rational sense. Since that's the case, we cannot really find the meaning of life unless we find it within ourselves. Thus, for Kierkegaard, in order to become an authentic human being, we must find our own meaning.

The linchpin of Kierkegaard's philosophy is his concept of the three stages of existence. As we know from Chapter 9, Kierkegaard equated the process of a person moving from one stage to the next (aesthetic to ethical to religious) with our pro-gressive development as individuals. This principle helped us understand how Sisko developed as a character over the course of *Deep Space Nine*. Though visibly uncomfortable with his role as Emissary to the Bajoran people when the series first began, the captain eventually grew to accept his responsibility, to the point where (as we saw for ourselves in "The Reckoning") he takes a "leap of faith" and becomes a man who exists purely on a religious level. True, the values the captain embraces aren't exactly Christian. They are, however, certainly theistic. For that reason, let's refer to Kierkegaard's philosophy as "theistic" exis-tentialism.

Voyager also exhibits a streak of theistic existentialism in "Sacred Ground" (*VGR:* #43), in which Janeway finds she must also take a "leap of faith" in order to save Kes' life. While visit-ing an alien planet governed by the Nikani, a religious order, the away team observes monks passing in and out of a sacred chamber. A curious Kes tries to explore the chamber herself, only to be stricken by a powerful force field that leaves her comatose and near death. Soon we learn the force field is actu-ally an intense biogenic field. When the Doctor can't revive Kes, the monks tell Janeway the only way to save her is for the captain to undergo a religious ritual and converse with the ancestral spirits. Though a total skeptic by nature, Janeway agrees, hoping that some physiological change will occur dur-ing the ritual to make withstanding the force field possible.

Besides, she says to Chakotay, "I imagine if we scratch deep enough, we'll find a scientific base for most religious doctrines."

At this point, Kierkegaard would say, Janeway is behaving like a person living at the ethical level—displaying the virtue of a good friend hoping to find a practical cure to a life-threatening dilemma. With the help of a guide, she allows herself to be taken through the motions of the ritual, and is eventually taken to a small room where a woman and two old men are sitting on a bench. Though she wonders if they're also going through the ritual, they confound her by saying they're just sitting and "waiting." When the trio mock the captain for her scientific bias and supreme confidence in rationality, Janeway becomes impatient and bursts out of the room. Janeway becomes even more confused when her guide insists that the entire ritual is "meaningless"—the only thing that matters is finding her connection to the spirits. After surviving a rock-climbing ordeal, Janeway is presented with a nesset, a snakelike poisonous creature that bites the captain and causes her to fall into a trance that will last 39 hours. While entranced, she pleads for Kes' life, only to be told by her guide that her request "is inconsequential. You have what you need to save her yourself." But for that to happen, the guide continues, Janeway must surrender reason along with her need to be in control. She must have faith.

This, of course, sets the stage for the sort of crisis Kierkegaard believed is inevitable for the person who exists purely on an ethical level. There comes a time when such a person realizes how impossible it is to satisfy all aspects of moral law, or encounters phenomena that are impossible to explain by purely rational means. At this point, the ethical person finds himself at a crossroads: either remain at the ethical level, or move onto the religious level by an act of total commitment—indeed, a "leap of faith" that surpasses all rationality or morality.

Janeway is at such a crossroads when she finally realizes everything she went through was in fact "meaningless"—the ritual challenges were merely concocted to satisfy her need for a challenge. For Kierkegaard, coming face-to-face with meaninglessness can often jolt people from their certitude, making them aware of the limitations of reason. Until we acknowledge the meaninglessness of our existence, we can never be in a position to fulfill ourselves.

Kierkegaard contrasted the impersonal objectivity of reason with a committed subjectivity to faith. There is no objective truth in life, only a personal truth found in the act of commitment to a choice. At this point in "Sacred Ground," Janeway could be characterized as what Kierkegaard called the "serious" person who relies on her detached understanding to solve problems. He argued that the serious person is unable to take a genuine risk:

> If he does not get certainty, our serious man says in all earnest that he refuses to risk anything, since that would be madness. In this way the venture of our serious man becomes merely a false alarm. If what I hope to gain by venturing is itself certain, I do not risk or venture, but make an exchange.

To become a truly human being (or a "subject," as Kierkegaard would put it), Janeway must choose and act in the absence of reason. Until she does, she is not really risking anything.

Janeway decides to go through the ritual again—only this time, she acknowledges her ignorance, telling her guide she's flat-out confused. That's a good sign, says the guide: "Now you're ready to begin." As Socrates once taught, and as Kierkegaard would undoubtedly agree, true wisdom starts with admitting that you know nothing. Reentering the room with the three old folks—who she now realizes are the ancestral spirits—Janeway waits when she is asked to wait. Mocking the captain's unconditional trust in her ability to reason things out, one of the spirits observes, "Even when her science fails right before her eyes she still has full confidence in it. Now there's a leap of faith." Perhaps despite herself, Janeway tries to open her mind to the possibility that something more than science is at work in the religious rites. Her love of truth, an Aristotelian virtue, leads her to move to the religious level.

The spirits then tell Janeway the only way to save Kes is not just by going beyond logic, but by outright defying reason. The captain must carry Kes back through the shrine's energy field. If she truly believes, the spirits insist, Kes will be cured—but if she has the slightest doubt, they both will die. Chakotay, representing reason in this case, insists this is tantamount to suicide—after all, the ship's sensors indicate that the force field is lethal. Even Kierkegaard would say Janeway is about to engage in a genuine risk. Nonetheless, she surrenders all reason and takes a leap of faith. Though she doesn't understand why ("That's the challenge," she admits to Chakotay), her faith in this instance is unshakable. Moments after carrying her friend back into the force field, the captain's faith is rewarded—Kes awakens. Though the holographic Doctor will later offer an ironclad naturalistic explanation for Kes' recovery, Janeway for once is not so sure that science had anything to do with it.

Although we never again see Janeway acting at the religious level, it's worth noting the remark she makes to Seven at the end of "The Omega Directive" (*VGR:* #89): "If I didn't know you better, I'd say you had your first spiritual experience." Presumably the captain recognizes in Seven what she herself went through in "Sacred Ground," where not even she could deny the theistic nature of this particular existential experience.

EXISTENCE PRECEDES ESSENCE... OR, A FEW WORDS ON THE NATURE OF PAPER CUTTERS, REPLICATORS, AND HOLOGRAPHIC DOCTORS

Kierkegaard and Nietzsche prepared the way for Jean-Paul Sartre and 20th-century existentialism by rejecting all past ethical theories—none of which, they believed, expressed any interest in the existence of the human individual. Like his predecessors, Sartre was deeply concerned with the nature of the choices we make in our daily lives. Unlike Kierkegaard, however, Sartre and Nietzsche were atheists.

Sartre (1905–1980) won but refused to accept the Nobel Prize for literature. You could say he was exercising his power of choice—after all, the French philosopher and novelist argued that first we exist, then we choose the essence or nature we will have. In the case of the human being alone, Sartre claimed that "existence precedes essence." The fact that we exist before we know how our characters will turn out makes us unique among other existing things.

Sartre held that the nature of human beings cannot be explained in the same way we describe a manufactured article. Just consider your standard, ordinary paper cutter. Sartre argued that long before the paper cutter exists, long before it's even been made, the manufacturer already conceives it as having a definite purpose, and as being the product of a definite process. If we were to consider the "essence" of the paper cutter to mean the procedure by which it was made and the purpose for which it was produced, then the essence of the paper cutter would indeed precede its existence. This, of course, is the complete opposite of "existence precedes essence." For Sartre, this radical difference between human beings and manufactured items illustrates how little the two have in common. In terms of ethics, this suggests that we owe no moral obligation whatsoever to paper cutters and other household tools and appliances—in other words, things whose essence is designed for the sole purpose of fulfilling certain human needs.

If this sounds a little abstract, think back to Chapter 6 and the situation Janeway faces in "Latent Image" (*VGR:* #105). An error in the "feedback logic" between the Doctor's cognitive and ethical programming caused the continual replay of a traumatic moment: faced with two equally critically injured patients (Harry Kim and Ensign Jetal), but with only enough time to save one of them, the Doctor chose to rescue Kim simply because he knew him better. Because the Doctor had become destructively obsessed about this particular memory, to the point where he could no longer function properly, Janeway deleted it from his system—without consulting him. Eighteen months later, with the help of Seven of Nine, the Doctor learns what the captain did and demands to know why. However, because Janeway fears a full explanation might cause the conflict in the Doctor's ethical programming to recur, she tells him he will simply have to accept her decision.

Naturally, Seven challenges Janeway's judgment and confronts her about it—in the middle of the night: "I am having trouble with the nature of individuality." Though the captain tries to put off the conversation ("There's a time and a place for philosophical discussion, Seven"), her protégée persists in her belief that the decision regarding the Doctor was wrong. Resigned to defending herself there and then, Janeway uses an analogy that also illustrates Sartre's point about the nature of paper cutters. Ordering a cup of "hot coffee" from the replicator, only to find her drink lukewarm, she complains that regardless of how often she specifies the temperature of her coffee, the replicator "just doesn't seem to want to listen—almost as if it's got a mind of its own. But it doesn't. A replicator operates through a series of electronic pathways that allow it to receive instructions and take appropriate action, and there you go—a cup of coffee, a bowl of soup, a plasma conduit, whatever we tell it to do." The holographic Doctor, she explains, "is more like that replicator than he is like us."

Using the terms of Sartre's principle, the replicator's essence precedes its existence because it was manufactured by a certain procedure for a specific purpose. The process by which it was made and its purpose for being were present in the manufacturer's mind before the actual replicator existed. Likewise, Janeway insists, the Doctor's essence preceded his existence insofar as he was designed by someone who followed a certain procedure for a specific purpose. Unlike humans, the paper cutter and the Doctor do not have a choice as to how they will ultimately function. Accordingly, neither is entitled to the kind of moral obligation a human being would ordinarily expect. (This, of course, is the same argument Riker has to use when forced to prosecute the case against Data in "Measure of a Man," *TNG: #35*.)

Seven doesn't buy that. Given her Borg hardware, she's just as much a manufactured item as the Doctor is. Why is her autonomy respected and the Doctor's not? Apples and oranges, says Janeway: "You're a human being. He's a hologram." Though it may seem the captain is stating the obvious, she's really emphasizing Sartre's basic point: there's a vast difference between a being who determines her own purposes and one whose purpose is determined by others. Janeway, like Sartre, suggests that the gap between the two types of beings justifies respecting the autonomy of humans while disregarding it in the case of holographic doctors, replicators, or any other preprogrammed being.

But Seven reminds Janeway that although she was originally a preprogrammed being while part of the Borg Collective, she was ultimately allowed to evolve into an individual. More to the point, Seven adds, the captain also allowed the holographic Doctor to evolve, "to exceed his original programming. And yet, now you choose to abandon him."

These words strike a nerve in Janeway, to the point where she seriously questions the wisdom of her decision. "There's a battle going on between the Doctor's original programming and what he's become," she confides in B'Elanna Torres. "I decided to end the battle. But what if I was wrong? We allowed him to evolve, and at the first sign of trouble... We gave him a soul. Are we allowed to take it away now?"

Though Torres tries to assuage the captain ("We gave him personality subroutines—I'd hardly call that a soul!"), her words have no effect. Janeway realizes that once she allowed the Doctor to evolve as a personality, she gave him the power to choose his essence as an individual—much the same way, Sartre would add, that we as humans choose our own essence.

This sets the stage for another conversation between Janeway and Seven that mirrors their existential dialogue from earlier in the show. This time, it's the captain who awakens the protégée because she is having "trouble with the nature of individuality."

"You require a philosophical discussion," observes Seven dryly, using the captain's own words against her.

Though Janeway gets Seven's drift, that doesn't stop her from pulling rank. "There's a time and a place for it. This is one of them." She then cuts to the chase: "After I freed you from the Collective, you were transformed. It's been a difficult process. Was it worth it?"

"I had no choice," deadpans Seven.

"That's not what I asked you," says Janeway.

Seven, of course, knows this, and proceeds to ask herself the captain's real question: "If I could change what happened, erase what you did to me... would I?" After giving the matter a great deal of thought, Seven finally replies, "No."

Sure enough, the "feedback logic" error plagues the Doctor again when the memory of his trauma is restored. This time, however, rather than "ending the battle" for him by erasing the unpleasantness from his life, Janeway decides to help the Doctor work through his crisis himself. Over the next two weeks, she keeps a round-the-clock vigil as the Doctor works his way through his anxiety, pondering possibilities that create more pathways than his program can follow. When Janeway falls asleep one night from exhaustion, the Doctor finally snaps out of his existential crisis by insisting that she go to sickbay. Though the captain waves him off ("Doctor, I'm a little busy right now—helping a friend"), he assures her that he'll be all right and urges her to get some rest.

AMNESIA ON THE *ENTERPRISE* AND SELF-CREATION

Before we bid adieu to "Latent Image," there's one last element of the episode that's pertinent to our discussion. When Janeway leaves for sickbay at the end of the show, the Doctor picks up the book she dropped when she fell asleep. It's the same book, as a matter of fact, she was trying to read when Seven interrupted her at the beginning of the story: *La Vita Nova* (A New Life), Dante Alighieri's classic tale of rebirth.

A new life, according to Sartre, depends on the decisions we make and the actions we take. Life is a constant challenge, because we all are constantly creating ourselves as we live our lives. Each of us is a work in progress—we make ourselves the way we are, and we have the ability to remake ourselves at any time, if we so choose. Oftentimes our choices can take us in a different direction than we'd imagined. Long before they were Children of the Sun, for example, both Septimus and Flavius were active members of the Roman establishment—Septimus was a senator, while "Flavius Maximus" was one of the most popular gladiators in the televised Roman arena. Once they heard the message of the Son, both men rejected the values of their old lifestyle and remade themselves in a new light.

Septimus and Flavius are not the only characters in "Bread and Circuses" who reinvented themselves after rejecting the values of their previous lives. Though prohibited from attempting a rescue mission by Condition Green (the secret code Kirk had relayed to the *Enterprise* indicating that he is in trouble), Scotty manages to save the captain anyway by disrupting the planet's energy supply just as Kirk is about to be executed on live television. When Kirk uses the confusion to extricate Spock and McCoy from their cell, Merrick gets a glimpse of how a true starship captain is supposed to act in the face of danger. Rather than deciding that his nature was chosen for him by his previous choices, the man known as "the Butcher" chooses to re-create himself and rescue the *Enterprise* three. Having stolen Kirk's communicator from the proconsul, Merrick uses it to have the captain, Spock, and McCoy beamed off the planet—an act of treachery that costs him his life. (Claudius Marcus, for that matter, also had an opportunity to re-create himself by sparing Kirk once he grew to respect him. However, by electing to execute the captain in order to save face, he ultimately decided his nature was in fact chosen for him.)

"Conundrum," of course, illustrates the concept of remaking oneself even more dramatically. When the Satarrans drain them of their short-term memories, the crew of the *Enterprise* are forced to re-create themselves through their decisions and actions. Because of their amnesia, they can make themselves completely different from what they were before. For example, though Commander Riker and Ensign Ro Laren are normally at each other's throats, in their "blank slate" state they become friends—and then lovers! Of course, Sartre would remind us that we don't need to lose our memories in order to create who we are and who we will become. We're capable of doing this every moment of every day of our existence.

Sartre also believed that as we choose to make ourselves into a certain sort of person, at the same time we also choose for all people—that is, as we create our own values, we also create an image of human nature as we believe it should be. "In fact, in creating the man that we want to be," Sartre writes, "there is not a single one of our acts which does not at the same time create an image of man as we think he ought to be. To choose to be this or that is to affirm at the same time the value of what we choose."

In other words, when we make choices, we must also ask ourselves whether we would be willing (or "rationally will," to use Kant's phrase) for others to choose the same action. Whether we realize it or not, we become role models for others through the choices we make. By choosing to pursue a sexual relationship with Ro, Riker is telling the rest of his crew (as well as those of us watching at home) that he believes sleeping with your coworkers is perfectly okay for all of us, too. Similarly, when I recycle my newspapers, cans, and bottles every week, or choose vegetarianism over eating meat, these are more than just my personal values—these are values I believe to be important for all others, and that's why I want others to choose them as well.

Because the individual choices we make concern not only ourselves but all of humanity, Sartre would say that we are endorsing our choices as virtues that all people should follow. Whenever we chose a particular course of action (be it vegetarianism, recycling, or interoffice dating), we approve the value of what we have chosen. Sartre emphasized this very point as follows:

Certainly, many people believe that when they do something, they themselves are the only ones involved, and when someone says to them, "What if everyone acted that way?" they shrug their shoulders and answer, "Everyone doesn't act that way." But really, one should always ask himself, "What would happen if everybody looked at things that way?" There is no escaping this disturbing thought.... A man who lies and makes excuses for himself by saying "not everybody does that," is someone with an uneasy conscience.

This passage makes us reflect on how easy it is to rationalize our actions, and how often we do it. Yet Sartre insisted that people who attempt to do this actually know "deep down" that they are responsible for their actions.

Which brings us back to the image with which we closed the previous chapter—Sisko anguishing over the choices he made in "In the Pale Moonlight" (*DS9:* #143). Though the captain acted like a utilitarian throughout the episode, and tried convincing himself that he could "live with" his choices because the ends justified the means, the man we see at the end of the show is clearly "someone with an uneasy conscience." Sartre would say that Sisko forced himself to consider "What would happen if everybody looked at things that way"—and found the answer immensely disturbing. For these reasons, we can safely assume that the captain does not endorse the choices he made as virtues all of us should follow.

EXISTENTIAL ANGST... OR, PICARD AND KIRK ARE CONDEMNED TO BE FREE

Sartre insisted we have an absolute responsibility to ourselves and to each other. No matter how tempting it is to shirk this responsibility, we cannot blame anyone else (as much as we may want to) for the sort of person we've become or the kind of choices we've made—not our parents, not our teachers, not our friends, not our family, not television, the movies, nor any other aspect of society. Each of us is responsible for our character and our situation in life.

Since we can't blame anyone but ourselves for our choices and actions, that means our sense of responsibility is heightened immensely. This is why Sartre believed the extreme responsibility of our choices is experienced in anguish—a deep and inescapable sense of uneasiness. The anguish over our choices, as well as the despair at not having access to absolute answers, causes the "existential angst" with which all of us, Sartre said, must live.

Sisko experiences existential angst in "In the Pale Moonlight," as does the Doctor in "Latent Image." Likewise, Janeway is frequently wrought with anguish due to a critical decision she made in "Caretaker," *Voyager*'s premicre episode. Upon taking *Voyager* into the Badlands to track down a Marquis ship, the captain chose to destroy the Caretaker's array—the ship's only way home—in order to save the Ocampa planet. This leaves *Voyager* stranded in the Delta Quadrant, 75 light-years away from home. Instead of blaming the enemy, Janeway assumes full responsibility for her decision—a burden that erupts into full-blown existential angst in "Night" (*VGR:* #95), wherein she castigates herself for the "error in judgment" that, in her mind, has left her crew lost in space. While the captain's self-reprobation perhaps goes a bit too far (as we know from our last chapter, she hides herself from her crew for several weeks), it certainly underscores Sartre's point that in making our own choices, we also choose for all people. Indeed, Sartre would say that Janeway's admission and angst shows us that she lives "authentically," shouldering the burden of her responsibility and not making excuses.

In "Conundrum," after the Satarran operative MacDuff convinces Picard to destroy a Lysian vessel, he likewise faces the inescapable anguish of which Sartre spoke. The Satarrans, as we know, have manipulated the amnesiac captain into believing the Lysians are a genocidal race responsible for what has happened to his crew. Shortly after crossing the Lysian border, the *Enterprise* scans what appears to be a Lysian destroyer—only to find it poorly armed and barely shielded. The vessel hails them, but MacDuff discourages Picard from responding: "No! Their new weapon—whatever it is that erased our computers and memories. Maybe this is how they do it—over communication channels!" With no apparent choice, Picard fires on the Lysian ship, wiping it out with a single shot.

Though MacDuff assures Picard that obliterating the vessel was the right thing to do, the experience leaves the captain deeply disturbed . . . and grasping for answers. Surely the Federation could not have warranted an attack on an "enemy" whose weapons technology is so blatantly inferior, and whose 53-member crew was dwarfed by that of the *Enterprise*. At this point, Picard begins to seriously doubt the morality of his "mission"—destroying the entire Lysian command post. Sartre would say this is not a decision that can be made lightly by a person of conscience. Such a person may experience a profound sense of uneasiness, since he doesn't know beforehand if he will make the right decision.

Picard knows he is free to make his own decisions. This is important, because he could have identified so strongly with the role of a Starfleet captain that he could have just as easily forgotten it is only a role. He could have easily forgotten that he had to make a major decision that would be his responsibility, since he was free to accept Starfleet's order or reject it.

Sartre maintained that in personal matters no one can make our decisions for us. To illustrate this point, Sartre once told an audience about a student who came to see him during the German occupation of France. The student was caught in a dilemma between two fundamentally conflicting kinds of morality: a morality of personal devotion and a morality of defending society. Because the boy's mother was sick and elderly, she was totally dependent on him. Though the boy desperately wanted to help his mother, he also wanted to go to England so that he could join the Free French Army and help fight the Germans. Anguished over what to do, he sought Sartre for advice. Sartre then told the audience the following:

> Who could help him choose? Certainly not Christian doctrine, since both choices satisfy the criteria of a Christian choice. Nor again Kantian ethics, for he cannot consistently treat everyone as an end, for someone will have to be treated as a means. I had only one answer to give. "You're free, choose..."

Sartre's anecdote serves to remind us that being totally free means we can only choose in anguish and alone, without anyone else—an existentialist principle Picard put into practice in "Ethics." Torn between his respect for Worf and his personal beliefs against suicide, a despondent Riker asks the captain what to do when the Klingon seeks his help with the *Hegh'bat* ceremony. Though Picard clearly feels Riker's pain, he reminds Number One that he must ultimately decide for himself.

For Sartre, freedom is the source of all value and meaning. This means we are radically free, since at any moment we can choose to become a new sort of person, psychologically as well as (to some extent) physically. We don't need a self-help guru to remind us we all have the power to change our lives. Would you like to lose weight or tone your body? Want to be kinder, gentler? How about becoming more intellectual, or more creative? No one can stop us from reaching these goals but ourselves. We set our own limits.

The Anthony Robbinses of the world refer to this concept as "empowerment." Sartre, however, used a much different term: he said we are "condemned to be free." This is an odd expression, insofar as freedom, the way most of us think of it, implies a lack of condemnation. But the way Sartre saw it, we are "condemned" as human beings because we did not choose to be born in a particular situation. And yet, once we're thrown into existence, we are free. We must live with the burden of choice forever.

Sartre also believed that although we're free to choose, we are not free to refrain from choosing. As he put it: "I ought to know that if I do not choose, I am still choosing." We see this existentialist concept expressed in "The Omega Glory" (*TOS:* #54), wherein Kirk discovers that Captain Ron Tracey of the Starship *Exeter* violated the Prime Directive by using his phaser on the natives of planet Omega IV. Though Federation regulations clearly require Kirk to arrest Tracey, our hero can't quite decide what to do. After all, Tracey's use of his phaser was the only way to ensure his own survival as well as the survival of a peaceful village. Reflecting Sartre's principle that we cannot avoid choice, Spock pointedly reminds the captain that if he doesn't act, "we will be considered equally as guilty."

Like Spock, Sartre knew that if we try to deceive ourselves into thinking we don't have to make a choice, we've actually made a choice: namely, to let others choose for us. Attempting to avoid commitments is no different from any other choice we make. Like recycling, eating vegetarian, mentoring a child, or donating to charitable causes, it's an expression of value that implicitly "involves all mankind," and for which we must "take full responsibility." We cannot avoid making choices that have value implications that could impact the sort of persons we become. For Sartre, a human being is "nothing else than the ensemble of his acts, nothing else than his life," whose unrealized "potential" counts for nothing. Therefore, we must always be involved in, and committed to, action.

SHOULD PICARD FOLLOW HIS ORDERS?

Sartre emphasized there is no escape from freedom — or, as the Borg would put it, resistance is futile. Now, what could that possibly mean? We've heard of escaping from captivity, but who would want to resist freedom?

Just about anyone, said Sartre, if they knew what freedom actually means. In fact, Sartre believed we don't really want to be free because of the responsibility it entails. More to the point, we want the best of both worlds: we want the benefits of freedom, but without the burden of responsibility. We don't really want to have to choose who we are and what we become, so we try to escape our freedom by shirking responsibility. We may not realize it, but we do this every time we say things such as "I don't have time for this," "She makes me so mad," "Everybody else does it," "It's none of my business," "He told me to do it," "That wasn't me—it was my evil twin," and so forth.

That freedom entails responsibility holds true not only on a very personal level, but also in our relationship to society. Rather than blaming society as an abstraction, we should work to change it. Sartre insisted that our "dreams, expectations and hopes" that things were somehow different count for nothing: "For instance, unless we say 'no' to an immoral order from authorities, we are just as responsible as the person who gave the order is." In other words, by choosing to hide behind the old standby "I was just following orders," we're only fooling ourselves into thinking that we had no choice in the matter. We're deceiving ourselves by choosing to believe that we can only be what our parents, our friends, our society, or our superiors want us to be.

We know, however, that Picard is not one who usually deceives himself. With that in mind, let's return to "Conundrum" to see how he handles his freedom and responsibility. Concerned about the lack of corroborative evidence from the Federation, and increasingly suspicious about the precise nature of his ship's missing data files (not to mention the strangely specific memory loss suffered by his crew), Picard tells MacDuff that he has "grave concerns" about their mission and doubts "whether or not it can be justified." As we can see from the following exchange, the captain takes his responsibility to society very, very seriously:

> MACDUFF: I'm sure our superiors feel our orders are justified.
> PICARD: Orders we can't even verify.
> MACDUFF: Orders we can't ignore.
> PICARD: I also can't ignore that we have greatly outclassed the one enemy vessel we've encountered. I feel as though I've been handed a weapon, sent into a room and told to shoot a stranger. Every possible shred of information which might shed light on this has been conveniently eliminated. Well, I need some moral context to justify that action—and if I don't have it, I'm not content simply to obey orders. I need to know that what I'm doing is right.

The duplicitous MacDuff humors Picard by saying, in effect, wouldn't it be nice if all our questions were answered. But the Satarran spy, intent on carrying out *his* mission, continues to try to goad the captain into action: "Is it right to allow prolonging the war—to allow the needless deaths of thousands on both sides—solely on the basis of our moral discomfort?" This is the same question that Sisko asked himself in the episode "In the Pale Moonlight."

Leaving Picard alone to ponder his decision, MacDuff then goes into Plan B. Summoning Worf to his quarters, he tries appealing to the Klingon as a fellow warrior "born to combat." Sartre would say that MacDuff is trying to convince Worf that he was born with a nature (or an essence) that he cannot change. The Satarran wants Worf to believe the mission to destroy the Lysian command post must succeed, and that their warrior skills make them uniquely qualified for the battle ahead. Given Picard's vacillation on the issue, they might have to take matters into their own hands. This, Sartre would add, puts Worf in the position of making an important choice that will affect not only what happens to the Lysians and the *Enterprise,* but also the sort of person he will become. After all, like the rest of the crew, Worf at this juncture is still under Mac-Duff's spell—he doesn't remember who he is, or that he's part of a team that relies on each member's judgment in moments of critical decision. Will Worf's warrior tendencies determine his actions—that is, will he act as though his nature has already been determined? Or will he exercise his freedom to remain a loyal member of the crew?

Picard, of course, is not content to merely wish that his orders could be different. Nor will he be content to let Starfleet accept responsibility for the orders he believes it gave him. Indeed, he knows that if he follows these orders, he's just as responsible as Starfleet. Once he determines that the Lysian command station has very little by way of defensive capabilities, and that over 15,000 lives are at stake, he refuses to carry out the attack: "I do not fire on defenseless people."

Naturally, MacDuff tries to belay the order by insisting Picard has flipped his gourd. The Satarran spy seizes command and orders Worf to fire all weapons. Now it's time for Worf to make a decision that will determine the course of his life. Without any memory of where his loyalty lies, he must choose what sort of person he is: whether his nature was decided once and for all at birth, or whether he can choose the sort of nature he will have. He decides to refuse MacDuff's order. Though the Satarran makes a last-ditch effort to control the ship, Worf and Riker stun him with their phasers, exposing his alien identity in the process.

Sartre would say that Worf and Picard embrace their freedom—Picard feels free to go against an immoral order, while Worf demonstrates his freedom to contain his warrior inclinations. At the same time, they take responsibility for their own actions. Worf knows that he's not just a cog in Starfleet's wheel, but rather an individual responsible for controlling his inclinations and for the fate of both the Lysians and his fellow crew members. Meanwhile, Picard not only refuses to rationalize his plight by shifting the blame to Starfleet, he acknowledges his responsibility by apologizing to the Lysians for the tragedy of their lost crew and ship. Rather than saying "Mac-Duff made me do it" or "I was not in my right mind," he exercises his freedom as an individual by accepting responsibility for the mistakes he has committed. The captain knows that he doesn't have to continue making the same mistakes he made in the past, but instead is free to become a different sort of individual, at any moment of his life, according to the kind of choices he makes. And, Sartre insisted, so are we!

And now it's time for us to embrace a whole other kind of responsibility. We must choose among the various ethical theories we have examined to determine which indeed is the ethics of *Star Trek*. This responsibility cannot be avoided—resistance is futile. So without further delay, let's proceed at warp speed to the task at hand.

CHAPTER 16

THE ETHICS OF
STAR TREK

Now that we've explored every major ethical theory—relativism, virtue ethics (both Platonic and Aristotelian), hedonism, Stoicism, Christian morality, Hobbes' social contract, duty ethics (encompassing Kant's philosophy, Regan's principles, and Ross' prima facie duties), utilitarianism, and existentialism (Kierkegaard's theistic values, as well as Sartre's atheistic view)—it's time to figure out which of them most adequately reflects the overall ethics of *Star Trek*.

The operative word here is "adequately." Though many theories are quite able to account for normal situations, if we can't apply them to circumstances that are unusual, then their inadequacy becomes apparent. Just as a careful starship captain should always anticipate the unusual course of events, so should a careful thinker be alert to those cases that deviate from the ordinary. Because the *Star Trek* characters are always finding themselves in situations where they have to make snap judgments about what's right and what's wrong, the ethical theory on which they rely must always succeed in providing them with the guidance they need from circumstance to circumstance. Of course, this depends on the scope of the theory. The wider the scope, the greater its range of application; the narrower its scope, the narrower the application. Therefore, the ethics of *Star Trek* should be a theory with a scope broad enough to deal with the unusual situations so regularly depicted in the series and films.

Since adequacy is so crucial, we might as well get rid of any theory that definitely does not represent the views of more than one major *Star Trek* character. We've already discounted ethical relativism because it's fraught with contradiction. The social contract principle is also out, since that's clearly endorsed only by the Ferengi. Though many characters like to vacation on Risa, hedonism as a way of life is uniformly rejected by each series, so we can say *hasta la vista* to that. Finally, given Gene Roddenberry's views on organized religion, we'll have to eliminate Christian values per se (although we'll still consider the theistic aspects of Kierkegaard's existentialist philosophy). That leaves with us five finalists: virtue ethics, duty ethics, Stoicism, utilitarianism, and existentialism.

Next, we'll take a look at each *Star Trek* series and determine the ethical bias of the major characters—Kirk, Spock, and McCoy from the Original Series; Picard, Riker, and Dr. Crusher from *The Next Generation;* Sisko, Odo, and Worf from *Deep Space Nine;* and Janeway and Seven from *Voyager.** Then we'll try to identify each series with one (or more, if more apply) of our five theories. Once we come up with an ethical theory that adequately represents the ethics of *Star Trek,* we'll test its consistency to make sure the theory's principles fit together in a logical way.

One final note before we begin. Bear in mind that as noble as they are, none of the *Star Trek* characters are saints. Just because they embrace a particular ethical theory doesn't necessarily mean they always embody it perfectly. The characters may be heroes, but they also have the same kind of flaws that

---

*We're limiting ourselves to the major players so as to avoid overcomplicating matters. Perhaps we can take a more detailed look at the ethics of the other characters in the next book.

you, I, or any other human being has. This means, of course, that there may be times when their behavior doesn't represent any particular ethical theory at all.

THE VIRTUES OF THE ORIGINAL SERIES

Now, that we've narrowed things down a bit, let's start with the Original Series and determine the ethics of Captain Kirk by first discarding any theory among our five candidates that he himself would reject. For one thing, we know the captain disavows the utilitarian concept of "the greatest good for the greatest number," based on his actions in "The *Galileo* Seven," "The Mark of Gideon," *Star Trek III,* and many other occasions. Combine that with his great disdain for hedonistic utopias ("Maybe we're don't belong in paradise," as he observes in "This Side of Paradise"), and it's safe to say that he doesn't agree with utilitarian ethics. Existentialism doesn't really apply in Kirk's case, either, since he never seems to anguish over the decisions he makes (unless, of course, he's been split in two!).

What about duty ethics? We know for sure he takes his obligation to protect his crew and his ship seriously at all times. But he's not exactly Kantian, given his willingness to bend the rules occasionally if he needs to. The captain's maverick reputation (17 different temporal violations, umpteen breaches of the Prime Directive) undoubtedly stems from his days in the Academy, when he was the only cadet ever to beat the final exam, the insoluble *Kobayashi Maru* scenario. As we know from *Star Trek II,* the *Kobayashi Maru* is a simulated transport ship that has unintentionally crossed into Klingon space. The cadet, acting as captain, receives a distress call indicating that Klingons are about to attack and destroy the ship. If the cadet crosses into Klingon space to attempt a rescue, he's a dead duck, because the Klingons in this exercise have more weapons and more personnel. But if he does nothing, then all 81 crew members and 300 passengers aboard the vessel will more than likely die. In other words, it's your classic no-win situation. What did Kirk do? After two failed attempts, he reprogrammed the simulation computer so that he could succeed. Though the young Kirk won a commendation for original thinking in the line of duty, Kant would clearly disapprove of this action, given his mandate that all moral duties are absolute.

While Kirk certainly takes his obligations seriously, he also believes there are times when conflicting duties rule out acting according to absolute moral laws. In order to reconcile his respect for duty in general with those occasions where even an oath to Starfleet must occasionally be overridden by more pressing concerns, the captain has implicitly adopted Ross' notion of prima facie duties. In episodes such as "Amok Time," he uses reason to decide which of his duties must prevail in a particular situation. More often that not, he chooses to act on the prima facie duties of non-maleficence and gratitude over his loyalty to Starfleet.

This isn't to say Kirk takes his duty of fidelity to Starfleet lightly. As we saw in "This Side of Paradise," the captain, upon looking at one of his medals, chooses his duty to Starfleet over his duty of beneficence to his crew, all of whom want to stay on Omicron Ceti III after succumbing to the effects of the spores. Though remaining on the planet would give everyone immense pleasure, Kirk decides that his oath to Starfleet is more important—just as Ross believes we have a duty to improve the virtue, intelligence, and pleasure of others. He uses a similar justification for intruding in the affairs of Gamma Trianguli VI ("The Apple"). "We do what Starfleet tells us," he says to McCoy.

As a rule, though, whenever Kirk does breach his fidelity to Starfleet (particularly when it comes to obeying the Prime Directive), it's out of deference to an overriding duty of beneficence. Kirk feels that he has an obligation to help individuals act freely and acknowledge their individual responsibility. If he can help them accept their freedom and responsibility, he has helped to improve their virtue. If the situation is such that the captain believes he has a more urgent duty than fulfilling his obligation to Starfleet, he doesn't hesitate to act on the prevailing duty. In other words, he considers duties as prima facie— that is, conditional.

Given Kirk's approach to duty, it shouldn't surprise us to say that he has an Aristotelian take on justice—particularly with regard to equity. Like Ross' philosophy of duty, Aristotle's virtue ethics insists that we take all relevant factors into account when we decide what to do in a particular situation. The captain does this all the time—even when he can't quite make up his mind! Remember how ever-mindful he was in "The Enemy Within" of the shivering conditions Sulu and the rest of the landing party faced on Alpha 177, despite the fact his ability to decide was literally taken away from him.

Kirk also tries to modify his responses by the Aristotelian mean—the intermediate between two extremes of emotion or action. That he relies heavily on the advice of both Spock (extreme reason) and McCoy (extreme emotionalism) shows us how seriously he believes in the importance of achieving the mean in all he does. We've seen Kirk exhibit Aristotelian virtues in many episodes, including mercy to the Gorn ("Arena") and the Horta ("Devil in the Dark"), compassion to Odona ("Mark of Gideon"), altruism and self-sacrifice ("City on the Edge of Forever," "The Savage Curtain," *Generations*), justice ("I, Mudd," "Plato's Stepchildren," "The Cloud Minders"), proper pride ("The Ultimate Computer," "This Side of Paradise"), not to mention courage and friendship on numerous other occasions. In short, the captain's ethical code is drawn from Aristotelian virtue ethics and Ross' prima facie duty ethics, with virtue exerting the greatest pull on him.

Can we say the same for Mr. Spock? Well, the Vulcan certainly has a solid grasp on what "achieving the mean" means. Aristotle believed that while our emotions play a major role in determining virtuous actions, they must always be held in check by our reason. Spock, as he reminds McCoy in "The Enemy Within," manifests this philosophy every day of his life: "I have a human half, as well as an alien half, constantly at war with each other. I survive it because my intelligence wins out over both, makes them live together." Spock also has a keen understanding of equity and friendship, having risked his career for Captain Pike in "The Menagerie," as well as sacrificing his life for Kirk and his friends in *Star Trek II*.

Though duty is also important to our Vulcan friend, he's probably a little more Kantian about it than Kirk. As we know from "The Apple," "Bread and Circuses," and other episodes, he's always quick to remind the captain when he's about to violate the Prime Directive. Spock also recognizes the intrinsic worth of all animals ("Devil in the Dark," *Star Trek IV*), indicating an appreciation for Regan's duty ethics. (Kirk respects the no-harm principle, too, but usually after Spock reminds him about it.)

Spock really differs from the captain, though, in two areas. He's the lone utilitarian of the Original Series, a man who truly believes that "the needs of the many outweigh the needs of the one." As we saw in "The *Galileo* Seven," the lives of two people count for more than his own life, just as the lives of six people count for more than the lives of one. His consideration for the consequences of his actions goes beyond sheer numbers, embodying a deeper-seated empathy for suffering and death than perhaps most humans have. His concern with the pleasure or pain he might cause is also a utilitarian characteristic — though, of course, he usually hides these feelings from the rest of the crew.

Which brings us to the second difference. While Kirk tends to be rash and impetuous, Spock's constant repression of his emotions in favor of reason makes him a natural Stoic. The Vulcan personifies the four qualities that the Stoics believed were essential to living a good life: simplicity of habits, endurance, self-restraint, and dedication to the community. Equally important, he has the wisdom to know the difference between the things he can control and those he can't, a Stoic philosophy that sometimes rubs people the wrong way (as we saw in "The *Galileo* Seven," "Journey to Babel," and other episodes). Therefore, it's logical to conclude that Spock combines utilitarian principles with a Stoic disposition.

What does this mean in terms of the ethics of the Original Series? If we consider only Kirk and Spock, the ethical foundation appears to be a "mean" between virtue/duty ethics and utilitarianism/Stoicism. But there's a third part of the equation—namely, Leonard "Bones" McCoy. Whenever there's a philosophical difference between Kirk and Spock, McCoy sides with the captain more often than not. Case in point: though Spock believes Kirk's destruction of Vaal in "The Apple" would devastate the humanoids of Gamma Trianguli VI, Bones insists that it "will be the making of those people." McCoy's constant needling of Spock also suggests that the views expressed by the Vulcan do not reflect those of the crew as a whole.

Thus, we must conclude that the moral foundation of the original *Star Trek* is a hybrid of Aristotelian virtue and prima facie duty principles. That being said, however, Spock's "Stoic utilitarianism" is nonetheless treated with respect (certainly by Kirk, definitely by the show's writers) as it serves to accentuate the ethics of the series overall.

DUTY ABOUNDS IN *THE NEXT GENERATION*

As we turn our attention to *The Next Generation*, let's ask ourselves whether Jean-Luc Picard would have cheated on the *Kobayashi Maru* scenario. Answer: not on your life! The captain of the *Enterprise*-D staunchly believes that, unless we're dealing with serious exceptional circumstances (such as an actual life-and-death situation), rules are made to be followed. Thus, even though he's breached the Prime Directive himself a few times, he has more frequently advocated its strict interpretation — perhaps because he understands the ramifications of General Order No. 1 more than any other *Star Trek* captain. In "Pen Pals," for example, Picard convenes a meeting of his officers to determine a course of action after Data inadvertently breaches the Prime Directive by communicating with young Sarjenka. Though Data wants the *Enterprise* to intervene upon realizing the girl's planet is in danger, Worf believes they should butt out ("The Prime Directive is not a matter of degree, it is absolute!"). When Dr. Pulaski objects to this kind of "rigidity," Picard defends the Prime Directive by bringing out the implications of her response: "So we make an exception in the deaths of millions. Is it the same if the situation is an epidemic, and not a geological calamity?"

"Absolutely!" says Pulaski, which is precisely the kind of response Picard would expect from a dedicated physician.

But the captain takes it a step further. "What about war? If generations of conflict is killing millions, do we interfere?" When Pulaski has no answer, the captain sighs: "Ah, well! We're all a little less secure in our moral certitude. And what if it's not just killings? What if an oppressive government is enslaving millions? You see, the Prime Directive has many different functions, not the least of which is to *protect us* — to prevent us from allowing our emotions to overwhelm our judgment."

All things considered, Picard seems a bit more respectful of rules than dear old Captain Kirk. You could look it up: Picard rarely breaches the Prime Directive, and has far fewer temporal violations on his record than his predecessor. Given his willingness to heed the rules, that makes the leader of *TNG* far more Kantian in his approach to duty than Kirk ever was. Picard shares Kant's views on personhood (as we know from "I, Borg" and "Measure of a Man"), and believes that because all rational beings have intrinsic worth, they should never be used as a means to achieve an end ("Man of the People," *Insurrection*).

Picard is not alone among the *TNG* crew when it comes to his Kantian approach to obligation. We know that Riker, for one, seriously believes that an oath is always inviolable. Faced with conflicting responsibilities in "A Matter of Honor," he walks the tightrope between his oath to Starfleet and his duty to the Klingons without breaking either. Pressed into duty in "Measure of a Man," Number One argues the case against Data to the best of his ability, although he clearly doesn't want to. Similarly, though he desperately wants to see Deanna become a bridge officer in "Thine Own Self" (*TNG:* #168), Riker cautions that he cannot help her if she is not qualified ("As much as I care for you, my first duty is to the ship").* He shows an astute understanding of Kant's two-step barometer for measuring one's duty in "Ethics" when he refuses to help his friend Worf commit suicide (a principle he could "rationally will" to all people). Not even the power of Q can sway Riker's commitment to duty, as we saw in "Hide and Q." Though a utilitarian would argue that a gift of superpowers could ultimately bring about the greatest good for the greatest number, a person like Riker with strong Kantian principles knows he can overcome such a temptation by sheer force of will.

Granted, as we know from "The Outcast" (*TNG:* #117), sometimes Riker's libido gets him into trouble. He also questions the Edo's strict interpretation of the law when Wesley's life is on the line in "Justice" ("When has justice been as simple

---

*Of course, Deanna is ultimately promoted to full commander by the end of the show.

as a rule book?"), an attitude that's clearly more compatible with prima facie philosophy than Kant's "no exceptions" policy. As a rule, though, Riker believes in the Kantian notion that duty should always come before our personal inclinations.

Kant's influence also extends to Dr. Beverly Crusher, the only crew member in "I, Borg" who acknowledges Hugh's intrinsic worth from the very beginning (though Picard and Geordi eventually recognize the young Borg as a rational being, they initially see him as a means only). Similarly, she is aghast at Toby Russell's utilitarian approach to medicine in "Ethics," arguing that a physician's intention is what ultimately matters, not the consequences of his or her actions. Given all this, it seems safe to say that the ethics of *TNG* is rooted firmly in Kant's system of morality.

Yet as our look at Commander Riker clearly suggests, *TNG* is not completely Kantian. Picard also challenges the Edo god in "Justice" by observing "There can be no justice so long as laws are absolute. Life itself is an exercise in exceptions." Both Aristotle and Ross would say that the captain has a sensitivity to what is just in particular circumstances that goes beyond absolute rules of morality. Indeed, as we know from "Pen Pals," Picard eventually allows Data to save Sarjenka (provided her memories of the *Enterprise* are erased) because he knows that there are some obligations, such as friendship, "that go beyond duty."

Like Captain Kirk, Picard knows that sometimes prima facie duties such as friendship or justice must prevail over his fidelity to Starfleet—an awareness directly tied to his belief in the Aristotelian virtue of equity. Aristotle knew it was unrealistic to exact absolute rules of morality across the board when everyday living itself is an inexact science. While there's a proper course of action for every situation we face, exactly what we should do will always depend on the context—or, as Aristotle put it, "at the right times, on the right occasions, toward the right persons, with the right object, and in the right fashion." Though written law tries to cover all the bases, sometimes a situation comes along that goes beyond the parameters of the law as it was first conceived. Just as Ross' prima facie philosophy provides us with an option to consider when duties conflict, Aristotle's concept of equity allows for the consideration of extraordinary circumstances in our application of justice.

Picard exhibits many of the same virtues we've seen in Kirk, such as courage, compassion, proper pride, and justice. Though somewhat more aloof than Kirk, Picard is no less willing to go to bat for his friends whenever they need him. He fights for Data's daughter, Lal, in "The Offspring" (*TNG*: #64), defends Riker's integrity in "Hide and Q," pleads for Wesley's life in "Justice," argues the case for Data's autonomy in "Measure of a Man," and risks his life to save Data again in *First Contact*. The captain even manifests a virtue that's not always so evident in Kirk: wisdom. While Kirk thrives on his swashbuckling image, Picard usually comes across as a wise king. We see how much he values wisdom, for example, in "Measure of a Man," when he tells his former lover, JAG officer Phillipa Louvois, that she's "always enjoyed the adversarial process more than truth." When Louvois can do no more than sigh in response, Picard hopes that she's "learned some wisdom along the way."

As much as Picard shares Kirk's inclinations toward duty and virtue, he is clearly less willing to bend the rules than his counterpart on the Original Series. This is probably because the captain also adheres to existentialist principles—values that are clearly absent in Kirk's ethical code. Despite his Kantian leanings, Picard cannot completely subscribe to Kant's system because he doesn't believe in absolute rules. At the same time, not having access to absolute rules often leads him to moments of existential angst, as we clearly saw in "Conundrum." Indeed, the captain's private, introspective nature is very compatible with existentialism, which relies heavily on the anguish of choice and the despondency over no absolute rules. Though Picard seems to rely more on atheistic principles than theistic philosophy, we can get a good picture of the captain's ethical development by way of Kierkegaard's three stages of existence.

In "Tapestry," for example, we learn that young Ensign Picard lived his life at what Kierkegaard calls the aesthetic level. Guided strictly by his emotions and impulses, the only thing that mattered was enjoying the pleasures of the senses: he dated two women simultaneously, engaged in frequent barroom brawls, and was given to many youthful indiscretions. However, after being stabbed through the back, Picard abandoned his attitude of selfishness and detachment and moved on to the ethical level, where he develops a code of ethical conduct formulated by reason. Yet as a person motivated by ethical choices, Picard is disturbed by the fact that sometimes he must deliberately violate the Prime Directive to effect justice. His guilt presents him with a new choice: either remain where he is and exercise ethical responses with even more devotion, or choose to exist at the religious level. Unlike Sisko, who made the leap of faith to the religious level when faced with a similar crossroads in *DS9,* Picard chooses to further his commitment to ethical programs and remain at the ethical level.

Picard's atheism, as well as his firm belief that his officers should make their own life-choice decisions without his help, strongly suggests that his personal existentialism more closely reflects the teachings of Sartre. We have noted his profession of atheism in "Who Watches the Watchers?" (*TNG:* #52). After the Mintakans mistake him for their god, Picard tells them, "We haven't had that kind of belief in hundreds of years."

All told, the ethics of *The Next Generation* clearly reflect those of its captain: a solid foundation of Aristotelian virtue ethics, existentialist sensibilities, and Kantian principles that nonetheless allows for prima facie exceptions.

EXISTENTIALISM WEIGHS HEAVILY ABOARD DEEP SPACE NINE

In a sense, *Deep Space Nine* truly does "boldly go where no one has gone before." Unlike the crews of the other three *Star Trek* shows, who "seek out new life and new civilizations" (except when they're worming their way out of black holes), the Federation team aboard the space station Deep Space Nine develops an ongoing relationship with only one civilized world: the spiritual people of Bajor. As we've discussed, the premise of the show can be clearly understood by the kind of ethical theory Benjamin Sisko represents—Kirkegaard's theistic existentialism. The evolution of the man who would be Emissary from a skeptic who resisted being perceived "as an icon, religious or otherwise" (as he said to Kira in "Destiny") to a full-fledged man of faith is a picture-perfect illustration of Kierkegaard's three-stage existentialist development. Though he once referred to the beings the Bajorans worship as "the wormhole aliens," by the end of the series even he believes them to be the Prophets.

Sisko's commitment to life on a purely religious level is put to the ultimate test in "The Reckoning," an episode that closely parallels the saga of Abraham and Isaac—the biblical story which, as we know from Chapter 9, Kierkegaard used as the basis for his book *Fear and Trembling*. The captain's faith in the Prophets is so steadfast that he's willing to sacrifice everything he holds dear, even the life of his own son. Naturally, Kierkegaard would applaud Sisko's actions, reminding him that it isn't enough to follow the rules and be what Starfleet wants him to be—he must take on responsibility for himself. The only way to do that is by making the leap of faith into the religious level. In order to become a truly "authentic" person, Sisko must leave the standards of Starfleet behind (including his love for reason and for things to make sense), choosing to trust in the divine instead—which, of course, he does.

We saw how deeply Picard's Kantian foundation runs throughout the other major characters on *TNG*. Is Sisko's theistic existentialism likewise reflected in his senior officers? We certainly know from "Accession" and "The Reckoning" that Kira is willing to trust in the divine over reason. That would make her, like Sisko, an "authentic" human being in the Kierkegaardian sense. Worf also has a theistic side, based on his support of Kira in "Rapture" during an argument with O'Brien and Jadzia. When Jadzia snorts "Since when did *you* believe in the Prophets?" Worf simply replies, "What I believe in is faith."

But while Kira and Worf understand Sisko's religious commitment, Jadzia, O'Brien, and Dr. Bashir often find it troubling. Jadzia and Bashir, for example, thought Sisko was crazy for letting "The Reckoning" take place instead of allowing them to emit the chroniton particles that would have exorcised the spirits from Kira and Jake's bodies. At the same time, however, many of the captain's officers certainly understand the existential angst he goes through in weighing his choices. Besides being wracked with guilt when his fidelity to Starfleet conflicts with his friendship with Liam Bilby in "Honor Among Thieves," O'Brien is subjected to anguished, guilt-filled memories of a 20-year prison sentence when he is falsely accused of espionage in "Hard Time" (*DS9:* #91). Similarly, the realization that he has been genetically engineered gives Bashir cause for existential anguish in "Dr. Bashir, I Presume?" (*DS9:* #114).

So while Kierkegaard's existentialist teachings may not be the predominant ethical point of view aboard Deep Space Nine, it's pretty clear that existentialism in general certainly abounds. Indeed, Sisko and his officers are conflicted, anguished, tortured individuals with problems that must be solved from within. Many of the choices they make are choices about their own inner states.

Take Odo, for example. As a character, the shape shifter typifies the lost individual who neither understands his role in life nor his own nature. "All my life," he confides in Kira in "Emissary," "I've been forced to pass myself off as one of you . . . always wondering who I really am." Odo's very name comes from the Cardassian word "odo ital," which translates into "nothing" ("Heart of Stone," *DS9:* #60). Since existentialism claims that we are born as nothing, that we have no definite nature, and that we must create our nature by our actions, the shape shifter's name fits in very well with this theory. We can account for Odo's deep feelings of alienation, a distinct characteristic of Sartre's existentialist philosophy, by his own recognition of his "nothingness." As he once told Kira (in "Necessary Evil"), the reason everyone comes to him with problems is because he is "the outsider." Though he frequently comments on the absurd, often petty nature of humanoid behavior, Odo is nonetheless attracted to human beings—much as Kierkegaard himself was attracted to Christianity because of its "absurdity."

In "Broken Link" (*DS9:* #98), Odo finds others of his own kind in an ocean known as the Great Link. Though momentarily attracted to their unity, he soon becomes tormented by clashing responsibilities and indecision. The lure of joining his people, thereby escaping his estrangement, is very tempting. That choice appears to be taken away from the constable, however, when the shape shifters strip him of his powers (thereby giving him further cause for feeling alienated). And yet, as Sartre taught, deceiving ourselves into thinking we have no choice is itself a choice to let others decide for us. Odo knows he's still free to choose between remaining isolated or living as a human among other individuals. Odo chooses to live among humans, even after his powers are restored in "The Begotten" (*DS9:* #110).

There's also evidence of Nietzsche's existentialism on the space station. As a Klingon, Worf exhibits values Nietzsche would associate with the master morality. Worf certainly "takes pleasure in subjecting himself to severity and hardness, and has reverence for all that is severe and hard." We see this, for example, in "Let He Who Is Without Sin," when he chooses to remain in his Starfleet uniform while Jadzia and the others wear clothing much more conducive to Risa's tropical climes. The Klingon also has a "profound reverence for age and tradition," as well as a "belief and prejudice in favor of ancestors and unfavorable to newcomers." Jadzia basically makes the same observation to Worf in "Looking for *par'Mach* in All the Wrong Places" (*DS9:* #101): "You know, for a Klingon who was raised by humans, wears a Starfleet uniform, and drinks prune juice, you're pretty attached to tradition." However, Worf's existentialism is mitigated by his Stoic principles. The Klingon officer's dedication to the community, simplicity of habits, self-restraint, belief in suicide, and endurance (just think of his prenuptial ceremony!) bolster his Stoic ethics to the point where they're nearly as strong as his existentialist streak.

Similarly, though neither Odo, O'Brien, nor Bashir show any theistic existentialist traits, they all integrate their individual existentialism with a strong sense of duty ethics. That should come as no surprise in the case of O'Brien, considering his long tenure under Captain Picard in *The Next Generation* (and, of course, his ethical decision in "Honor Among Thieves" is completely based on Ross' prima facie principles). Odo's approach to duty, on the other hand, is strictly Kantian. There's also a little hedonism in Bashir and O'Brien, given their mutual preoccupation with darts, holosuite programs, and their model of the Alamo.

Nonetheless, despite this influx of Stoicism, duty, and hedonism, the overall ethics of *DS9* is clearly existentialist. Advocates of existentialism ethics are concerned with understanding the anguished human(oid) condition, as well as charged with the necessity of making commitments in order to fulfill our individual potential. As existentialists, Sisko and his officers presuppose that human(oids) have the power to decide about their lives. They know that free will means we can choose the sort of person we want to be and become the person we choose.

THE COLLECTIVE ETHICS OF KATHRYN JANEWAY

So far, we've found that each *Star Trek* series can be characterized by one dominant form of ethics. Will the same pattern hold true for *Voyager*? Let's find out by looking at the ethical code of Kathryn Janeway.

Though she can be as impetuous as James T. Kirk, *Voyager's* captain has a calm, unflappable demeanor not unlike that of her counterparts on *TNG* and *DS9*. We've seen her in the role of patient teacher to the Malon, the simulated Leonardo da Vinci, the holographic Doctor, and her protégée, Seven of Nine. Though occasionally stubborn, she's not afraid to admit her mistakes if she knows she acted rashly or judged a situation too quickly ("Scorpion, Part 2," "Latent Image"). That's the sign of a person who's not only aware of a mean in ethical action, but attempts to achieve it. That, in turn, makes Janeway a person who values Aristotelian virtue ethics. We've certainly seen her display the virtues of courage, mercy, generosity, friendship, compassion, as well as patience, many times throughout the show.

Like Kirk and Picard, Janeway has also demonstrated that virtue ethics can smoothly blend with the ethics of duty. We can see this in "In the Flesh" (*VGR:* #98), for example, during yet another difference of opinion with Seven of Nine. Engaged in a face-off with Species 8472 after they have captured Chakotay, Janeway orders her protégée to target 8472's weapons array. When Seven suggests targeting their power systems as well, the captain refuses: "I don't want to risk shutting down their life support. If we can end this without casualties, so much the better." Naturally, Seven disagrees ("This species does not deserve our compassion!")—an understandable reaction, given the Borg's innate hatred of 8472. But Janeway still has the final word ("You picked a lousy time for an ethical debate") and orders her to knock out their weapons. The captain's compassion for 8472 reflects her understanding of Directive 0101, which came into play earlier in the story: "Before engaging alien species in battle, any and all attempts to make First Contact and achieve a nonmilitary resolution must be made." This is one duty to which Janeway is wholeheartedly committed. She uses it as a guiding principle, one that she could "rationally will" that everyone would follow. Her virtue of compassion supports and strengthens her resolve to carry out this duty, even if it means disarming *Voyager* when 8472 is clearly about to fire on them.

Dog lover Janeway has a particular affinity for Regan's duty ethics. Her actions in episodes such as "Scientific Method," "Prey," "Night," and "In the Flesh" reflect an understanding of Regan's "harm," "respect," and "worse-off" principles. Like Spock, she believes that all subjects-of-a-life have intrinsic value, not just rational beings. True, it takes some lobbying on Seven's part before the captain is totally convinced that the Doctor is a subject-of-a-life ("Latent Image"). To her credit, though, once Janeway realizes the Doctor has beliefs and desires, perception/memory and a sense of his own future, the ability to feel pleasure, pain and other emotions, and the ability to state preferences and pursue goals—in other words, the four criteria for a "subject-of-a-life"—she affords him the moral consideration she knows he deserves.

The captain is also an existentialist who, like Sartre, knows that when she makes a choice for herself, she also chooses for all people. She often anguishes over the decision that ultimately kept her crew lost in the Delta Quadrant. (Of course, had she made another choice, "*Voyager* the series" wouldn't exist...but that's another story.) She plays midwife to the Doctor during his dark fortnight of the soul at the end of "Latent Image." She even shows a streak of Kierkegaard's philosophy, surrendering all reason and taking a leap of faith in order to save Kes in "Sacred Ground."

But Aristotelian virtue, existentialism, and an allegiance to duty-based principles aren't the only ethical values alive and well on *Voyager*. As we discussed in Chapter 5, Janeway is the most Platonic of the *Star Trek* captains, in that she has overridden the personal rights of her own crew members more than Kirk, Picard, and Sisko combined. To make these decisions in good conscience (and as an existentialist, Janeway is very much attuned to her conscience), she has to believe she has greater wisdom than the people whose rights she overturned. That makes her the prototypical "philosopher-queen." For wisdom, in Plato's book, doesn't simply mean good judgment, but also the ability to plan and deliberate in accordance with policies designed for the common good. Only the Guardians in Plato's ideal society have the proper training and temperament to reason on behalf of the entire community. A wise Guardian is a philosopher invested with supreme governing authority—a philosopher-king (or philosopher-queen, in Janeway's case). In order for the community to achieve harmony, those who lack the proper ability to rule should always defer to the judgment of the philosopher-king.

Given how Janeway perceives her role as captain, it's fitting that her protégée is also someone who sees things from a distinctly Platonic perspective. As a former Borg, Seven of Nine began life believing in the subordination of the individual for the collective good. Though she still believes in maintaining the harmony of her "collective" (*Voyager*) by deferring to the judgment of her "queen" (Janeway), she nonetheless revels in her newfound individualism (often by challenging the captain). Seven also shares Plato's fascination with perfection, which he expressed in the world of the Forms. While Seven may not yet have found perfection, it's not for lack of trying: "The lure of perfection is powerful," she tells Janeway in "Drone" (*VGR:* #96). We see Seven's attraction to perfection explicitly expressed in "The Omega Directive," an episode that also illustrates Plato's notion that moral error is the result of ignorance (an idea that stems from the Allegory of the Cave). Seven also fights bravely to distinguish reality from illusion in "One" (*VGR:* #93), when nebular radiation causes her to hallucinate. Though someone with less faith in the power of reason might have given up, Seven reasons her way out from the nebula's control, as a true Platonist would.

Given how pervasive Platonism is on *Voyager*, it's fitting that the overall moral foundation of the show is itself a kind of "collective." Whereas each of the first three *Star Trek* series has a distinct ethical personality of its own, the ethics of *Voyager* is an amalgam comprised of existentialism, various duty principles, and both Aristotelian and Platonic virtue. This eclecticism is perhaps most apparent in "Death Wish" (*VGR:* #30), wherein a member of the Q Continuum asks Janeway to grant him asylum so that he can commit suicide.* As we look closely at this episode, we can see each component of *Voyager's* ethical foundation in action.

---

*Interestingly enough, this episode not only has a premise similar to the *TNG* segment "Ethics," it also features Jonathan Frakes as none other than Will Riker.

Janeway learns that "Quinn," one of the Continuum's greatest philosophers, has been imprisoned for over 300 years because he wanted to kill himself.* When Q appears, and Quinn demands asylum, Janeway is forced to arbitrate the issue. Both sides agree to the hearing, on the following conditions: if Q wins, Quinn must return to confinement; if Quinn wins, the Continuum must remove his powers so that he can then kill himself. This puts Janeway, who personally opposes suicide, in the thick of a moral dilemma that would make Ross squirm. Her virtues of mercy and justice have put her on a collision course with the Prime Directive. Naturally, Q can't resist rubbing it in: "Will you send him to prison for an eternity, or assist him with his suicide plan?"

Knowing that elderly, infirm Vulcans practice ritual suicide, Quinn wants Tuvok to represent him. Though Tuvok believes the end of a life such as Quinn's would be a waste, he nonetheless assures Quinn that he will represent him to the best of his ability. The Vulcan then stipulates that his client's existence as an immortal has become impossible to endure; if his path leads to death, he should be entitled to that choice without interference. Q, on the other hand, argues his case on the following utilitarian grounds: (1) by putting his own wishes above the welfare of the Continuum, Quinn is not thinking of the greatest good for the greatest number; and (2) Quinn's suicide "would have all sorts of unknown consequences to the Continuum." Though Q also declares Quinn to be "mentally unbalanced" for wanting to kill himself, Tuvok refutes that point by citing several examples of cultures that do not consider suicide to be evidence of mental illness. The Vulcan also requests an inspection

---

*Though known as "Q2" throughout the original shooting script, the character named himself "Quinn" near the end of the episode. The name Quinn, of course, brings to mind Karen Ann Quinlan, whose condition first ignited the death-with-dignity movement in 1976.

of the conditions Quinn has endured during his confinement, arguing that Janeway should consider the quality of life to which his client would be subjected if she rules for the Continuum. The captain agrees, and together they find themselves inside a dark, very cramped environment surrounded by sheets of ice.

Janeway then begins her analysis by citing the only principle she knows in regard to the ending of suffering: "the double effect principle on assisted suicide that dates back to the Bolean Middle Ages." This standard, which sounds an awful lot like the rule developed by St. Thomas Aquinas in the 13th century, states that "a single act may have two effects, of which one alone is intended, while the other is incidental to that intention. But the way a moral act is to be classified depends on what is intended, not on what goes beyond such an intention, since this is merely incidental thereto."*

Meanwhile, Q decides to cover all bets by offering Janeway a bribe—he'll return *Voyager* to Earth if she rules for the Continuum. Again, a classic utilitarian argument: the captain gets her fondest wish, making her entire crew happy, all at the cost of imprisoning one individual for eternity. We know Tuvok has already subordinated his inclinations to his duty. Will Janeway do the same?

We'll see how the captain chooses to act in just a moment. First, though, based on what we know so far about the story, we clearly have ourselves a veritable potpourri of ethical posi-

---

*Aquinas' principle of double effect is the moral experience of conflicting choices and consequences, some good and others evil, of the same action. The "bad" effect is the unfortunate circumstance of a single act intended to be good. Aquinas intended the principle as a means of providing moral guidelines under which such an action may or may not be permitted. The Catholic Church has applied this principle in such areas as abortion and euthanasia. Though Aquinas was specifically addressing the issue of self-defense, his double effect principle uses the same form of argument that Janeway invokes in her ruling.

tions. Quinn, fraught with existential angst, wants to achieve harmony by ending his life—which, as you'll remember from "Ethics" and Chapter 11, also reflects Stoic philosophy. Quinn's isolation also reminds us of Socrates, another great thinker who was ostracized by his own people. Q's utilitarian argument also smacks of the totalitarianism advocated by Plato. Though Tuvok personally opposes Quinn's position, he nonetheless fulfills his duty to defend him, as Kant says we should. We've also got a little Christian philosophy thrown in, for good measure.

When the hearing resumes, Tuvok again requests an inspection of the living conditions that led to his client's suffering. Soon everyone is whisked to a place so empty, one could die of terminal boredom rather quickly. Quinn then implores Janeway to "Look at us! When life is futile, meaningless, unendurable...it must be allowed to end." The existentialist in Janeway understands this completely, especially after Quinn brings up the "meaninglessness" of such an existence.

The following day, Janeway announces her ruling—a decision that clearly did not come easily, given her conflicting feelings on the matter (her personal aversion to suicide versus her compassion for Quinn). "I've tried to tell myself that this is not about suicide, but about granting asylum—that I am not personally being asked to perform euthanasia. And as technically true as that may be, I cannot escape the moral implications of my choices." Indeed, no existentialist could!

Nonetheless, the captain knows that she must also weigh the good of society against the rights of the individual. Since the consequences to the Continuum are unforeseen (and therefore cannot be predicted), and since Quinn is suffering intolerably, Janeway grants him asylum aboard *Voyager*—a decision that rejects the utilitarian argument in favor of Regan's "harm," "respect," and "worse-off" principles and Ross' prima facie duty of non-injury. In addition, the captain's compassion, mercy, justice, gentleness, open-mindedness, and honesty all indicate her allegiance to virtue ethics.

Janeway also beseeches Quinn to try to find meaning in his new life as a mortal, a request that reflects Sartre's existentialist ideas. However, she soon discovers that Quinn, indeed, has killed himself by ingesting a rare form of hemlock—the same drink Socrates used to end his life 3,000 years before. Though the utilitarians would take Janeway to task over how things turned out, Kant would assure the captain that her actions were morally worthy. Not only was her intention pure, she based her decision on a principle (we should try to find meaning in life by continuing to live) she could "rationally will" for all people to follow.

Besides incorporating just about every moral theory we've discussed in our journey, "Death Wish" clearly shows us the eclectic ethics of Janeway and *Voyager* at their best. That makes it a particularly appropriate final episode to consider, especially since (broadly speaking, anyway) each individual *Star Trek* series embodies not only its own but each of the others' major ethical principles as well.

THE ETHICAL TAPESTRY OF *STAR TREK*

Overall, we can say that the Original Series most clearly reflects Aristotelian virtue; *The Next Generation,* the ethics of duty (particularly those espoused by Kant's system of morality); *Deep Space Nine,* existentialism; and *Voyager,* Platonic virtue. Yet as ethically diverse as *Star Trek* may seem, there are some principles drawn from each of these theories that all four shows have in common. From Kant's duty theory, we see that each series respects the principle that a rational being should always be treated as an end and never as a means only. Each show places a high value on the autonomy of the individual and the importance of following our duties over our desires.

Each endorses the pursuit of altruism over egoistic concerns. Finally, all four shows recognize the importance of intention over the consequences of an action when evaluating the morality of an action.

Each of the *Star Trek* series respects all forms of sentient life, as well as both the "harm" and "worse-off" principles—all of which comply with Regan's duty ethics. They also uphold all seven of Ross' prima facie duties: reparation, fidelity, gratitude, self-improvement, justice, beneficence, and above all nonmaleficence (non-injury).

Each show also agrees that the end does not always justify the means—a rejection of utilitarian values that comes straight out of Aristotelian virtue theory. It is not justifiable to use a bad means to accomplish a good end. All four incarnations of *Star Trek* concur with Aristotle that in any particular situation there is always a right thing to do. However, in considering the proper course of action, we must also take into account all the factors relevant to a particular situation—another key Aristotelian idea that each series shares. All four shows also recognize and strive to realize the virtues of compassion, courage, justice, equity, friendship, and temperance.

Now, you could argue that some parts of Aristotle's ethics aren't valued by any of the *Star Trek* characters. You'd be right, in the sense that many critics of Aristotle consider the virtues in his system to be antiquated. In other words, while virtues such as liberality, magnificence, and wittiness may have been highly regarded by the cultivated Greeks of Aristotle's time, they're not necessarily valued by contemporary society (let alone the 23rd- and 24th-century worlds of *Star Trek*). Of course, Aristotle anticipated this by avoiding the extremes of Kantian moral absolutism and cultural relativism. Though Aristotle believed there is one right way to act in a particular situation, he also maintained the importance of considering the context of each individual situation, as well as the individuals in each situation. The rules for right action can never be absolute. For that reason, he knew we must also consider cultural differences, since moral values are not derived independently from nonmoral factors of human living.

With that in mind, let's modify Aristotle's list of virtues to comply with those moral states admired by our friends in the *Star Trek* universe:

DEFICIT [VICE]	MEAN [VIRTUE]	EXCESS [VICE]
Cowardice	Courage	Foolhardiness
Inhibition	Temperance	Intemperance
Peevishness	Friendliness	Obsequiousness
Poor-spiritedness	Gentleness	Irascibility
Groveling	Cooperativeness	Antagonism
Bias	Justice	Legalism
Vacillation	Open-mindedness	Intolerance
All-forgivingness	Mercifulness	Unyieldingness
Submissiveness	Respect for others	Contempt for others
Lying	Honesty	Blabbermouth
Spinelessness	Compassion	Ruthlessness
Pacifism	Peacemaking	Bellicosity
Back-stabbing	Loyalty	Sycophancy

The first four virtues, as we know from Chapter 6, are the same as the first four on Aristotle's list. While he knew justice and honesty are virtues, for some reason he didn't include them in his discussion of the mean.* Nor did he discuss any of the other seven (cooperation, open-mindedness, mercy, respect, compassion, peace, loyalty), except either indirectly or in passing. Perhaps he felt they were self-evident. In any event, Aristotle never claimed to have offered an exhaustive list of virtues. The point is, each of the *Star Trek* series extols these virtues, while frowning on the excesses on either side of them.

---

*Aristotle does, however, list truthfulness.

Turning to existentialism, all four show the value of the importance of freedom and responsibility. We should accept responsibility for who we are and all that we do, without ever hiding behind excuses. Our choices are to be taken seriously—they impact not just our personal lives, but indeed all of society.

Because it seems no one theory clearly defines the overall ethics of our four series, perhaps we can say that the principles of virtue, duty, and existentialism, when taken as a whole, comprise an "ethical tapestry" of *Star Trek*. That would certainly work, in terms of the criteria we've used to evaluate each theory—after all, we've already demonstrated how each principle more than adequately applies to each series. But as a whole, are these principles consistent with one another? Since each of these ideals come from discrete ethical theories, it's conceivable that one or more could cancel the others out. Will they work together in harmony and form one picture?

Consider, for example, that if we eliminated the "no exception" rule from Kant's duty ethics, then the principles he espouses would actually be consistent with those promoted by Regan and Ross. Not only that, the guidelines Regan and Ross provide would make Kant's theory even more user-friendly. You see, the problem with Kant (at least among philosophers) is that his system of morality doesn't contain enough content to provide practical ethical direction for our everyday lives. That would no longer be a problem, though, if we supplemented his ethics with the principles and duties endorsed by Regan and Ross.

Ah, you say, don't Kant and Regan disagree over what sort of individuals ought to be extended moral consideration? Well...yeah, technically speaking. Except that Kant's principle that rational beings should always be treated as an end and never only as a means doesn't preclude Regan's requirement that all subjects-of-a-life must be treated with respect. In fact, if we combine Regan's and Kant's principles into one theory, we actually expand the boundary of our moral concern (or, if you prefer, narrow the range of individuals we're ethically justified to exploit). Regardless of how you see it, this merger gives us a new moral rule: "Act so that you treat subjects-of-a-life, whether in your own person or in that of another, always as an end and never as a means only." Would *Star Trek* agree to this? From what we've seen ("Devil in the Dark," "Gamesters of Triskelion," "Ethics," "I, Borg," "Captive Pursuit," "Scientific Method," among other examples), the answer is yes.

Further, Regan's theory is highly compatible with Ross' teachings. Regan's "harm" and "worse-off" principles are both similar to Ross' duty of non-injury. Moreover, both Regan and Ross characterize our duties as prima facie—that is, duties that may be overriden in the event of a more pressing moral demand. This idea, as we know, is highly compatible with Aristotle's notion of equity. All of which, of course, is very useful to *Star Trek,* particularly with regard to General Order No. 1. If we look at the Prime Directive as a prima facie duty, we can understand that its frequent violations are hardly immoral, but rather a practical example of what morality sometimes requires.

In fact, once we remove the inviolability from Kant, supplement his system with Ross' and Regan's principles, and expand the range of beings to whom we owe ethical consideration, we could actually consider Kant's theory to be one of the cornerstones of the ethics of *Star Trek*. Let's call this a "modified Kantian ethics."

While following this modified Kantian ethics, *Star Trek* shows us how we can develop our moral virtues, as well as the direction we should take once we develop them. Indeed, virtue ethics is quite consistent with the ethics of duty, once "inviolability" is out of the picture. Once applied, the very same moral laws in Kant's system could easily result in a virtuous character. In addition, both Aristotelian virtue ethics and our new Kantian ethics claim that a person is not morally good unless he or she cares about doing what is good simply because it is right. Likewise, both claim that a person who only does what is right incidentally is not morally good.

Also, both Aristotelian virtue and our "new, improved" Kantian ethics insist that we use reason to decide what to do in a particular situation, as well as emphasize the role of context in determining what we should ultimately do. Depending on the circumstances, prima facie duties may be overridden by other moral duties that are more pressing. This also is quite compatible with the Aristotelian principle that virtue is an action or feeling responding to a particular situation at the right time, in relation to the right people, with the right motive, and in the right way. Additionally, both concepts agree on the importance of governing our emotions with reason, particularly with regard to controlling violent emotions that might interfere with our ability to achieve noble goals (such as peace).

Existentialist teachings are also in harmony with the principles of Aristotle and Kant. Existentialism's demand that we not run from our personal freedom, nor our responsibility to society, accentuates the serious implications of the ethics of duty and virtue. Sartre's emphasis on personal and societal responsibility complements Aristotle's view of the human being as both individual and social in nature. Moreover, both Sartre and Kant affirm that before performing a certain action, we should always consider what would happen "if everyone acted that way." Both hold that we are free to oppose external pressures. We're even free to disobey what others tell us to do, if we know the law to be inequitable (as Picard showed us in "Justice") or believe there's no moral context to justify that action ("Conundrum").

Aristotle and Sartre also agree that we form our own character by our actions and choices. This idea complements Ross' duty of self-improvement—after all, if we're responsible for our characters, it's reasonable to believe we have a duty to improve ourselves. Choice is integral to all three theories: Aristotle believes one important condition for an act to be virtuous is that we choose the act for its own sake; Kant insists that we make autonomous choices; while existentialism is concerned with choice, *period.*

So at last, we've found it. Our ethical tapestry is no hodge-podge of arbitrary moral standards, but rather a unified theory that accounts for the action or choices taken or made by every character, in every segment, in every series or film in the *Star Trek* universe. Just as Thomas Aquinas created his own theory by synthesizing Aristotelian and Christian philosophy, *Star Trek* has created a distinct moral code by bringing together the most judicious principles of virtue, duty, and existentialist teachings. Better yet, by unifying these principles of different ethical theories in a coherent way, *Star Trek* has formulated a new brand of ethics powerful enough to stand on its own.

Do you think a society based entirely on *Star Trek* ethics could possibly prevail in the future? Why not? The rules are practical to follow and easy to understand. *Star Trek* has already provided us with the blueprint.

It all comes down to one thing. As Jean-Luc Picard might say, only we can "Make it so."

SUGGESTED READING

RESOURCES ON ETHICISTS

Aristotle. *Ethica Nicomachea.* Translated by W. D. Ross. In *The Basic Works of Aristotle,* edited and with an introduction by Richard McKeon. New York: Random House, 1941.

Augustine, St. *Fathers of the Church.* Edited by P. J. Defarrari et al. Washington, D.C.: Catholic University of America, 1948–62.

Epictetus. *Discourses and Enchiridon.* Based on the translation of Thomas Wentworth. Higgonson, N.Y.: Walter J. Black, 1944.

Epicurus. *Letters, Principal Doctrines and Vatican Sayings.* Translated by Russel Geer. New York: Macmillan, 1985.

Hobbes, Thomas. *Leviathan.* Edited by Michael Oakeshott. New York: Collier, 1962.

Kant, Immanuel. *Fundamental Principles of the Metaphysics of Morals.* Translated by Thomas K. Abbot. Indianapolis: Bobbs-Merrill, 1949.

Kierkegaard, Søren. *A Kierkegaard Anthology.* Edited by Robert Bretall. New York: The Modern Library, 1936.

Nietzsche, Friedrich. *The Portable Nietzsche.* Selected and translated by Walter Kaufmann. New York: Penguin Books, 1976.

Plato. *The Collected Dialogues of Plato.* Edited by Edith Hamilton and Huntington Cairns. Princeton: Princeton University Press, 1961.

Regan, Tom. *The Case for Animal Rights.* Berkeley: University of California Press, 1983.

Sartre, Jean-Paul. *Existentialism.* New York: Philosophical Library, 1947.

RESOURCES ON *STAR TREK*

Atkins, Dorothy. "*Star Trek:* A Philosophical Interpretation." In *The Intersection of Science Fiction and Philosophy: Critical Studies,* edited by Robert E. Myers. Contributions to the Study of Science Fiction and Fantasy, no. 4. Westport, Conn.: Greenwood Press, 1983.

Blish, James. *Star Trek.* Vols. 1–11. New York: Bantam Books, 1967–75.

Engel, Joel. *Gene Roddenberry: The Myth and the Man Behind "Star Trek."* New York: Hyperion, 1994.

Gerrold, David. *The World of "Star Trek."* New York: Ballantine Books, 1979. 2nd ed., Chappaqua, N. Y.: Bluejay Books, 1984.

Greenwald, Jeff. *Future Perfect.* New York: Penguin, 1998.

Hanley, Richard. *The Metaphysics of "Star Trek."* New York: Basic Books, 1997.

Harrison, Taylor, Sarah Projansky, Kent A. Ono, and Elyce Rae Helford, eds. *Enterprise Zones.* Boulder, Colo.: Westview Press, 1996.

Hertenstein, Mike. *The Double Vision of "Star Trek."* Chicago: Cornerstone, 1998.

Okuda, Michael, and Denise Okuda. *The "Star Trek" Encyclopedia: A Reference Guide to the Future,* 2nd ed. New York: Pocket Books, 1997.

Richards, Thomas. *The Meaning of "Star Trek."* New York: Doubleday, 1997.

Whitfield, Stephen, and Gene Roddenberry. *The Making of "Star Trek."* New York: Ballantine Books, 1968.